THE LIFE AND TIMES OF
EDWARD MARTYN

The Life and Times of Edward Martyn

AN ARISTOCRATIC BOHEMIAN

MADELEINE HUMPHREYS

IRISH ACADEMIC PRESS
DUBLIN • PORTLAND, OR

First published in 2007 by Irish Academic Press

44 Northumberland Road,	920 NE 58th Avenue, Suite 300
Ballsbridge,	Portland, Oregon,
Dublin 4, Ireland	97213-3786

www.iap.ie

British Library Cataloging in Publication Data:
An entry can be found on request

ISBN 978 0 7165 2923 1 (cloth)

Library of Congress Cataloging-in-Publication Data:
An entry can be found on request

Typeset by Carrigboy Typesetting Services
Printed by Biddles Ltd., King's Lynn, Norfolk

For Eddie, Niamh and Fiona, with love

Frontispiece: Pen and Wash drawing of Edward Martyn by John B. Yeats, 1899

Contents

List of Illustrations		ix
Acknowledgements		xi
Introduction		xiii
1	Smyths and Martyns	1
2	Christ Versus Apollo	14
3	The Soul in Crisis	24
4	'Strength without hands to Smitc'	39
5	The Best of Times	53
6	All Things Irish	69
7	A 'Celtic' Theatre	86
8	Controversies	99
9	A Literary Theatre	113
10	Political Drama	128
11	The *Leader*	144
12	Sacred Art and Music	161
13	1904	174
14	King Martyn and the Martynettes	188
15	Melancholia	202
16	Hardwicke Street	215

17 Easter 1916 230

18 The Final Curtain 246

Notes 260

Bibliography 276

Index 279

List of illustrations

Frontispiece: Pen and Wash drawing of Edward Martyn
        by John B. Yeats, 1899   vi

1   Loughrea, Co. Galway, 1850 (courtesy of the National
     Library of Ireland)   2

2   Masonbrook House, Loughrea, Co. Galway.
     (Provenance unknown)   5

3   Eyre Square, Galway, *c.*1900 (courtesy of NLI)   9

4   Spa House and Baths, Lisdoonvarna, Co. Clare
     (courtesy of NLI)   13

5   The Norman Tower at Tillyra.
     (*Galway Arch. & Hist. Soc. Journal*; courtesy of the NLI)   29

6   Shelbourne Hotel, Dublin, *c.*1900 (courtesy of NLI)   31

7   St. Stephen's Green, Dublin, *c.*1900 (courtesy of NLI)   33

8   Edgar Degas: *Two Ballet Dancers* (courtesy of the National
     Gallery of Ireland)   41

9   Portrait of Eric Stenbock (*Stenbock, Yeats and the nineties*,
     Provenance unknown)   59

10 Portrait of Nevill Geary (*Nigeria under British Rule*;
     courtesy of NLI)   70

11 Dunguaire Castle, Kinvara, Co. Galway (author's collection)   73

12 (a) Arthur Symons *c.*1895 (courtesy of the NLI)   74
     (b) W.B. Yeats *c.*1895 (Provenance unknown)   75

13 (a) Edward Martyn (Gaelic League Portrait, 1899)   80
     (b) Edward Martyn and Susan Mitchell, 1899
        (courtesy of NLI)   81

14 Tillyra Castle, 1907 (*Galway Arch. & Hist. Soc. Journal*;
     courtesy of NLI)   83

15   Florimonde deBasterot's modest house at Durus. July 1897   89

16   Review of *The Heather Field* with sketch of Edward Martyn
     (Henderson Collection, NLI)   101

17   Edward Martyn's agreement to underwrite the debts
     of the Irish Literary Theatre (Henderson Collection, NLI)   110

18   The Antient Concert Rooms, Great Brunswick
     (now Pearse) Street, Dublin (author's collection)   115

19   'Mr. Yeats and Mr. Martyn', cartoon by Max Beerbohm
     (Henderson Collection, NLI)   119

20   Augusta Gregory, 1904 (courtesy of NLI)   125

21   George Russell (Æ), *c.*1900 (courtesy of NLI)   129

22   Cover of *Beltaine*, 1900: doodles by Jack B. Yeats
     (by kind permission of Michael Yeats)   139

23   Cartoon of George Moore by Max Beerbohm
     (Henderson Collection, NLI)   153

24   Vincent O'Brien, Director of the Palestrina Choir, 1917
     (Joseph Holloway Collection, NLI)   154

25   Saint Brendan's Cathedral, Loughrea (author's collection)   171

26   Kildare Street Club *c.*1900 (courtesy of NLI)   191

27   Grace Gifford's cartoon of Edward Martyn 'having
     a week of it in Paris'   205

28   Edward Martyn and others in Killarney, July 1914
     (courtesy of the *Examiner*)   217

29   Poster for the Irish Theatre, 4–9 January 1915.
     (Henderson Collection, NLI)   221

30   'Cupid and Psyche' (George Moore and Susan Mitchell),
     by Grace Gifford (courtesy of NLI)   227

31   (a) Thomas MacDonagh in Volunteer Uniform, *c.*1916
          (courtesy of NLI)   233
     (b) Sackville (O'Connell) Street in ruins, April 1916   234

32   *Romulus and Remus* at the Irish Theatre, 21 December 1916
     (Henderson Collection, NLI)   237

33   Yeats's Tower at Ballylee Co. Galway   239

34   (a) Edward Martyn by Sydney Davis, 1917
          (Holloway Collection, NLI)   242
     (b) Grace Gifford by Sydney Davis, 1918
          (Holloway Collection, NLI)   243

Acknowledgements

I SHOULD LIKE TO EXTEND warm thanks to the many institutions and individuals that have helped me with the publication of this book. The staff of the National Library of Ireland must come first for their unfailing courtesy and helpfulness; Rodney Phillips and later Isaac Gewirtz, Curators of the Berg Collection in the New York Public Library; Gary Lundell, University of Washington Libraries, Seattle; Tara Wenger at the Harry Ransom Humanities Research Center, Austin, Texas; University of Delaware Library; the University of Reading Library; Department of Special Collections, Stanford University Archives; Tricia Andrews at the British Library and Jane Maxwell, at Trinity College Dublin Archive; David Sheehy, Dublin Diocesan Archive; Galway Diocesan Archive; Bill Gannon at the Land Commission and the staff of the Land Registry, Dublin.

It is unlikely, however, that the book would or could have been written without the continuous help and support of Dr Deirdre McMahon of Mary Immaculate College, University of Limerick. It was through her research that I stumbled on Edward Martyn in the first place and our periodical discussions on him over the years have always been both helpful and enjoyable. My daughter Niamh Humphreys also has an interest in the history of the period and has been a willing reader and editor throughout. Special thanks must also go to Professor Fergus D'Arcy of University College Dublin whose wonderful teaching, twenty years ago, instilled the confidence in me to write historical biography.

Among others to whom I am indebted are Jonathan Williams; Michael Yeats; Lord Hemphill; Jerry Nolan; Elizabeth O'Brien; Sister Marie-Thérèse Courtney, Sister of Mercy; Patrick Melvin; Sheila Donnellan; Joseph Murphy; Colin Smythe; Sister de Lourdes Fahy of the Kiltartan Cultural Society; Toni O'Brien; Judith Hill; Pauric Dempsey; Professor John A. Murphy; Professor Michael Laffan; Professor Mary Daly; Professor Hugh Gough; Kevin Barry; Diarmaid Ferriter; Daire Keogh; Fabian McCormack of the Discalced Carmelites, Dublin; Brendan Kilcoyne of Tuam; Anne de Valera; Professor Lucy MacDiarmid; David Norris; Sinéad McCoole and Carla King.

Thanks to my husband Eddie Humphreys who travelled many miles with me around Galway in the footsteps of Edward Martyn, and my daughter Fiona who often listened when she didn't want to. I am grateful to all.

Introduction

AFTER THE PUBLICATION OF the first book of George Moore's masterpiece *Hail and Farewell* in 1911, the satirist Susan Mitchell reflected on Edward Martyn's reaction. 'He held his ground bluffly', she tells us, 'against all the ill winds that cousinly venom could direct against him; using the consolation of a religion he had fashioned for himself out of music and the drama.' This is an extraordinarily apt observation of Edward Martyn, who found it necessary from a very early age to re-imagine himself. Born into the south Galway gentry in 1859, Martyn was destined to become a conservative Catholic landlord. But turning his back on this life, he became, instead, a nationalist and a leader of the Irish Cultural Renaissance. And yet he is little more than a footnote in Irish history.

In 1929 Denis Gwynn published a life of Edward Martyn which gives us the public man but tells us almost nothing about his private life, or that of his family. It was a respectable biography, for its time, but there is no way of knowing if Gwynn could have done better because, soon after the publication of the book, Martyn's personal archive was lost. The papers had been left in the safe keeping of Cyril Ryan, Provincial of the Discalced Carmelites in Dublin. It is possible that Ryan destroyed the papers, given that they may well have revealed the complexity of Edward's sexual nature or even his latent paganism, but if he did, it is unlikely that he had the co-operation of Denis Gwynn.

Then Moore published his great trilogy and laid bare his cousin's private life as he saw it. It did not cause a particular stir at the time because the novelist portrayed Martyn as a somewhat lovable duffer. He gave the reader 'Dear Edward' and, in the process, discounted his cousin's genuine and serious contribution to the artistic movements of the era. But in truth Edward Martyn was a sophisticated European with a proud pedigree. He also had a classical education from Oxford University which, in the end, taught him how to live. It was only possible to perceive this by treating his life as a jigsaw and filling in the pieces as they presented themselves, through exhaustive research.

Setting out on that research, it was gratifying to discover boxes of Martyn papers in the Land Commission of Ireland. The information there confirmed my belief that the European dimension in his life did not just come from his education. It was a part of his genetic heritage through his maternal grandmother's family. And the well-kept registers of the Land Registry, together with the research of Patrick Melvin, showed that James Smyth, Edward's maternal grandfather, generally described as a 'peasant' who greedily made money out of post-Famine Ireland, was actually from a professional family. He had acquired his wealth in the early nineteenth century some years before Edward's mother was born. From Board of Guardians records, held at the Galway County Library, a kinder, more responsible John Martyn (Edward's father) emerged, rather than the rake and philanderer who has previously been described. The discovery in the Galway Diocesan Archive of a sole letter from Edward's brother, John, to his mother was gold dust for it confirmed that Annie Martyn and her sons had a good relationship and that they had loved one another.

Friendship was supremely important in Edward Martyn's life. Shortly after he came back to south Galway from Oxford in the 1880s, his neighbour, William Gregory, brought his relatively young bride, Augusta Persse, to Coole Park. This was the beginning of a friendship that sustained Martyn for the rest of his life. Gregory's copious diaries (at given times Edward figures in them every day) bear witness to this friendship. When they are juxtaposed with the multitudinous letters of W.B. Yeats during the years of the Irish Literary Theatre, they give us a vivid and compelling picture of Edward's life at the time. Martyn's own letters to Augusta Gregory, held in the New York Public Library, are also highly revelatory of his feelings and, to an extent, his dependence on her friendship.

For Edward Martyn, man and boy, was lonely. After the death of his mother and brother, his life lacked intimacy. There is no evidence that he ever accepted the responsibility of physical love and all his early writings suggest a strong aversion to women. Such sentiment was well suited to Oxford University in 1879 where the cult of Hellenism was the *Zeitgeist*. Edward read for a degree in *Literae Humniores* (which he did not achieve), where the emphasis was on the work of Johann Joachim Winkelmann, who believed that true beauty must always be male and never could be female. For a long time a pattern revealed itself in Martyn's creative work which can be traced back to the influences he absorbed at Oxford, even after the upset of being accused of 'Paganism' in the pages of the *Catholic Register* in 1902.

He was a difficult landlord. It was a role he hated. Relations between the Martyn family and their tenants in south Galway were traditionally bad. Annie Martyn was blamed because, supposedly, her own 'peasant' background made her a 'hard woman'. In the Martyn papers in the Galway Diocesan Archive, however, there is an affidavit, throwing a completely different light on this issue and showing that the bad blood went back two generations to Edward's paternal grandfather. This discovery was extremely important, for Martyn's poor relationship with his tenants not only permeated his early plays but contributed to his bafflement when the Abbey Theatre decided to use what he considered the 'peasant play' to represent the ideal in Ireland.

As a young man, Edward Martyn's great heroes were Richard Wagner and Henrik Ibsen. After a mental breakdown in the 1880s, he retreated from his Hellenism and adopted an extreme form of Catholicism. But by the time he published his first creative work, *Morgante the Lesser*, a utopian novel, in 1890, he had returned, to some degree, to his former principles. In the years following the publication of *Morgante*, he travelled regularly to Germany to listen to, and write about, the great Wagnerian operas. There he stumbled on the plays of Henrik Ibsen. The later psychological work of the Norwegian proved highly personal to Edward, for they helped him to make sense of the inner world he had created for himself after his breakdown. When he came to write his own first play, *The Heather Field*, it was largely autobiographical, despite being based on the failed marriage of a fanatical idealist.

In writing this play, Edward Martyn had some help from George Moore and, a few years later, when he was leaving the Irish Literary Theatre, this proved a contentious issue. It came to light at a time when Moore had taken hold of Martyn's third play, *The Tale of a Town*, and made it his own. The fracas that ensued was high drama offstage. Yeats wrote of it in his *Autobiographies* in the 1930s, but the abundance of personal letters available to the biographer today reveal a subtly different story to that of the poet's suspect narrative.

Being shy and sensitive is not the same as lacking confidence. Edward Martyn had the fundamental confidence of the well-born 'aristocrat'. Out of his love for the work of Richard Wagner came his need to create a great cathedral choir for the city of Dublin. The clergy did not want it but Martyn, who was anti-clerical, was highly abrasive in his very public argument and showed respect only for the hierarchy. The latter had both respect for Edward's argument and for his money, and the Palestrina Choir was founded in 1901. The correspondence surrounding the struggle is well preserved in the Dublin Diocesan Archive.

In his forties Martyn became a missionary for art. With his help Sarah Purser founded her stained-glass studio, An Tur Gloinne, in Dublin in 1903 and together they organised the decoration of Saint Brendan's Cathedral in Loughrea, County Galway, making it a gem of Irish art. In the process they became firm friends and through his letters to her we become aware that, by middle age, he had shed the misogyny that blighted his early life. His involvement with the Gaelic League, the Feis Ceoil and the foundation of the Abbey Theatre 1904 all led him into becoming a public man. Gathering the evidence for these years was not difficult and it was easier still when he became president of Arthur Griffith's Sinn Féin.

Brought up as a unionist, Edward Martyn's nationalism had been growing all his adult life. It was, however, an unexamined nationalism. He was fundamentally anti-democratic and, although he was highly attracted to the European dimension in Griffith's 'Hungarian Policy', he was extremely uncomfortable in his quasi-political organisation. David P. Moran, who hated Arthur Griffith, used this knowledge to abuse Edward, almost on a weekly basis, for two years in the pages of his newspaper, the *Leader*. He was especially bombastic when Martyn took an action against the Kildare Street Club, which had expelled him for his lack of respect for the political beliefs of the other members. Moran's hyperbole was often very funny but it took its toll, and by the time Edward Martyn had resigned from Sinn Féin in 1908, he was suffering from acute depression.

The following years are well charted in his correspondence with John J. Horgan, held in the National Library of Ireland. He went back to writing plays but he also wrote and published some very self-revelatory poetry. There was a continued apprehension, shared by Dublin's literati, regarding the contents of George Moore's forthcoming book. When it was published, Susan Mitchell's reflection on Edward's reaction was uncannily accurate. This can be verified by his own treatment of the subject in his *Paragraphs for the Perverse*, an introduction to a book of essays that he intended to publish before his death, discovered in the Galway Diocesan Archive.

In 1914 a new, and very happy, era opened for Edward Martyn when the poets Thomas MacDonagh and Joseph Mary Plunkett approached him to partner them in the opening of an art theatre. They planned to bring European masterpieces to Irish audiences, as well as staging experimental Irish work that had nothing to do with the 'peasant play'. The inaugural performance was Edward's own play *The Dream Physician*, a satire on his relationship with Moore and Yeats. Less than eighteen months later, as he sat in his rooms in South Leinster Street and listened to the guns of the 1916 Easter Rising, he thought the good times were all over. A combination of Martyn's letters to Augusta Gregory and John MacDonagh and the diary entries of Joseph Holloway afforded me a fresh and fascinating glimpse of that poignant week in Irish history; the immediacy of a view from the footpath.

It wasn't all over. John MacDonagh, who was soon released from jail, took up where his brother Thomas, the mainstay of the company until his execution for his part in the Rising, had left off. With John's help, Edward kept the Irish Theatre in Hardwicke Street going until 1920 and in 1950 Mícheál Mac Liammóir admitted that it had blazed a trail for his own Gate Theate. William J. Feeney's *Drama in Hardwicke Street* is a *tour de force* on this little theatre.

The Irish War of Independence and the Civil War, spanning the years 1920–23, brought to an end the cultural explosion that had reverberated throughout Edward Martyn's life. They were also the years when his health broke and he found himself trapped in his castle in south Galway when he really wanted to be in Dublin at the centre of things. Elizabeth O'Brien, daughter-in-law of Vincent O'Brien, Director of the Palestrina Choir, generously allowed me to read the letters between Vincent and Edward for that period and they helped enormously in dealing with the last years of Edward's life. A consummate man of the theatre to the last, Martyn was also writing to the American impresario,

Barrett H. Clarke, and to Sarah Purser. He was writing to Purser even after he could no longer hold a pen, having Owen Linane, his man-servant and secretary, transcribe his thoughts. Still, it was Augusta Gregory's diaries that brought it all to life; even the tragedy of Edward's death and his burial in a pauper's grave.

In the end I did not complete the book I had set out to write. I wanted to know why Edward Martyn, a great patron of the arts, a playwright, a journalist and the first president of Sinn Féin, should always be a mere footnote in history. The answer was too easy. The Irish Cultural Renaissance is not a period well served by Irish historians. Individuals, however, including Martyn's friends W.B. Yeats, Augusta Gregory and George Moore, are very well served and are giants in their fields, highly acclaimed for their contribution to the development of the Irish cultural heritage. Edward Martyn was not a great writer; not an artist. He could not covet any such acclaim. But he knew what he could do. At a very early age he understood the purpose of art. Knowing himself to be 'not like other people', he used it to live a difficult life, and he quickly conceived of the notion that if dramatic art could do that for him, then it could also be used to develop the Irish cultural psyche. He was determined to have a theatre. The same motivation was behind all his artistic enterprises. He used his money, and his position, to make the most of what the newly emerging cultural nationalism had to offer to ameliorate the lives of his fellow citizens, and so he achieved his status.

Writing in her diary in 1930, Augusta Gregory remarked that Edward Martyn had represented for her the bridge between the old and the new Ireland. There is much truth in this observation and it made necessary a wide reading of that period in Irish history when radical change was the impending dynamic. The historical background of an Irish Catholic landlord in south Galway, awakening to the coming demise of his class, is no less compelling than allowing the imagination to conjure up a picture of Edward Martyn's bulky form sitting in his flat over Purcell's tobacconist's shop in South Leinster Street, Dublin, listening to the guns of 1916. The completed jigsaw covers a broad canvas with a diverse set of characters and each in their own way contributes to the Irish historical narrative.

1 • Smyths and Martyns

THE WINTER OF 1859 was a hard one. Annie Martyn did not attend the 'Grand Ball and Supper' at Kilroy's Hotel on 17 February to 'commemorate the rising commercial prosperity of Galway'. It was only a few weeks since her confinement, and she had carried her baby through the famously hot summer and autumn of 1858. No doubt the birth of her first son, Edward Joseph, on 31 January was a great relief. Tucked away in her father's house, Masonbrook, up the treeless hill and out of the town of Loughrea, she enjoyed 'the rising commercial prosperity' of the county in other ways. Cardinal Paul Cullen's ban on polkas and 'all other such dances repugnant to the purity of Christian morals'[1] would hardly have fazed her. She was 28 years old. Her family, the Smyths of Masonbrook, were second-generation landed gentry and the largest cattle ranchers in the country. She had brought a dowry of £20,000 to John Martyn. He was thirty years her senior and she was in no hurry to move across the county to Tillyra – the Martyn ancestral home. In Loughrea in 1859 the Martyn–Smyth family was safe and intact.

'The Catholics of this place differ from any I have yet seen,' wrote Edward Wakefield of the inhabitants of Loughrea in his *Account of Ireland Statistical and Political* in 1812. 'All the bankers are Catholic', and so were the bulk of the landed gentry. The origin of the Smyth family is obscure but James Smyth, gentleman, leased a 'dwelling house, office houses, yard and garden in the main street of the town of Loughrea'[2] in 1824. Two years earlier he had been witness to his brother John's admission to the King's Inns in Dublin. John later worked as a solicitor in Loughrea. His brother Robert was editor of the *Western Star* in Ballinrobe. At the time they were living with their father at Ballydugan,

1 Loughrea, Co. Galway, 1850, where all the bankers and
most of the landed gentry were Catholics.

an ancient deBurgo seat, in west Galway.[3] Then James married
Charlotte MacDermott and the blood of an old Galway family mingled
with that of the newcomer.

Charlotte MacDermott was the daughter of Major Anthony James
MacDermott, who had been an officer in the Austrian army.[4] The
widespread tribe of the MacDermotts had lost their estates in the
Jacobite rebellions of the seventeenth century. Like many of the other
'wild geese', they went abroad to seek their fortune in military and
commercial life. They were prominent in the wine trade. Some returned
to Ireland and, back in Galway in the nineteenth century, their
descendants took up the threads of an old way of life. James
MacDermott, Charlotte's brother, bought the Ramore division of the
old Daly estates (the Dalys are, perhaps, the oldest Galway family),
which was then in the hands of 'Jamaica Kelly'.[5] The family also owned
property in County Roscommon. In their different ways the religious,
military and commercial legacies of the MacDermotts were strong in
Annie Martyn and in her two sons.

Despite an outbreak of cholera in Loughrea in 1832, the town was still thriving when James Smyth bought the Masonbrook estate in 1834. It was a fitting demesne for Charlotte MacDermott and no less so as the birthplace of her grandson, Edward Martyn. Masonbrook had been built by a descendant of Robert Mason, a Cromwellian grantee, and it had housed many lovers of literature and art, including Sarah Monck, whose *Poems for Miranda* were published by her grandfather, Lord Molesworth, while her son John, a member of parliament, Revenue Commissioner and member of the Privy Council, was also a well-known commentator on Shakespeare and editor of *Massinger*, a literary magazine. The house was a large square building with an imposing portico and a carved stone staircase. It had on its grounds two fairy forts, Rathsonny and Rathannagroath, and a long stone rath. Robert Monck-Mason sold it to Denis Bowes Daly, the MP for Galway, but he failed to maintain it. The estate eventually went into chancery. Annie had been born in the town three years before, almost certainly in the dwelling on the main street quite close to the new Carmelite Abbey, in whose graveyard so many of her family later rested.

As the town of Loughrea evolved, so too did its connection with the Carmelites. Their presence there went back to the fourteenth century, when Richard de Burgo founded a monastery for the White Friars. The Carmelites had a learned and aristocratic background, often providing confessors to kings. They were already established in Dublin in what became Whitefriars Street. In July 1820 a new church at the Carmelite Abbey in Loughrea was dedicated, and a nunnery and chapel were completed in 1829. In 1837 a thousand children were being taught in three schools by the Carmelites.[6] It is unlikely that Annie Smyth was one of them. James Smyth could afford to educate his daughters at home. At the other end of the town from the Abbey, life was enhanced by the arrival of Charles Robert Maturin in 1834, gothic novelist and great-uncle of Oscar Wilde. He was the curate in the old Saint Brendan's church, where Lady Gregory worshipped in the days when she was merely Augusta Persse. In those years a second Catholic church was also built beside the cattle mart, where the Thursday markets were always well stocked with Smyth cattle.

While the Smyth family continued to prosper, the town did not. A downturn in the economy had set in before the end of the 1830s. The Clanricarde family, who owned Loughrea and vast acres surrounding it, were cast in the classic mould of bad absentee landlords. This was unfortunate since Ulick John de Burgo, who in 1827 was created marquess of Clanricarde by his father-in-law George Canning, the Whig prime minister, had an intimate connection with the area through his mother, who was the daughter of Sir Thomas Burke of Marble Hill, County Galway. (The Smyths and Martyns also married into the Burke family.) The Clanricardes, too, had been the main stabilising force among the Galway gentry reaching back to the seventeenth century. De Burgo was 'a tall thin aristocratic man, bald and bland wearing tight pantaloons, striped silk socks and pumps'.[7] He was also described as 'immensely rich with a fondness for low company'. As Under-Secretary of State for Foreign Affairs and Ambassador to Russia, he was kept well occupied, leaving little time to spend at the lovely seventeenth-century Renaissance-styled Portumna Castle. But he was neither popular nor particularly intelligent and in February 1858, when he was appointed Lord Privy Seal by the Prime Minister, Viscount Palmerston, the appointment lasted no more than three weeks. It was considered outrageous for many reasons, but mainly because of Clanricarde's personal life. He had an illegitimate son tucked away in Dublin. When it looked as though this piece of information might well bring down the government, the injudicious appointment was cancelled.

But Ulick John de Burgo cannot be held entirely responsible for the 'rapid progress to ruin of a once happy and prosperous town'.[8] This had its genesis in the destruction of a large proportion of the cottage industries by the overall effect on the Irish economy of the Act of Union in 1801. The Industrial Revolution had started in Britain and mass production had a devastating effect on cottage industries. Still, the depth of the decline was unexpected. A leading article in the *Tuam Herald* in January 1841 declared that it was 'at a loss to ascertain the causes which have led to the decay of a town so well circumstanced as Loughrea'.

James Smyth's profile was high. He was held in great esteem by 'the liberal press' in Galway. At home, Annie's birth was followed by that of her sister Louisa and then by the birth of the first son, John, in 1835. Two more sons, James and Anthony, followed. Growing up in the comfort of Masonbrook, the children were not shielded from the hardness of poor people's lives. In January 1841 their father's herdsman, Joseph Kelly, and his wife were drowned when the ice broke on a river they were crossing. They left behind them five young children, for whom

2 Masonbrook House. Edward Martyn was born here in January 1859. It had housed many lovers of literature, including Sarah Monck, whose *Poems for Miranda* were published by her grandfather, Lord Molesworth.

James Smyth took responsibility. It is easy to imagine tragedy on the land around Masonbrook, where Annie and her brothers and sister played. It was not rich, fertile arable land but mere scrub, suitable only for the grazing of sheep; a land that evoked images of starving peasants seeking shelter. The snow in the winter of 1841 was widespread. It stuck in the crevices and ridges of this rough land, making life difficult for a people already distressed but little imagining the misery that would befall them before the decade was out.[9]

The years of the Potato Famine brought degrees of hardship to almost everyone. James Smyth, however, continued to buy land.[10] He bought it in three different counties while, at the same time, playing his civic role as a member of the gentry by sitting on the Grand Jury for Galway and taking the chair on the Loughrea Board of Guardians. Significantly, he did not attend Poor Law Repeal meetings with his fellow landlords.[11] At these he was deliberately absent. His wealth is reflected in what he brought to market in Loughrea in April 1848. This included 300 ewes, 400 2-year-old ewes, 400 2-year-old wedders, 900 hoggets, 100 3-year-old heifers, 40 3-year-old bullocks and 40 2-year-old heifers.[12] Such abundance at the height of the Famine seems obscene, but the sale came about as a result of his surrendering two farms previously leased. The attention to business in the midst of chaos was a genealogical trait that was not lost on his daughter and grandson.

At 59 years old, John Martyn would not have gone to the 'Grand Ball' either. But he was no stranger to Kilroy's Hotel in Galway. In fact, for many years he had been listed annually among their 'most fashionable arrivals'. In choosing John Martyn, Annie Smyth had married a man with a past. According to local lore, he was a rake with a reputation for something close to profligacy. But a more critical gaze reveals a contradictory nature and a kindly man. His experiences during the Famine years mellowed his appetite for pleasure and then, of course, for the aspiring Smyths there was the question of his pedigree.

At the time that Richard de Burgo was building his monastery for the Carmelites in Loughrea, the Martyns were setting themselves up as merchants in Galway 'Cittee'. The first known Martyn, Geoffrey, is mentioned in an inquisition held in Athenry in December 1333. But it was to Oliver Martyn that Richard III granted armorial bearings.[13] Oliver had accompanied him on his Crusade to the Holy Land and 'had distinguished himself there by his valour'. As the city developed – it got its first charter in 1484 – the Martyns became one of the leading families; an oligarchy commonly known as 'The Tribes'. There were fourteen Tribes and, mostly claiming English descent, they were in control of Galway. Their loyalty to the crown was amply rewarded by a succession of generous charters that freed them from much government control and taxes. Galway was the principal support of the English interest in Connaught.[14]

Between 1590 and 1609 there were three mayors and four bailiffs by the name of Martyn in Galway. In 1634 Richard Martyn, a lawyer and 'rank papist', was MP for Athenry. In the parliament he was described as 'one that carried himself obstinately and indeed malevolently all through the parliament'.[15] This demeanour resulted from his anger at Charles I's plans for the plantation of Connaught. Galway loyalty counted for little with the Crown forces, and in the years that followed the hand of Richard Martyn can be traced in most of the rebellions in the city before the final defeat in the 1650s.

During this period Richard lived at Dunguaire Castle, a castle that remained in the Martyn family until after Edward Martyn's death in 1923. It had been built by Rory Moore O'Shaughnessy on the site of the royal rath of Guire Aidhne, at Kinvara. But at this time it is likely that the family also owned Tillyra, a property that they had almost certainly acquired through intermarriage with the de Burgos. Richard's son Oliver lived there, although perhaps not until the very early eighteenth century. Oliver was a member of parliament for Galway in 1689 and after the Williamite victories it was granted to him that he be exempted from the laws of attainder, whereby most of the neighbouring gentry lost their land. The Martyns of Tillyra were 'by special enactment exempted from their operation and secured in all their rights as citizens, proprietors and Catholics'. This was granted to Martyn because he was 'a person who during the rebellion behaved himself with great moderation and was remarkably kind to many protestants in distress, many of whom he supported in his family and by his charity and goodness saved their lives'.[16]

John Martyn carried his heritage lightly. By the time of his birth in 1801, the family were largely reduced to the status of mere landowners. This was unfortunate, for they had been far more successful as a merchant class than they would ever be as farming stock. By the middle of the eighteenth century large portions of the extensive lands attached to Tillyra Castle were being sold off to meet the demands of creditors. As sections of the Galway gentry moved out of the city to south Galway, it was often from the Martyns, who had been there a century before them, that they acquired their land. Coole Park, the home of the Gregory family, was carved out of Martyn land, as was part of Walter Taylor's Castle Taylor, and the Dalys of Calla benefited from unpaid mortgages on Martyn property. Exchanges of land often came about through marriage settlements. The gentry of south Galway married each other at an almost alarming rate, thus ensuring that Edward Martyn enjoyed a widespread *cousinage*,[17] a *cousinage* that supported him emotionally throughout his life. In 1798 there is no evidence that the marriage of his grandfather, Edward, to Mary Brown of Mount Hazel, County Galway, was anything other than a love match.

There were other reasons, however, for the year 1798 to prove a significant one for the Martyns and their posterity. It was the year of the rebellion of the United Irishmen. Edward Martyn, known as Éamon Bui Mairtín, was chief magistrate for the county of Galway. A Catholic landlord utterly loyal to the Crown, he showed little mercy when the rebels were caught and brought before him. 'Dominating lesser men such as Lambert of Cregaclare and Gregory of Coole', his harsh treatment of the insurgents reverberated through south Galway. Unfortunately, his behaviour brought with it a reputation that, for generations, blighted the relationship between the Martyns of Tillyra and their tenants.[18]

The animus the chief magistrate had for the fledgling revolutionaries did not interfere with his role of good husband and father. There is evidence that he enjoyed a happy home life, albeit a short one, with Mary Brown. She died in 1811 at the age of 36. Edward was 'disconsolate' and erected a large tomb to her memory in Kilmacduagh graveyard. The details of Edward's last will and testament show him to have been a good-natured man.[19] He and Mary had five children, three sons and two daughters. John, the eldest, was only 10 years old when Mary died. But by the time of Edward's death in 1836, most of the family were well launched into their own lives. In the light of the priorities of the times, three of them made very good marriages. Andrew, the second son, married Mary Dolphin of Turroe, thus bringing together two of the oldest Norman families in Galway. Jane, his elder daughter, married Richard Corballis, who had an estate at Rosemount, Dundrum, in south County Dublin, while Mary Anne married James Balfe of Runnymeade, County Roscommon. The women were granted large dowries from the Martyn estate which, unfortunately for John Martyn, were not paid before his father's death.

John's money troubles began immediately he came into his inheritance. He proved an unlikely person to deal with them. In time, his sisters put a lien on the estate, as did his brothers Andrew and Peter, to whom John owed almost £12,000, described simply as 'personal debts'.[20] Ultimately they registered their claims in the Court of Common Pleas, but there is no evidence of any great animosity in the family resulting from this.[21] Ignoring the problem, John simply made matters worse by

3 Eyre Square, Galway *c.*1900.

mortgaging large parts of the estate to facilitate his flamboyant lifestyle. He had little problem in finding people willing to loan him money, including his friend Thomas Reddington, Under-Secretary of State for Ireland, who loaned him £6,000 in 1841 at a rate of 6 per cent interest.[22]

John Martyn and Thomas Reddington were very typical Galway landlords. They had a shared interest in horseracing and fox-hunting. In the grand jury room in Galway in March 1839 they established the County Hunt. They also organised the Loughrea Races on an annual basis. Help with these endeavours was always forthcoming from William Gregory of Coole Park and Burton Persse of Roxborough Castle, both of whom were 'avid gamblers'. Out at Marble Hill, John's friend, and later witness to his marriage to Annie, Sir Thomas Burke, was also a gambler. He funded 'The Marble Hill Stakes' at the Curragh in County

Kildare and was well known to be neither 'prudent nor business-like'. With such friends, there was little chance that John, who started out in an impoverished state, was ever likely to get his life in order without help. Most of his friends 'married money', while it appeared that he was in no hurry to marry at all. Once, when collecting folklore in south Galway, the poet W.B. Yeats claimed to have talked 'to one of John's peasant mistresses', who said of him that he would chase a girl across the county on a horse just for a kiss.[23] It is likely that the young man named 'Patrick Martyn', residing at Tillyra at the time of the first Edward Martyn's death, and for whose presence there is no explanation, was John's illegitimate son.

Living the high life did not stop John Martyn from performing his civic duty. This became very onerous after 1846, when he was brought face to face with the despair brought on by the potato blight. As chairman of the Board of Guardians for Gort, he had the monthly chore of finding food for the people. Unlike many of his fellow land-lords, he had little patience with the promotion of public works. Watching the people of Ardrahan, his own immediate townland, turning to alcohol and crime and dying in the streets, he wanted the food to be given directly to them.[24] At Gort the local authority was almost overwhelmed by the numbers of people in distress and in 1847 John, with the help of his friends Lord Gort and Captain Shawe Taylor, was forced to raise £1,000 among the landlords to keep the workhouse open.[25] With Shawe Taylor he also succeeded in raising money to buy meal that could be sold cheaply to the starving people. By May 1849 he must have been near the end of his tether when he discovered that his herdsman at Tillyra had found a young woman killing a lamb on his land and had locked her in a stable while he went for the police. She hanged herself with her apron. John sacked the shepherd.[26] Beside this report in the *Galway Mercury*, it was noted that people were 'still dying in droves in the workhouse in Loughrea'.

By 1854 the town was slowly regaining its prosperity. Louisa Smyth, Annie's younger sister, entered the Sisters of Mercy in Loughrea on 24 October. A splendid *déjeuner* was given in her honour. The streets of the town were still in a 'muddy filthy condition', according to the *Galway Mercury*. Annie was 23 years old. Two years later Louisa was professed as Sister Mary Gonzaga, but we have no sight of Annie. She would have known John Martyn as a child and a young woman. Their social circle was small and intimate and John regularly sat with James Smyth on the grand jury and the Board of Guardians throughout the 1850s. John was familiar with Masonbrook even before the Smyths got there. When Denis Bowes Daly had been in possession of it he had brought his stud there from the Curragh – a mighty attraction for the young John. Now an elderly man, he was appointed a High Sheriff of Galway; he was a presence in the county. Even so, in 1857 he was 56 years old to Annie's 26. Did she choose him? Almost certainly. Later glimpses of Annie show her to be a strong, purposeful woman with, George Moore the novelist tells us, 'a clear practical intelligence'.[27] Her sister was gone from her. Her young brother John was a captain in the Connaught Rangers and there must have been a fear that he would be required to fight in the Crimean War, like many other Galway men. No doubt James and Charlotte wanted grandchildren. There is nothing to suggest that John Martyn was not a lovable man. Certainly he was a familiar one, but was he also a sick one?

The marriage settlement between John Martyn and Annie Smyth was a carefully constructed document. It was administered by six trustees, mostly Annie's uncles. By its terms John Martyn had all his debts paid and was left with a residue of £1,730 for his own use. Annie got the rents from various lands, which gave her a personal income of £600 per year. It is the settlement with regard to prospective children that makes us ponder the state of John's health. A sum of £6,000 was put in trust for any children of the marriage, whether they be born 'in the lifetime of the said John Martyn or after his decease'.[28] As it happened, he died just seventeen days after the birth of their second son, John.

It is an unsolved question whether or not John Martyn married Annie Smyth for her money. Accepting that most marriages in this class in post-Famine Ireland were economic contracts, it is tempting to believe that this couple was different. It is not beyond the bounds of possibility. John, after all, had lots of opportunity to save Tillyra, while Annie was still a mere child. It is possible that he felt a responsibility for the debts he owed his brothers and sisters, but it is not very likely. They were, by this time, all wealthy people in their own right. Perhaps he loved Tillyra and wished, in the end, to save it? Again, an unlikely premise; no affection for this demesne comes down to us through the pages of history from the Martyns. Certainly John and Annie's first born, Edward, by the time of his death hated it, albeit for myriad reasons. They had been in no hurry to go back to it after their wedding, which took place in the chapel at Leitrim, near Masonbrook. It was officiated by the Right Reverend Doctor D'Arcy, Lord Bishop of Clonfert, on 17 February 1857. John's best friend Sir Thomas Burke of Marble Hill and Sophie Bricknell (presumably a friend of Annie's) were witnesses.[29] The couple spent much of their time at Masonbrook and Annie's father and husband continued to perform their civic duties as magistrates in the area. Almost exactly two years later, Edward, soon to be know as Eddy but only by the family and very close friends, was born. At his baptism in Loughrea, his Smyth and MacDermott uncles were the main sponsors. The family cherished their Martyn heir. In March 1860 their second son, John, was born.

If John Martyn was not expected to live long into his marriage, it might have been assumed that Annie would continue to have the benefit of a strong male influence in her life in the shape of her father. This was not to be so. At the beginning of a very cold April in 1862, the *Loughrea Illustrated Journal* reported on 'the dangerous illness of James Smyth'. James had had a stroke while dressing for mass the previous Sunday. Grave fears for his ultimate recovery were entertained. The very best doctors and Surgeon O'Reilly from Dublin were in attendance. By August, however, when the Loughrea Regatta, an event often organised by John Martyn in the old days, was in full swing, the *Journal* could report 'a marked improvement in James Smyth's health'. James and Charlotte had spent the summer at the Lisdoonvarna Spa in County Clare where the more severe effects of the stroke were considerably relaxed. In the immediate years following, they lived a great deal of their time in their rented house at 103 Saint Stephen's Green, Dublin. No doubt the reason for this was to be close to James's doctors. But it was Charlotte who died there in 1867.[30]

There are few glimpses of Charlotte Smyth in the research of Edward Martyn's life. After his birth, when Annie had finally moved to Tillyra, mother and daughter were often to be seen together going about their charitable duties in various parts of south Galway. This stopped after James was taken ill, and we lose what little sight we have of her. Her death was a great blow to James, who, after returning to Masonbrook, died within the year. Annie still had her brothers and they had Masonbrook, but it was time to turn to the world beyond south Galway. Young Eddy had to be groomed for his inheritance.

4 Spa House and Baths, Lisdoonvarna, Co. Clare. The more severe effects of James Smyth's stroke were washed away in the sulphur baths.

Writing about Edward Martyn's sexuality in *Hail and Farewell*, George Moore reflects that the greater part of man's making is done before he comes into the world. Leaving sexuality aside for the time being, this is an apt observation. For the MacDermotts and Smyths had strengths to outweigh the Martyn 'weaknesses' and Edward inherited some of these strengths in spades. He needed them, for Annie, with the best will in the world, seemed to start him out on the wrong foot.

2 • Christk Versus Apollo

IN THE SPRING OF 1870 Annie set out for Dublin with her two young sons. She ignored the newly opened Athenry and Ennis railway, for which her father and husband had so strenuously campaigned. Instead, she took a canal boat from Limerick. Perhaps this was because she had a lot of luggage, including her carriage and horses, or maybe it was just more fun for the boys. It was a significant move. Edward's formal education was about to begin. The boy was no stranger to Dublin. He had spent time there with his grandparents at their house on Saint Stephen's Green. The summer holidays of 1868 had been enhanced by a visit to his Aunt Jane at Rosemount in Dundrum, under the purple tips of the Dublin mountains. That year, too, he made his first Holy Communion and was brought to Switzerland. It seems likely, however, that the bracing air of the Swiss Alps was more for the benefit of his little brother, John, whose health was a constant cause of concern. It was the start of European travel for the boys and Edward knew he liked it. Up until then, their education had been entrusted to governesses. Mrs Clancy was at Tillyra, while Miss Challoner was on call from Herbert Street when they were in Dublin. Edward's own voice from that time gives us some idea of his feelings when he remembered being 'forcibly dragged to Monsieur Garbois' Dancing Academy where I made scarce any progress beyond being taught to walk like a hen around the room'. But he also remembered that Monsieur Garbois 'dazzled my imagination with his talk of hunting and shooting and his rooms in Vienna and Paris'.[1]

In Dublin Annie settled into a large Victorian house at 47 Raglan Road, Ballsbridge, and promptly enrolled Edward at the Jesuit College in Great Denmark Street. Saint Francis Xavier's school, which did not become Belvedere College until the 1890s under the directorship of Father Thomas Finlay, had started out in Hardwicke Street in 1832 (a street where, in middle age, Edward Martyn would find his true spiritual home with the establishment of his own theatre). But by 1870 the school was well settled into Belvedere House in Dublin's north inner city.

'If I had been put on the right lines from the start', Edward once remarked to his cousin George Moore, 'my life might have been different'.[2] It is likely that he was talking about his Jesuit education. To a nature such as his, both mystical and independent, the Jesuit objective of fighting the world with the weapons of the world would never be an agreeable aspiration. As a previous biographer has remarked, an education with the Benedictines, whose great love of music and art matched Edward's, would have been a far more congenial option. However, Annie Martyn could not have been expected to know this. She relied on the advice of her friends and neighbours among the Galway gentry, some of whom believed that a good classical education was a necessary grounding for a landed Irish Catholic gentleman. It might have worked, had he been left in Belvedere. The image of the school that comes down to us from that period is one of relative comfort and kindness. It was populated by the sons of gentlemen, and around Dublin each morning the 'Belvedere Omnibus' trotted, picking up its 'fares' and delivering them safely to Great Denmark Street. There they entered the grounds of the magnificent eighteenth-century Georgian mansion through a small door in the wall.

At the age of 11, Edward Martyn, the embryonic aesthete, would have appreciated the large gracious rooms and the wonderful stuccoed ceilings of this beautiful building. And he certainly would have enjoyed Father John Green, the organist, who regaled the boys with his tales of miracles and marvels. Unfortunately he was not allowed to stay there. Belvedere was a mere stepping stone. There was not one Catholic school in Ireland that was regarded by the Irish gentry as good enough for the education of a wealthy landowner. So to England Edward must go. He was enrolled at Beaumont College (another Jesuit school) near Windsor in Buckinghamshire, where many of the titled sons of Catholic Europe were ensconced. So too were his cousins Augustus and Julian Moore (younger brothers of George) and a distant cousin, George de Stackpoole. He became very unhappy, not only as a result of his schooling.

'If you had been brought up as severely as I was …', Edward often said to George Moore in later life when excusing some timidity in his nature which might have given rise to an acerbic comment from Moore, leading us to believe that Annie had been a hard taskmaster; for Annie had the making of him up to the age of 11. Living on her own in Tillyra, after the death of John, she often had her brothers to stay. With both of her parents dead, she must have looked to them for advice. They were military men, as was Edward's Uncle Peter on his father's side. They knew the history of Edward's father. Did they fear for the boy? Did they constantly watch for signs of 'family weakness'?

Life in post-Famine Ireland was dramatically different to the Ireland of John Martyn's youth. It is possible that Annie looked back with horror on the life her husband had led before his marriage to her. Now, in the latter part of the nineteenth century, Victorian values, including those of sexual repression, abounded among the new Irish rural bourgeoisie and the gentry. They were valued by people and Church alike. It is likely that it was in these years that Edward Martyn developed his aversion to sex and especially to women, although never to mankind in general, something previous biographers have asserted. There is no evidence, however, that he ever accepted the responsibility of physical love, either of the homo- or heterosexual kind. It is most unlikely that the whole blame for this can be laid at the feet of Annie Martyn. In his late twenties, when Edward was at a particularly low and lonely period of his life, he wrote (but never published), among much other senti-mental poetry, the poignant lines

> … mysterious child
> oh would thou could'st live on undefiled.
> Gross manhood with angel genius wars
> Thou'lt change – alas

reflecting, perhaps, a more stressful childhood than that endured by the mere common experience of a dominant, albeit highly conventional, mother.

Since he was not happy, it is hardly surprising that Edward failed to shine at Beaumont, but all was not lost. The emphasis that they placed there on Latin and Greek stood to him all of his life. As soon as he was settled, Annie set up house at 8 Onslow Square in Kensington. This was a short distance from 39 Alfred Place, where the Moores of Moore Hall in County Mayo had their London establishment. The two families from the west of Ireland were naturally close and, although Edward's friendship was destined to be with George, the eldest and heir to the estate, in these early years he was generally in the company of the younger Moore brothers, who were contemporaries at Beaumont. The cousinship between the Moores and the Martyns was one not of blood but of marriage, and it reached back only to the marriage of George Henry Moore to Mary Blake in 1851. By 1870 Mary Blake Moore was also a widow, but her eldest son was 18 years old and already an embryonic sophisticate. He would soon leave home to follow a career as a painter in Paris. In the years to come, however, it was Moore the writer who would cause scandal to Annie Martyn.[3] In the meantime she was very glad of this family's friendship, and it is only through George Moore's gossipy letters to his mother and through his short early novels that we get to know Annie in middle age.

The school years were often interrupted by bouts of illness. In Edward's case they were never very serious, but this was not so for John, who joined him in Buckinghamshire two years after his own start there. In his diary for 1874 Edward notes 'John sick at Beaumont'. From then on his little brother stayed at home in Onslow Square and was tutored by 'Old Brown'. The diary is also revealing for these years in that it shows the Martyns taking almost all the long vacations in northern spa towns such as Harrogate or Scarborough. The year 1876 was an exception. They returned to Tillyra and, later that year, Annie's younger brother, James, died at the early age of 36. He was a childless widower living at Masonbrook and the cause of death, as stated on the certificate, was 'nervous exhaustion from days of convulsions'. This was almost certainly a euphemism for consumption. It was also the great fear for young John.

Annie's problems that year were aggravated when she was asked to remove Edward from Beaumont. His cousin George de Stackpoole was also expelled, as well as another Irish friend, George Hayden. The boys were removed because they attempted to burn down the dormitory in retaliation against the strict rule of no access to these quarters during the day.[4] The truth of this story is impossible to verify and the question remains: was there more to it? Naturally it was an experience that stayed with Edward Martyn. In his fourth play, *An Enchanted Sea*, the young protagonist, Guy Font, is expelled from school for causing the drowning of one of his schoolfellows.[5] But the fact that Edward was accompanied by two others in the expulsion shows us that he was not without friends in these years. And the friendship with George de Stackpoole, an amiable good-natured man who became a regular visitor to Tillyra, lasted long into middle age.

Edward got a good education at Beaumont. It was obvious, throughout his life, that he was a 'well-educated' man. Not merely 'well-read', but sharp in all the basics that a good education provides. This cannot be said of his friend Julian Moore, to whom brother George wrote in the 1880s, à propos a job for the former, 'you will be expected to write at least one language correctly can you do this'?[6] Edward did not pass any examinations. Nor did he go on to do a final year at Stoneyhurst, the most well known of the Jesuit schools in the English-speaking world, for a course in philosophy before going up to Oxford. This was usual for boys of his class. Perhaps they wouldn't have him or maybe it was merely owing to Annie's deep distrust and dislike of the Jesuits.[7] This dislike, which was probably enhanced by their treatment of Edward may, all the same, have its genesis only in her deep admiration and love of the Carmelites. As it was, Edward found himself with almost a year to kill before going up to Oxford. The diary merely states 'London'.

In May 1877 he matriculated to Oxford. Christchurch was the chosen college. When he got there, Oscar Wilde was still at Magdalen, albeit not in residence in his 'beautiful rooms'; he had failed to return in time for the first days of the Easter term in 1877, so the authorities had reassigned them. Wilde had been in Greece and would later complain that he was sent down for 'being the first undergraduate to visit Olympia'.[8] He was, of course, not 'sent down' and it was in 1877 that he developed his friendship with Walter Pater, the aesthete, novelist and critic, a friendship that Wilde's friend J.E.C. Bodly claimed had turned the youthful Oscar into an 'extreme aesthete'.[9] Pater and John Ruskin were the giants of the 'aesthetic movement' in Oxford at the time; a movement that looked to the past as a guide to the future. It stressed Britain's links with its European and, in effect, Catholic past. In these years Oxford gathered a disproportionate number of the best talents from Britain and abroad.

Walter Pater's belief that an aesthetic education offers us 'our one chance in life' would have been of great interest to even a young

Edward Martyn. Pater believed in aestheticism at its most fundamental level, that of sensation. Edward was in sympathy with these feelings.[10] It must have been very comforting for a young man from Loughrea to see how Pater loved the Carmelites for their aspiration to preserve the lofty charm of the Middle Ages. Although we have no voice to guide us from this period, the pattern of Edward's life afterwards paints a clear picture. He took no degree with him from Oxford, but it was during the years he spent there that he cultivated the aesthetic dimension in his life. Ultimately, this is what made that life bearable.

In common with everyone else at Oxford, especially the small Irish community, Edward was well aware of Oscar Wilde. There is no evidence that he admired him (Denis Gwynn, Edward Martyn's first biographer, tells us that Edward regarded Wilde as a 'poseur'), but Wilde believed that art could influence an improvement in society. If Edward, as a particularly young student, did not, at first, comprehend this, he learned quickly. He knew that Wilde was right. It seems highly likely that when the great aesthete went on to win the coveted Newdigate Prize and subsequently read his essay in public, the 19-year-old Edward, if he was in the audience, and he almost certainly was, would have experienced more than a frisson of pleasure. Not just because of the content of the lecture but because, at heart and throughout his life, he loved flamboyance.[11]

Choosing Christchurch was a fairly predictable move for Annie Martyn. The surprise was that she sent Edward to university at all. Over at Alfred Place, Mary Moore did not feel the need of a formal university education for her sons. Nor did many of the Galway gentry, especially the Catholics, who were, no doubt, cognisant of the displeasure such moves invoked among the hierarchy. Annie, however, was as much interested in social status as religion and the most influential family in south Galway, the Reddingtons, had sent their son, Christopher, to Christchurch. It was also the favoured college of the Clanricardes. Christopher Reddington's diaries of Oxford in the 1860s reveal that life for a young man from the west of Ireland, and a Catholic with it, could be almost exotic – certainly pleasurable. When Edward got there in the late 1870s, things were even better.

By then, Oxford University was far from anti-Catholic. John Henry Newman's reforms, which sought to put the university in touch with its medieval roots, had been in place for almost a generation. The 'pastoral principle', which encouraged older men to become mentors and protectors to their young students, operated in tutorial, and celibacy was encouraged. Benjamin Jowett was the Master of Balliol and liberalism was the *Zeitgeist*. This had not come about without a struggle. What was regarded as Newman's 'perversion' to Rome[12] had caused a backlash throughout the 1850s and 1860s and, in the wider arena, the Industrial Revolution was moving apace. There was a drift towards anti-intellectualism and materialism. The Crimean War and the great deficiencies in the British army, such as the abuse of enlisted men, were brought home to people as they had never been before. It was difficult to know how or what to think. At a level of idealism and intellectualism, Britain seemed to be losing its way. Some believed that its greatest danger lay in its dearth of ideas.

Then the liberals discovered Hellenism.[13] The Ancient Greeks had believed that they knew the best way to live. In Britain in the mid-nineteenth century many people, especially those at Oxford, came to agree with them. John Stuart Mill and Matthew Arnold, in particular, wanted to use Hellenism to lift Britain out of what they considered to be the uniformity and stagnation brought about as a side-effect of the Industrial Revolution.

At Oxford Jowett was the main agent for change. At his instigation, the curriculum shifted the Greats (the study of classical philosophy and history) from an emphasis on Latin towards Greek. Henceforth, anyone reading for a degree in *Literae Humniores* was likely to be steeped in Hellenism, as was Edward Martyn. His tutor was R.W. Macan, a scholar whose *magnum opus* was a voluminous translation of Herodotus. Macan later came to teach at Trinity College Dublin and much of his work made its way onto the shelves of the National Library of Ireland. He had hardly graduated himself when he became Edward's tutor (this was unfortunate for Edward, who would have greatly benefited from the influence of a mature mentor). Macan was very much involved with his own work; work that he approached as an historian rather than as a philosopher. His inspiration was a Prussian cobbler's son, Johann Joachim Winckelmann,[14] and the extent to which Edward learned to love Greek art for its 'noble simplicity, quiet grandeur and lack of passion' would indicate that he, too, had a direct line to Winckelmann. But Edward would not have been going to Benjamin Jowett's lectures just because his tutor had sent him (Jowett's lectures were always attended by people inside and outside Balliol). There were other influences.

The Catholics at Oxford, whilst they were welcome, were few and tended to cling together. This was made possible at the tiny Oxford Catholic Club, a Mecca for the lost, the lonely and the different. In the late 1870s Terence Woulfe Flanagan was there. He was Edward Martyn's cousin and Flanagan's best friend was Benjamin Francis Con Costelloe, Benjamin Jowett's favourite pupil.[15] Woulfe Flanagan and Costelloe were both at Balliol and Jowett was close enough to Costelloe to attend his wedding and give it his blessing. It was not a marriage made in heaven and it reflected, to some extent, the mix of natures that populated Oxford at this time. Costelloe's wife was Mary Smith, daughter of Robert Pearsall Smith, the great Evangelist. Her mother, Hannah, had written a bestseller, *The Christian Secret of a Happy Life*. Moving in the literary circles of late nineteenth-century New York and Boston, Mary was also very close to Walt Whitman, who regarded her as his 'bright particular star'. She met Con Costelloe at Harvard University and immediately fell in love with the 'short, dark, bearded, rather serious Irishman'. But, even though they had two children,[16] she wasn't long married to him when she met Bernard Berenson, the art historian. She left Costelloe and went to live with Berenson in Florence. When Costelloe died in 1899, she married Berenson within the year. Con Costelloe was a Home Ruler. He was also a devout Catholic and wrote for the Catholic Truth Society. One of the main bones of contention in the marriage, Mary told her friends, was Con's insistence that she believe in hell.[17]

These, then, were the Irish people Edward Martyn knew at Oxford. At the Catholic Club they all had another very special and mutual friend, Count Eric Stanislaus Stenbock. Stenbock was more than unorthodox, he was exotic. A great Estonian landowner and aristocrat, Eric added colour and notoriety to the lives of all those who came into contact with him. As late as 1893, just over a year before his death from cirrhosis of the liver, he was at Tillyra with Edward and Terry Woulfe Flanagan. Stenbock, writes his biographer, was 'witty, imaginative, generous and very rich'. He was also 'a pervert and a sick man'.[18] The Symbolist Arthur Symons said he had 'a vain desire to penetrate the core of evil', and, given that Stenbock entitled one of his poems 'The Ballad of the Dead Sea Fruit on an Apple tree that grew on the ruins of Sodom', there has to be some sympathy for Symons's critique. But he also wrote *Cradle Song*, which was a perfect lyric, and he figured in Yeats's 'lost generation' of poets. Stenbock spent only four terms at Oxford and it was in the spring term of 1879 that he met Martyn. If they did not meet at the Catholic Club in Oxford, an encounter could well have taken place in the company of the Discalced Carmelites in Kensington, London where both young men had friends among the friars.

What the Discalced Carmelites thought of this very odd man who, in his rooms, kept a red lamp burning continually between a Buddha and a bust of Shelley, while Fatima, an enormous toad, sat on his shoulders,[19] is not known. All that we can be sure of is that Edward liked him and maintained a close friendship with him until he died on 26 April 1895, coinciding with the opening day of the first trial of Oscar Wilde. For that year Edward simply wrote in the diary – 'troubles'. A calmer influence and the closest friendship Edward made at Oxford was with Nevill Geary. Geary, who was studying law, was a Protestant and recognised the Protestantism and paganism in Edward Martyn's nature. As we shall see, he would prove to be a staunch friend in times of crisis.

Edward's imagination could not but be fuelled by these people. But it was not helping him with his studies. The Deanery Records show him as being either *non satis* or *vix satis* in Latin and Mathematics, but he was *satis* in his studies of the *Odyssey*.[20] It was hardly surprising. He was enjoying himself but he must have been confused. All his education to date had come from the Jesuits and now he was following the new curriculum for Greats at Oxford. He was reading widely and, at the heart of all the reading was Plato. And, for many, Platonism was being used as a surrogate for Christianity. Among Edward's new friends were those who perceived Christianity to be a failing belief. Platonism also suggested the possibility, and the legitimacy, of love between men. Not, however, for Benjamin Jowett, who abhorred homosexuality.

Nevertheless, there was sexual ambivalence in Oxford Hellenism and, for many, homosexuality was a cultural ideal. Up until Oscar Wilde's catastrophe, Oxford Hellenism was considered to be a legitimising discourse for male love. Following the new curriculum meant reading Johann Winckelmann, who saw Plato in quite a different way from Benjamin Jowett. Winckelmann's affinity to Hellenism was not mainly intellectual but was enhanced by the fervent belief in romantic friendship between young men. For Johann Winckelmann, true beauty was male and never could be female. He considered that people who couldn't understand this could never understand true art. For the greater part of his life, Edward Martyn felt this. He also trod that fragile borderline which separated male bonding from homosexuality. The male club, which started for him at Oxford, became a sanctuary. If, on entering Oxford University in the spring of 1877, Edward Martyn had misogynistic tendencies, they had every reason to be greatly enhanced by the time he left the university in the autumn of 1879.

The backdrop to these Oxford years was one of land troubles and mounting violence in south Galway. William Gladstone's first Land Act in 1870, designed to give some protection to tenant farmers, largely failed because of a lack of co-operation on the part of landlords. But good agricultural prices had held up well into the middle 1870s and helped to maintain equilibrium between the two sides. By 1879, however, things had greatly deteriorated. Miserable weather conditions contributed to a very poor harvest. Grain prices tumbled and evictions owing to bankruptcy became commonplace. In August Michael Davitt founded the Irish National Land League, a mass movement of tenant resistance against landlords, with Charles Stewart Parnell as its first president. It landed in south Galway with a vengeance.

Returning to Tillyra in 1879, without a degree, the 20-year-old Edward Martyn was faced with these problems, mainly the non-payment of rents. This did not constitute, however, any shortage of money. Annie had shown herself a true daughter of James Smyth and had greatly increased his inheritance. Now she intended to spend £20,000. She had set in train extensive restoration work on the old house and castle, Tillyra. Edward was well aware of this for his neighbour, William Gregory of Coole Park, had made a special visit to him in Oxford to discuss it. In the prevailing social and political climate, Gregory did not think it was such a good idea. Edward, however, had little choice in the matter. He was not accustomed to thwarting his mother. There were big plans afoot for the heir to the Martyn dynasty and Annie wanted a near palatial house. In her eyes it was a very necessary appendage to his status in the community. But even at this tender age, Edward Martyn knew that it was unlikely he would ever want such a house or anything to do with the life to which Annie aspired. As it happened, it wasn't all that long before he felt confident enough to put in place arrangements that curbed her ambition and made her look at her son with new eyes.

3 • The Soul in Crisis

WHILE MARTYN WAS endeavouring to settle down to life at Tillyra, George Moore returned from Paris to live in London. It was 1880 and Moore's return would prove highly significant in Martyn's life. Moore was under an obligation to take some interest in his land in County Mayo. He found this hard to do, and as he got to know Martyn better, he was often fascinated to watch the extent to which his young cousin understood the practicalities of land ownership. Moore affected to be a Liberal while Martyn was a strong Unionist and remained so until the early 1890s. The older man could see the injustices in the system but his feelings about the tenants were much the same as those of Martyn. He didn't like them and he had no sympathy for their plight. He was realistic, however, about the changes that were coming. The 1881 Land Act finally granted tenants fair rents and fixity of tenure and Moore saw the beginning of the end for the Irish landlord. He became an embryonic Home Ruler, who had no compunction, however, in exacting his rents with the help of the Royal Irish Constabulary. 'The degenerate son of a worthy father' is how the *Connaught Telegraph* viewed him.[1]

In fact Moore often wanted to be worthy of his father, George Henry Moore,[2] but whether Edward ever thought of John Martyn, or was conscious of the humanitarian impulses of the latter, remains a mystery. All the male influences in his life had come from the men on his mother's side of the family and they were inbued with the insecurities of the *nouveau riche*. Still, the gregariousness of John Martyn was not completely lost, for there is evidence that John junior was very popular with the people. On one occasion he led them to victory in a faction fight with the Persse family.[3] It is clear that John, as the younger son, had a lot of freedom and little responsibility. What probably attracted Annie Smyth to John Martyn in the first place is well reflected in the little we know of their second son, who appears to have had a more cavalier attitude to life than was ever possible in the nature of his older brother.

Soon after Moore's return to London, where he intended to turn himself into a writer, Annie Martyn begged a favour of him. Would he be willing to become a mentor to her son and help him develop his cultural interests? This was Annie using her basic good sense. Moore had first met Edward Martyn when he was 'a bulky youth from Galway' and a friend to his younger brother, Augustus. Now after his years at Oxford, where no member of the Moore family had gone, the ungainly lad had a particular interest in high culture. Taking advantage of his classical education, Edward had already travelled to Greece and was attempting to write an epic poem based on his experiences. Moore had much to teach him. The writer's education had, after all, been picked up in French cafés. He could bring a different flavour to Edward's life. So for the next thirty years he figured largely in that life, at a broad cultural level. He came to love his shy and awkward cousin. By the time Moore sat down to write his great trilogy, *Hail and Farewell*, which is based on his years in Ireland, Edward Martyn had become for him, in truth, 'Dear Edward', remaining so for posterity.

In that same year, 1880, Edward Martyn came of age, which is how he describes it himself in the diary. He was in possession of 5,000 acres of land. His neighbour and friend, William Gregory, had a similar holding at Coole Park and, over at Masonbrook, his Uncle John Smyth had twice as much.[4] In July William Gregory brought his bride, Augusta Persse, to Coole for the first time and she was given a rousing welcome. One hundred of the Coole tenants sat down to dinner with the bride and groom.[5] This was not the relationship Martyn had with his tenants. At Tillyra there had always been friction. The mistrust that had come into the landlord–tenant relationship during the magistracy of the first Edward Martyn had seeped down through the generations. There was ill-will and it was compounded by Annie Martyn's ungracious dealings with the tenantry. After her death in 1898, when Edward had set in train negotiations to sell the land to the Land Commission, the Piper Corley, a well-known local musician, described to Douglas Hyde what life had been like in the 'old days' at Tillyra. It was, he told the poet, 'an ordeal to go there with fear in your heart and weakness in your feet and a sixpenny or maybe a threepenny thrust out at you then through the window'.[6] As late as 1901, Augusta Gregory notes in her diary that 'Edward neglects gracious things like, for instance, he gives no firing [firewood] to the people as we are doing though his woods are full of decaying timber.'[7]

In 1880 it was hardly likely to have been much better elsewhere. Most of the south Galway landlords feared their tenants. Agrarian outrage was rife and it was not unusual for public speakers to call openly for the murder of landlords – to 'be shot down like partridges' was one particularly vivid metaphor used. The times were ugly for the owners of land. Many did not venture outside their demesnes. Martyn's neighbours kept him advised of their dealings with their tenants. Maintaining a united front was essential. Even tenants who were friendly and loyal to William Gregory collapsed under the pressure of the Land League. Coming to maturity in this fearful atmosphere was hardly conducive to the carving of a brave man out of a timid, albeit stubborn, nature.

Being Catholics in a land of Catholics did not help. The League made no distinction between Catholic and Protestant landlords. The Martyns, all the same, must have taken comfort from their friendship with the clergy. Father Considine, the parish priest at Labane, was a regular visitor to Tillyra. As a nationalist he was likely to have information on the League's activities and plans. Prior knowledge, however, that your barn was likely to be torched on a given day did not necessarily make life any easier. So the Martyns gave themselves relief by staying away from south Galway for long periods. In 1880, before the reconstruction of the castle had started, they went to Oberammergau in the Bavarian Alps for the passion play and in 1881 they travelled to Italy.

George Moore, who had not yet acquired Edward as a travelling companion, did not join them on these trips, and it is unlikely that John Martyn went along either. John, despite his weak constitution, had followed the Smyth family tradition and had joined the army. He was commissioned into the Third Dragoon Guards when he was 19. In September 1881 he wrote to his mother, who was staying at the Shelbourne Hotel in Dublin, telling her that he liked soldiering. There is a poignant tone to the letter, however, reflecting a weak and sickly young man. 'I havn't [sic] heard from Eddy,' he writes, 'but I have from Bob and James who have offered me a colly [sic] pup.'[8] His bill for champagne, he tells her, was nearly £40. A year later they were all together again in Tillyra for the Hunt. But the hunting was stopped for fear of Land League assassinations and soon after that John fell ill. They all left for Menton in the south of France. It is clear that they returned to Ireland for the summer, but Martyn records in the diary that he 'wintered alone' at Tillyra in 1882/83.

When George Moore first started visiting Tillyra in the early 1880s, he recorded a flourishing social life. The stables were filled with hunters and Edward Martyn was a good horseman. Annie was grooming him to be the leading squire in the county. In all practical matters he was his mother's son and quickly got a reputation as a harsh landlord. Even at such a tender age he held extremely anti-democratic views and looked on Gladstone's land reforms, and his ideas for Irish Home Rule, with dread. He was also utterly opposed to Parnell, a position that would change within a decade. He was not alone in these sentiments. The early diaries of Augusta Gregory reflected similar feelings at this time, although her quarrel with Gladstone had more to do with Egypt than it had with Ireland.

The castle, when the work was completed, was a castellated house of two storeys with regularly disposed mullioned windows, corner turrets and battlements. There were prominent gargoyle sprouts and a fine gothic hall. Symmetrical gardens fronted the property and the old Norman tower remained. Soon it would put to good use. The work was done under the direction of the church architect George Ashlin, and it did not start properly until 1882. Some of the inside decoration, most of which was done by John Dibble Crace, took until 1891 to complete. By that time Martyn had bought much fine art, including a Monet and two works by Edgar Degas. He had also commissioned some stained glass from Aubrey Beardsley for the staircase, but this was not completed before the artist's early death. There was also stained glass by Crace, including a window featuring the Martyn armorial bearings. In the winter of 1883 he was alone in the midst of building chaos when he got the news of John Martyn's death on 5 March. The body was brought back and buried in the Martyn tomb at Kilmacduagh.

It is easy to imagine Edward Martyn's loneliness through that dark winter at Tillyra. The house was surrounded by a high grey stone wall and the trees were filled with rooks and ravens. Depression was looming on the horizon. He was 24 years old and now was an only child. Annie was ever more anxious for him to perform his duty; to become the master of Tillyra; to marry and provide heirs to the estate she had saved from ruin; to have influence in the community. He was proving to be a very difficult young man; a man unsure of his sexuality; a man who had been somewhat seduced, but mostly bewildered, by the Hellenism that had surrounded him during his years at Oxford; a man with a highly imaginative temperament whose inner life bore no relation to the humdrum life of an Irish Catholic landlord.

However, despite the confusions and what would become contradictions, he was a far from hopeless case. Annie had reason to be optimistic. He had learned to be self-sufficient and solitary but, at the same time, he enjoyed the company of many who shared his artistic interests. Despite his apparent misogyny, this did not preclude women; women came to play a major and positive role in his life. He loved filling Tillyra with guests and began to make a mark as a gracious host. Daisy Fingall, wife of the eleventh earl of Fingall and a distant cousin of the Martyns, fondly remembered her early visits to this pleasing castle. She recalled, with pleasure, 'the plain living and the good wine and the brilliant talk and thinking'[9] and how Edward Martyn carved the enormous joints 'as generously as a parish priest'. This contrasts with life at Roxborough Castle, the home of the Persses, where Augusta Gregory records, with disgust, in her diary for 22 July 1882 'seven soldiers in the Harness room drinking whiskey out of cups'. Still, Annie's ambitions had to be curbed.

In the summer of 1883, just a few months after John's death and while the work on the castle went on apace, Martyn made a decision. If he must live in, and be the master of, Tillyra, he would do so on his own terms. He set about creating his own space. When Moore came for his visit in September, he discovered that his young friend had restored and furnished the ancient Norman tower. He had acquired 'a room of his own' or, to be accurate, three rooms. The first floor of the tower was converted into a private chapel with wooden furniture copied from the paintings of Albrecht Dürer, and tall candlesticks. The second floor contained a strong wooden desk and was lit by Pre-Raphaelite stained-glass windows, designed by Edward Frampton, with representations of Chaucer, Milton, Dante, Shakespeare and Plato. This was Edward's study. At the top, he had a bedroom with a flagstone floor, a *prie-dieu* and a very narrow bed. Annie was astonished. She did not recognise this

5 The Norman Tower at Tillyra, where Edward created 'a room of his own'.

budding medievalist and it would take her some time before she could come to accept the unlikelihood that he would ever exchange this 'monk's cell' for a marriage bed.

This religious fervour, nevertheless, was tempered with reason and Edward Martyn had every intention of making the world his monastery. While he often wrote of his loathing of the earth, it was a sentiment that was somewhat belied by his pleasure in being a part of it. Even then, he had a hankering to be at the centre of things, while at the same time remaining above the fray. He was enjoying his money and the freedom it gave him, especially in the realm of patronage. In 1884 a bell tower, funded by Edward, was added to the local church at Labane, Annie paid for the high altar of Sicilian marble. He was young, and he knew he wanted to be a writer. There was plenty of time to write the misery out of his life.

In middle age he published a poem entitled 'Youth':

> Oft in the sad and wayward youth of man
> Come moments full of pure and earthly peace
> Like Frankincense in stillness sweet
> Who can describe its short exquisite release
> From mental anguish lurching to despair
> Toiling youth thwarted from each wished for end
> And make it loath this fair earth, sea and air

What was 'each wished for end'? There is no knowing when he wrote this. Much of the poetry he published in the *Leader* in 1911 had been written at an earlier stage. He often told Moore that he could never do what he wished to do and yet it is not entirely clear what it was, in the long run, that prevented him doing anything he wished to do, other than, perhaps, his own fearful nature. He lacked guile and he was never good at hiding his feelings. George Moore admitted that it was Edward's 'psychological admissions that made him so agreeable a travelling companion' on their many trips to Europe.

Moore, who was carefully watching and listening, had no compunction at using his friends' lives for the making of good copy. George Russell (Æ) wrote of him: 'He gets every ounce of copy out of his friends that he can, regardless of their feelings.'[10] In 1887 he published *A Mere Accident*, a novella about a young Sussex squire. This is one of three novellas, all of which are based on the young life and thoughts of Edward Martyn. In *A Mere Accident*, the hero John Norton/ Edward Martyn is a young man who has a difficult relationship with his mother. She was a woman who loved her son in 'her own cold hard way'. She possessed a sharp, determined mind and taught her son to deal efficiently with all the business of running a large estate. More than anything else, she wanted him to marry well and to take his place in society. But John/Edward doesn't like women – 'I don't think I could live with a woman; there is something very degrading, something very gross in such relations. There is a better and purer life to lead,' he says.

6 Shelbourne Hotel, Dublin *c.*1900. The Moores and the Martyns were there for the 1884 'Season'. George Moore wrote his mother: 'marriage is of course the ruling topic of conversation and poor Eddy causes them all the deepest inquietude'.

Moore was studying his 'subject' even as he created him. In a letter to his mother from the Shelbourne Hotel, in February 1884, at the height of the 'Dublin Season', he wrote: 'marriage is of course the ruling topic of conversation and poor Eddy causes them all the deepest inquietude'.[11]

Forcing Edward Martyn to take part in the social life of Dublin in the 1880s must have been torture for the young man. Perhaps Moore tried to protect him, for in May 1884 his mother accuses him of 'having quarrelled with Mrs. Martyn'. He reassured her 'we are the best of friends possible – what you heard was only the scandal of Dirty Dublin'.[12] This Dublin is well documented in Moore's novel *A Drama in Muslin*, where he describes 'threadbare streets, broken pavements, unpainted hall doors, rusty railings' and the total vulgarity of the

'Dublin Season', which was nothing more than a marriage market where, he knew, Edward Martyn had no place.[13] Edward's celibacy, Moore wrote, was more than 'the whim of a young man who thinks that a woman might rob him of his ideals'.[14] Annie was a gregarious woman and she was enjoying 'the Season', an occasion she had been denied in her own youth. Always dressed in fashionably cut silks, she was, as well as keeping her eyes open for a bride for Edward, chaperoning Mary Martyn, his first cousin, eldest daughter of his Uncle Andrew. Mary was being launched in society. The women seemed, Moore wrote to his mother in July 1885, 'to be getting on very well in the social way. May has a knack for making friends.'[15] It wasn't until 1895, however, that Mary Martyn married. She chose Peter Hemphill and established a family connection with Constance Lloyd, the wife of Oscar Wilde. Peter Hemphill was a Protestant; sectarianism never had a role to play in the Martyn family.

'Edward is hard at work at his poems,' Moore also wrote in his letter to his mother in July. When they were not at Tillyra or at the Shelbourne Hotel, the friends lived in separate lodgings in the Temple in London. Edward was at Pump Court, living with Nevill Geary,[16] while Moore had rooms in Dane's Inn. In April they had been to Paris together, where Moore was endeavouring to interest Edward in current French painting. He was successful in so far as his 'student' eventually bought the Monet and the two paintings by Degas. In his role as mentor, however, Moore was prepared to go only so far. When, on 4 May, they met Emile Zola at the Palace of Industry, the writer did not introduce his young cousin. In the early years of his writing life Moore had regarded Zola as his maître and in 1885 he was still somewhat in awe of him. With his usual good nature, Edward told his friend Gerald O'Donovan of how he had been left to fend for himself while Moore promenaded the gallery with the great man.[17] Still, Moore was fairly assiduous in keeping an eye on his young protégé. When he found him wearing good strong Galway boots in the drawing rooms of Kensington, he recommended patent leather shoes instead. The 'bulky youth' from the West took the advice and acquired a pair of fashionable shoes but he soon went back to his boots. He didn't intend to frequent too many drawing rooms.

Drawing rooms, nevertheless, were where people met other people in this late Victorian era. And frequenting them, for George Moore at

7 St. Stephen's Green, Dublin *c.*1900.

this time, had a specific intent. He was looking for Walter Pater because he wanted Pater's approval for his work. This he never got, but he did get to know the man a little. He didn't introduce Edward. That Edward Martyn read Pater's great novel *Marius the Epicurean*, which was published in 1885, however, is certain. It was all the rage in literary circles. It is the story of a young man growing up and seeking some truth among the philosophies current during the reign of the Roman Emperor, Marcus Aurelius, in the second century AD.[18] The hero, Marius, is attracted to Christianity but, by the time of his death, is still in a confused state and not a committed believer. His father died when he was an infant and the boy had had a pious, unquestioning upbringing. When he came into his estate it 'had come down to him much curtailed through the extrava-gance of a certain Marcellus two generations before'.[19] He lived much in the realms of the imagination and was something of an idealist 'constructing the world for himself in great measure from within' and always 'with a certain incapacity wholly to accept other man's valuations'.[20] An emotionally self-absorbed young man, Marius moved from writing poetry to writing prose. (Before he became known for his prose work in 1893, Walter Pater burned all his own poetry.) With 'an habitual longing for a world fairer than that he saw',[21] Marius went through life with the fear of death always on him. This fear of death also dogged Edward Martyn throughout his life.

Did he, at the age of 26, identify with Pater's hero who, up to the time of his death, was wrestling a crisis of conscience on the validity of Christianity? What is certain is that in this period, the autumn/winter of 1885, when so many people were talking about Pater's book, Martyn burned his own poetry; the epic Greek poem that he had been working on since leaving Oxford. On 15 October George Moore had written to his mother: 'Edward is still writing poetry,' so the destruction came later in the year. Its failure brought him to the edge of a nervous breakdown and, for a period, over the edge. The diary reports that he spent the summer and autumn of 1885 in London and that he was 'ill'. But was it just the work? Writing his novella *A Mere Accident*, not much more than a year later, George Moore has his hero, John Norton/Edward Martyn, reading *Marius* and, as a result of reading it, claiming, 'I was made known to myself.' He learned that 'it was possible somehow to come to terms with life'. As we shall see, this did prove to be a liberating time for Edward Martyn. Well, a form of liberation at least.

By February 1886 Moore's correspondence reveals: 'I have just returned from Paris where I spent a pleasant fortnight with Edward. We saw a great many painters and pictures, writers and books. I persuaded Edward to buy two pictures.'[22] So the period of acute crisis passed relatively quickly.

But was the poem any good? There is little point in speculating. It is lost. Unlike his personal papers, which were left in the apparent safe-keeping of his friend Cyril Ryan, Provincial of the Carmelites, in Clarendon Street, Dublin and subsequently 'lost', this act of destruction was all his own work. There is no recorded reaction from Moore, but it shocked other friends. Henry Barnett, the editor of the *Court and Society Review*, wrote to Martyn: 'You have made a great sacrifice and one which I cannot think altogether wise or justifiable. Yet I do respect

you for it. There are few men who would have done what you have
done; and however much I must regret the results of it, I admire your
fortitude and conscientiousness.'[23] It is in a long letter from Nevill Geary
that we learn something of the state of Edward's mind at the time and
some understanding of what the poem was about. 'Your reasons', he
wrote to Edward regarding the destruction, 'are

> (1) The subject and philosophy are not compatible with your
> belief as a Christian and a Catholic and (2) That in future you
> wish to write 'only what is conducive to the Glory of God rather
> than to the poor gratification of personal vanity. Now I am not
> a Catholic', wrote Geary the lawyer, 'but I do believe in the
> existence of God, and I furthermore write as your friend as to
> (1) Whether any particular writing is or is not incompatible with
> a Christian's belief is just a question of fact. Now I would never
> advocate publishing anything directly contrary to Christianity,
> nor would I do so myself. So if you are thoroughly convinced
> that what you have written is directly prejudicial your duty is not
> to wait or to ask anyone's advice but to put it in the fire at once.
> As a matter of fact I perceived nothing whatever incompatible
> in your poems as far as I can read; how could there be in the
> Pheidias and Pericles?'
>
> 'If there is a *bona fide* doubt', Geary continued … , 'is it not a
> direct principle of Catholicism to submit your conscience to that
> of the priest … , why not consult some eminent theologian of
> your church thereon? This at all events is what Pascal did. As to
> (2) that you would only write what is conducive to the Glory of
> God and not to gratification of personal vanity – that is a broad
> assertion, it would stop all poetry by Catholics as you. If your
> proposition were universally applied, how would the world
> progress? Or are you going to leave its progress to be conducted
> by atheists? Further, is it not a little *presumptuous* to consider that
> anything you or the uninspired man would write would conduce
> to the Glory of God. Let a man improve the talents with which
> God has endowed him, and if it pleases God to make use of the
> result … will it not be reckoned to the advantage on the last day?
>
> I do not think your talent lies in the way of hymns or
> theology, but rather for poetry; all your object is to write poetry

to the best of your ability. You write it as poetry, not as theology, in which you are not an expert. Pascal showed the Voltairians and the Encyclopaedists of the eighteenth century that a man could be an exquisite reasoner and a good Catholic. Do you show the nineteenth century that a man can be an exquisite modern poet without a taint of infidelity. Poetry is indifferent in itself so long as there is no anti-Christian intention. You are not bound to force religion into things indifferent. There is a good old-cavalry maxim: "Commit your soul to God and charge home".

'I trust you will pardon this long argument', Geary concluded, 'but it seemed to me somewhat monstrous that you should cut yourself off from a harmless interest in life on account of a proposition which I can hardly consider to be theology, viz. that every man is bound to write nothing but that which he considers in his own mind will be directly conducive to the Glory of God in the mind of any reader.'[24]

Since, in the long term, there was no apparent attempt on Edward Martyn's part to write anything specifically for the Glory of God while, like many a writer, he wrote a great deal for the 'gratification of personal vanity', it is possible that he listened a little to Geary's arguments. For some years after, he continued to behave like a young man in crisis. He wrote a further letter to Henry Barnett on New Year's Eve 1885,[25] threatening to withdraw his subscription to the *Court and Society Review* if George Moore's new novel, *A Drama in Muslin*, which was being serialised by the magazine, contained any offence against faith or morals (this was six weeks before Moore brought him to Paris). Barnett, who desperately needed Martyn's money if not his friendship, was highly placatory. The serial version of the book did leave out much of the passionate sex scenes of one of the characters, May Gould, and glossed over the lesbianism of Cecilia Cullen, the heroine's best friend. And then there was the problem that the heroine was an atheist. There is no direct evidence of the extent to which Edward was upset by the book. In his vunerable state, perhaps he did not even read it, although there is ample evidence that he read most of Moore's work and was often a useful critic. Moore was in trouble, anyway, in south Galway; Annie Martyn had banned him from Tillyra because of his depiction in the novel of the parish priest, who was so obviously inspired by their own Father Considine at Labane. Indeed, Moore was never allowed to go to mass at Labane again. It was a great relief to him until he realised that he was still expected to go to mass if he stayed at Tillyra, only now he had to go all the way to the Catholic church in Gort.

In the event Martyn did not publish any poetry for over twenty years. His bizarre behaviour in the late 1880s continued with a formal request to his bishop that he be given permission to read books that had been condemned by the Vatican and placed on the *Index Expurgatorious*. Bishop MacCormack was a little surprised. It was generally accepted that a man in Edward Martyn's position would understand that this *Index* was meant as a warning against being influenced by the ideas in the books and not necessarily a bar to reading them. Edward explained to the bishop that his confessor advised him to seek exemption. He said they were given and he himself had had one from Rome. 'I hope you will not think that I ask this favour with a view of abusing the great privilege.'[26] The bishop did not feel competent to deal with the matter and referred him directly to the Vatican through the auspices of Dr Kirby, Rector of the Irish College in Rome, to whom Edward wrote: 'I have in my library books of general literature, philosophy etc., a few of which I have heard are on the Index ... it would, therefore, be of immense relief to my mind if I were to obtain an exemption from the rules of the Index. ... I am in my thirtieth year.'

The most surprising thing about this last letter is its date. By 1889 it appeared that Edward Martyn had settled down and had gone on to other things. He was living a good life and was writing in other genres. He seemed determined to cut himself off from, and to denigrate the work of, writers and artists of the aesthetic movement of the last quarter of the nineteenth century, where he might have been expected to find his natural home. In 1887 he wrote to George Moore's friend Edward Dujardin cancelling his subscription to the *Revue Indépendante* because he didn't like the contents of an article by Joris-Karl Huysmans entitled 'Le tableau de Bianchi au Louvre'. Dujardin was extremely perturbed and asked George Moore to intervene. Moore replied: 'I will write to Martyn with pleasure but I don't think there is the least use in doing so. Martyn is an intelligent fellow but when there is any question of religion he ought to be under lock and key.'[27] Huysmans, who started his writing career with some naturalistic novels, had moved into the realms of the aesthete. He created characters who turn their backs on the world as it is, like Des Esseintes in *À rebours*, to develop a world of sensuousness and artifice within which to cultivate extremes of self-awareness, profound selfishness. Just the kind of characters Edward Martyn, in time, would create.

Sensuousness and artifice went on to play leading roles in Martyn's life. It was his consciousness of this side of his nature and his belief that it came into conflict with his religion which made him so fearful. Some time in the 1880s he decided that he was going to live within, and strictly adhere to, the basic tenets of the Catholic faith. He decided that he needed to live inside certain boundaries and, because of his upbringing by Annie Martyn, those set out by the Catholic Church suited his public persona, if not his temperament or his cultural and artistic preferences. Whenever he perceived himself to have strayed, he would pull back. This stultified his art and would go on to make his life very difficult, for in Edward Martyn, as George Moore rightly observed, Christianity did not absorb the old paganism. They existed side by side within his nature, causing a need within him to constantly reassure himself that he was a 'good Catholic'. At the *fin de siècle*, he was living in an era of 'new truths'. He was not always able to close his mind. In the end it was the acceptance of 'new truths' which made him brave, although he had a long way to go.

4 • 'Strength without hands to Smite'

IN 1887 QUEEN VICTORIA celebrated her Golden Jubilee. By and large, the gentry of south Galway still respected her, but would not for much longer. In the spring Edward Martyn took a trip to the French Riviera and then to Paris, where he bought the painting by Claude Monet. Moore documents this purchase as taking place a year earlier, but 1887 seems more likely. It is the latter year that Martyn records in the diary. Throughout the summer months the social life of County Galway was very lively. The residents of Coole Park, Tillyra, Castle Taylor and Lough Cutra were in and out of each other's houses daily. Algernon Persse, of Roxborough Castle, had married Norah Gough of Lough Cutra in 1886, much to the displeasure of the Gough family. Not one of the Persse brothers was considered a good match. They were drinkers and gamblers and in the long run Algernon and Norah did suffer greatly at the hands of William Persse, Algernon's older brother. He gave them the estate at Roxborough to run after the death of the eldest Persse, Dudley, but he quickly took it back and then set out successfully to kill himself with drink. Both Dudley and William Persse died in madness. Melancholia was strong among the gentry of south Galway; they could see no clear future for their class.

Augusta Gregory documented these events in her diaries.[1] She wrote of William Persse: 'he could not resist and the mind was going and he would have brought shame and trouble on us all'.[2] Her own late marriage to Sir William Gregory was successful. She was glad to be in Coole Park with her little boy, Robert, and she was always happy in the company of 'Mr Martyn', who, in the following years, became for her 'dear kind Edward Martyn'. She was particularly friendly with his cousin, Comte Florimonde de Basterot, who often visited Tillyra from his summer home at Durus, just outside Kinvara. The Gregorys had a summer home in Finavarra and Augusta Gregory had known Florimonde's father, Bartholemew, all her life.

The de Basterots, whose connections with south Galway came about first through intermarriage with the French family and then through marriage into the O'Briens of Fairfield,[3] lived for the greater part of the year in Rome. In November 1887 the old Comte de Basterot, Bartholomew, who had been born in 1800, died there. Augusta Gregory gives us a vivid description of the requiem mass in San Luigi's, which was 'mummery, incense and gestures and indifferent choristers singing responses and a coffin with a cloth embroidered with skulls over it'.[4] She wrote that Florimonde ought to have been ashamed at asking them to witness it. Indeed, it hardly seems a fitting end for a member of such an aristocratic French family, whose ancestors had once headed the *Parlement* of Bordeaux. They had done much for south Galway. Florimonde's paternal grandfather, James, provided the land for the building of Kinvara parish church and then filled it with decorative art. He also built the quay at Kinvara which was later completed and extended by Robert Gregory.[5] These two men, with more imagination and ingenuity than the average landlord, planned a canal to join Kinvara to the Fergus river and worked hard to get local flour mills operated by wind power.[6]

Lady Gregory wasn't just angry with Florimonde. She was in a pugnacious mood all that winter. Her diary entry for 25 November reads: 'Dined at the Denbighs, rather dull, all catholics or perverts except Lady Louisa Legge.' On 4 December she records a tea party where there were 'too many women'. And on another occasion she 'fainted at dinner' and was grateful that 'only the Gearys were there'. She had constant headaches and then, to compound her misery, she got news, through de Basterot that her erstwhile lover, Wilfrid Scawen Blunt, was in prison in Loughrea. Blunt was an anti-imperialist who had been supported by her in his Egyptian nationalist campaigns in the early 1880s[7] and was now heavily involved with Irish nationalism and the Land League in the heart of what could be considered to be Augusta Gregory's own 'turf'.[8] An English landlord, diplomat and politician, Blunt considered the Land League's aspirations entirely legitimate. He

8 Edgar Degas: *Two Ballet Dancers.* It hung in the Rose and Gold Drawing Room in Tillyra, alongside the Corot and the Monet. W.B. Yeats had not expected Martyn to have such fine taste and was reluctantly impressed.

was addressing a meeting at Woodford, County Galway, when he was arrested. Initially he got out on bail, but in early 1888 he was committed to Galway jail and then to the prison at Kilmainham in Dublin. What started out as a novel experience soon became wearisome and difficult. He was very grateful when Augusta Gregory appealed to her fellow landlords, including her husband and Edward Martyn, who were members of the Grand Jury in Galway, for lenient treatment of him during his incarceration.[9] As a result, he did benefit from his class and status.

While the Irish landlords were sympathetic to Blunt at the level of friendship, they did not like his political activities. William Gregory had supported him for a while over the Egyptian nationalists[10] but in his capacity as an Irish landlord he held other views. He was also very keen to collect his rents. So was Edward Martyn, who was described in this period as being 'most extreme in his landlord views, and no man on the Galway Grand Jury – which he regularly attended always wearing his hat in the room – was more severe, strict and hard on the popular class, in measuring out compensation for malicious injuries'.[11] He was trying to live up to Annie's expectations but, as with drawing rooms, he would soon part company with jury chambers.

It wasn't all heavy weather. There was fun too. In this period Nevill Geary wrote him a highly appreciative letter of a visit he had recently made to Tillyra: 'It was perfectly delightful,' he wrote, 'every luxury of civilisation with the ease of bachelor life … everything to gratify every intellectual and bodily pleasure, the delightful soft Irish atmosphere, the stroll over the park down to watch the sun setting over Galway Bay, and those wild rides in the heather-covered mountains with the views over the level green plain … the easy placid mornings over fire and books: and then again I am harping over the wicked luxury of, after a day's hunt, the champagne rolling down one's gullet lovingly, and the skin tight with wine and meat, lying on the hearth listening to the organ wailing out some medieval chant of grief and triumph.' Then Geary went on with the gossip: 'I fear you will be greatly grieved to hear of a sudden and permanent catastrophe that has fallen on a friend of ours, F.R., he has become *engaged* to a young lady. He is very much in love. I have seen him several times in a state I can only compare to drunkenness.' He tells an anecdote about Oscar Wilde: 'In mixed company, the talk fell on Rome. Wilde said, very bored, "Oh don't talk of Rome. It's the Whitely of Art."' And of their old friend Barnett: 'he has again disappeared leaving a legacy to the *Court and Society Review* a libel action from a writing of his therein'.[12]

Martyn was settling in to life. He attempted to use his environment as a backdrop to the development of short-story fiction, setting scenes in great Irish houses on country weekends. One long attempt survived in his papers and was reproduced by his first biographer.[13] Like all embryonic writers, Edward wanted to put his feelings about everything into his story. His dialogue was poor (George Moore wrote in the margin 'did ever people talk to people like this?' Later E.M. would describe such dialogue as people 'talking essays to each other'), but his descriptive passages are atmospheric. The plot, such as it is, is the friction between landlord and tenant in Ireland and the situation is an idealised version of Tillyra. Gerald Crofton, the hero, is entertaining an old college friend in his demesne in south Galway, where 'the surrounding countryside looked less desolate than other parts of the west of Ireland. The few houses had a comparative air of prosperity and the rich green fields were fenced with neat walls.' Crofton's house was set 'in a small park furnished with huge old ash trees and spreading beech' and the house was 'built of a grey stone which age had encrusted with mellow orange-toned lichen'. Over the front door was the inscription *Welcome to all for this is the house of liberty.*

At this stage in his life, Martyn's notion of 'liberty' was a highly restrictive one. In the story the friends sit among great Impressionist paintings in a library that included well-thumbed editions of Plato, Schopenhauer, Goethe and Winckelmann, as well as 'all the great English writers'. The post-prandial conversation turned to the Italian *Risorgimento* that Crofton/Martyn hated. For the Italians he had, at this point in his life, nothing but irrational contempt. They were 'a people whose real genius consists in the drilling of ballet girls and the manufacture of *bonbons*'. He compared what he considered the degeneracy of the new Italian nation to that of the great Prussian nation which had been brought to greatness by men of genius 'with iron and blood and in spite of all opposition'.[14]

He uses his character, Crofton, as a mouthpiece to vent his own spleen on the Italians, whom he describes as 'vain, verbose, degenerate and utterly wanting in sentiment for art and beautiful things'. In this writing we see the start of the extravagant prejudices Martyn often indulged in when he took up his pen and which, when not modified by a ruthless editor such as George Moore, spoiled much of his creative writing. It also affected his critical articles, which otherwise had merit. In this instance, however, the extreme feelings are bound up with his loyalty to the Catholic Church. It had been under siege for some years from hostile Italian governments, often Liberal or left of centre, and supported in the main by public opinion.

There was also a north/south cultural divide to be considered. Martyn was, as his close friends knew even if he didn't recognise it himself, culturally more Protestant than Catholic. Despite the 'gloomy Protestant Churches' he visited on his travels, a part of him was attracted to the puritanical culture of Northern Europe. It was there he found his heroes in the shape of Frederick the Great, Albrecht Dürer, Henrik Ibsen and Richard Wagner. Thomas Carlyle, the nineteenth-century writer, biographer and polemicist, was also warmly admired. This was a difficult position for a man who had been born into, and nurtured by, the Irish Catholic Church; essentially a peasant church with little intellectual or aesthetic leanings. Where would he find his friends?

Martyn wanted to write about Ireland. He had an instinctive and sensuous feeling for the landscape and he was beginning to take some interest in politics on the broader scale. In his story, he abuses absentee landlords, describing them as 'flunkeys' who exchange their birthrights for London drawing rooms (this careless use of cliché is also something which continued to mar his work). When it is suggested to Crofton/ Martyn that he too spends time in drawing rooms, the hero protests: "Quite so! But I know my own country better than any other place, and I live here longer than elsewhere; and I am more in touch with my countrymen than with any others. It is a poor thing to be a stranger in one's own country. 'You are right', replies his friend, 'indeed you ought to be happy – apparently able to do what you like'. 'No, I am not', he answered with a quick look full of the most painful meaning, 'I am *never* able to do what I like.'"

The writer and historian W.E.H. Lecky was a regular guest at the Gregory dinner table in these years. It was reading Lecky's *History of Ireland in the Eighteenth Century* which Edward Martyn claimed had turned him into an Irish nationalist.[15] The book was first published in 1892 when Martyn's nationalism was beginning to blossom. But in the late 1880s, when they were meeting around the table, Lecky was as great a champion of the Unionist cause as his host and his fellow guests. Indeed it was he who remained so while his hostess, after the death of her husband, and many of his fellow guests, did not. In the 1880s Home Rulers were considered either fools or traitors by many of the Irish gentry.[16] Democracy was anathema; a threat to liberty and, above all, a threat to private property. Private property was regarded as the supreme political and social good; property owners were perceived to be the people who had the leisure and the education to devote to politics.

Parnellism was a combination of democracy, nationalism and socialism, and the Land League was regarded, by Martyn and his peers, as socialism in action in Ireland. It led to egalitarianism and, as an extremely reactionary Roman Catholic at this time, this was not an ideology with which he was likely to have any truck. Nevertheless his brand of Catholicism did not give rise to any problem for him when it came to Lecky's description of priestly despotism as 'scandalous'. And he agreed that the Home Rule leaders were backed by 'the most ignorant, the most priest-ridden portion of the community'.[17] He was staunchly anti-clerical. The Irish clergy were, after all, highly 'populist', and Martyn, a well-read man, looked back to the French Revolution, and the role the French clergy had played in it, with some knowledge and some dread.

Later in life Edward Martyn remarked that his principles were usually those of the company he kept. This was not true, but in the 1880s it nearly was. However, W.E.H. Lecky was on the liberal side of Unionism. So too were the Gregorys and many of the other south Galway landlords and some influential Catholic families such as the Reddingtons. Martyn, however, was not. The time was drawing near when he would stop being a Unionist, but he would never become a Liberal. In November 1885 Gladstone had been returned to power in Britain with a large majority. He had a personal commitment to Home Rule for Ireland. It was not shared by all the Liberal Party, which was split between Radicals and Whigs. The Whigs were the wealthy aristocratic landowners who believed they had been born to rule and with whom Gladstone had some sympathy. The Radicals were mainly made up of religious Nonconformists, who believed they could rule and transform society in alliance with the working class. It was surprising that Gladstone, a traditional Tory in many ways, threw in his lot with the Radicals. On the Irish Question, however, he was almost messianic and he believed he could carry a majority of the party with him. It was a great mistake. In 1885 the Whigs, led by the Marquis of Hartington, did not enter Gladstone's cabinet. And in March 1886 Joseph Chamberlain, a Radical, joined them on the outside. Chamberlain was in a position to persuade other Radicals against Gladstone on Home Rule for Ireland, which he did. On 8 June the Home Rule Bill was lost by thirty votes and the great Liberal Party of Britain was irrevocably split.

In late 1887 Christopher Reddington, then Under Secretary of State for Ireland, wrote to Martyn requesting that he throw in his lot with the Gladstonian Liberals. He got short shrift. The occasion arose in late 1887 when Lord Ripon and John Morley, who had been Chief Secretary to Ireland during the period of the doomed 1886 Home Rule Bill, were to visit Dublin. Reddington wanted Martyn to form a part of the reception committee. He pointed out to him that no one had spoken 'more justly or fairly on the Irish Land Question than John Morley'.[18] Martyn wrote in reply:

> On this morning I received your letter asking me to act on the Committee of reception in connection with the visit to Dublin of Lord Ripon and J. Morley. There is no influence that would persuade me so quickly as yours to take action in such cases in general, albeit I feel myself utterly unfitted to mingle in politics, for which I have consequently rather a distaste. But by filling the position to which you now invite me, I would be going against all my ideas of political and moral right, although at the same time I am fully cognisant of the insignificance of the importance of my ideas to everybody except myself. I am therefore obliged to refuse you with sincere regret. This is not the place to argue the merits or demerits of Home Rule. I will only say that I do not believe the people of Ireland really desire it; and that any attempt to rally the forces of the so-called National Party after the severe blow which they have received over here by the more or less efficient carrying out of the law, and in England by the success of the Hartington and Goschen meetings at Dublin, seem to me so mischievous that if I were to help on such an attempt in ever so small a way, I should always consider myself more or less responsible for the inevitable result of boycotting and murder which are certain to ensue upon the restoration of the League to its former vigour. I will, of course, keep your communication strictly private and hope you will excuse my being so outspoken to one who is older and of infinitely better judgement. However, I feel this to be a case where a man must judge for himself if he is ever to judge at all. I am no politician and belong to no party only I believe in Hartington and Goschen more than in Ripon and Morley.
>
> Yours very sincerely,
> Edward Martyn

It was hardly surprising that he felt like this in 1888. He was, to a very large extent, a born Whig. He believed in property and the rights and responsibilities that go along with ownership of land; all good Whig principles. But, even by this time, he had developed a nature that was full of contradictions, and in refusing to meet John Morley he was doing himself a disservice, for Morley was the kind of man who fascinated Edward Martyn. Having set his face so firmly against any form of Liberalism, this seems an unlikely prospect, but Morley was a complex character. He ploughed his own furrow fearlessly and never ceased to believe in the perfectability of man. He was no Victorian prig, although it was fashionable to refer to him as such (E.M. referred to him as a 'blasphemous prig'). He admired Walter Pater and George Eliot alike and he used his editorship of newspapers and journals to preach their gospel. If he was too hopeful, too rational, it was hardly a fault. Morley had a genius for friendship and, had they met, he might well have seduced Martyn, despite his belief that the world was disengaging from 'the shifting sands and rotting foundations of theology'.[19] Later, when he had more confidence about what might or might not influence his relationship with God, and had less animosity towards Liberalism, we find him and Augusta Gregory enjoying Morley's lecture on Frederick the Great, given to the Carlyle Centenary meeting in London in 1895. Gregory describes it as 'a great delight'.[20] It is likely that in 1888 it was more than just Morley's attachment to land reform and his abhorrence of the coercion tactics of the British government that stopped Martyn from wanting to meet him. It was the attraction of Morley's ideas and fear of his capacious mind.

From 1888 to 1890 the political tempo in Ireland quickened. Parnellism was at its height. Coercion was increased. Land troubles continued and Parnell's colleagues John Dillon, William O'Brien and Timothy Harrington introduced a scheme that came to be known as the 'Plan of Campaign'. Tenants were advised on 'collective bargaining', whereby they would ask the landlord to lower his demands voluntarily. If he did not, they would pay no rent but would contribute to an 'estate fund' which would be given to him when he changed his mind. Martyn was nervous but during this period he didn't take any pleasure in the part his cousin John Woulfe Flanagan played in what became known as the scandal, *Parnellism and Crime*. Woulfe Flanagan was editor of *The Times* in 1887 when it had published a series of articles, the purpose of which was to prove that Parnell and his party were behind much of the murder and mayhem of the previous years. Letters supporting this charge and purporting to be written by Parnell were also published. There was outrage. The government, on the insistence of Joseph Chamberlain, set up an inquiry. It was composed of three anti-Home

Rule judges, who saw to it that all the machinery of Dublin Castle was put at the disposal of *The Times* to enable it to smash Parnell. It didn't succeed. In February 1899 Richard Pigott, a Dublin journalist financed by the Loyal and Patriotic Union, was found to have forged the letters. A year later *The Times* paid Parnell £5,000 in damages. To many, it was a case of the Irish nation being vindicated.

In 1888 Edward Martyn went back to Greece. If his diary is an accurate record of his travels, then it is the last time he went there. Perhaps that was because the following year he rediscovered Bayreuth, where his love affair with all things German would be intensified.[21] However in 1888 he also 'wintered at home'. He was writing a book. It was not all written at Tillyra for on 22 March George Moore wrote his mother from the Temple: 'Edward Martyn is completing his great work. I have seen none of it but from what he tells me I expect it to be magnificent, but Geary who has seen some of it says it is nonsense. I am inclined to think it is good. I know the ideas are splendid, the conception fills me with enthusiasm, but Geary assures me it is absurd. I long to see it. Edward is to my thinking an immensely clever fellow and it is a pity if it should be another case of *strength without hands to smite*.' [author's emphasis][22] But what did Moore know of Martyn's 'ideas' at this point and what was the 'conception' of the book?

Morgante the Lessser is an attack on the materialism of the age and what the author considered to be its insidious undermining of Christianity.[23] It is written in the style of a prose satire and is modelled on the work of Rabelais and Swift. It opens with two quotations from Thomas Carlyle's *Sartor Resartus*, of which the second merits a full transcript:

> It is the night of the world and still long till it be day we wander amid the glimmer of smoking ruins, and the sun and the stars of heaven are as if blotted out for a season; and two immeasurable Phantoms 'Hypocrisy' and 'Atheism' with the gowl *[sic]* 'Sensuality' stalk abroad over the earth and call it theirs.[24]

Except that this is not the original full quotation. Carlyle continues: 'Well at ease are the Sleepers for whom Existence is a shallow dream.' It is not odd that Edward Martyn left this out, for though existence might be hell on earth, death was never, for him, a welcome option.

Indeed he had, Moore tells us, 'an intense and ever pulsatory horror of death'.[25]

Sartor Resartus, a prose poem written by Carlyle at the beginning of his career, is, by and large, a rejection of Voltaire, who was accepted as the universal genius of the Enlightenment. *Morgante the Lesser* also rejects Voltaire and the whole basis of liberalism. However, it is a satire, so for most of the story Morgante, Martyn's hero/giant, is in love with materialism. He can proudly trace his ancestors back to the Pharaohs, who, he believes, espoused the extreme materialism of paganism. A leading member of his family was *Protegoruss*, who held as his first principle that man is the measure of all things. Morgante loves what he regards as 'the degeneracy of the Greeks' and, for him, subjectivity reigned triumphant. During the Reformation the family supported the movement for Protestantism and believed it 'laboured to free the human mind from the trammels of authority; to make every man his own theologian and consequently of first importance to his own particular self; to foster irresponsible speculation; and generally to disorganize the forces of the Christian church.'[26] Morgante loved it all and, with his followers, the *Enterists*, pursued the goal of making the world as materialistic and as shallow as possible. Martyn's hero is grotesque and his chief physical characteristic, and that of the *Enterists*, is their size. They are excessively bloated from the amount of wind they carry in their stomachs. They drink in their own importance.

In this book which, for the most part, is taken up with a description of the background, birth and education of the hero, Morgante, Edward Martyn attempts, unsuccessfully, to satirise everyone and everything, with the exception of the island of Agathopolis, his Utopia, which he praises. Morgante's exploits, on his way to achieve his materialistic goals, are simply boring. It is satire devoid of any lightness of touch. The writer never sugars the pill. The prose is turgid and the clichés abound; the politicians are always 'puppets' and a 'young don' falls in love with the hero. Women are constantly belittled and abused (happily Martyn's misogyny abated somewhat after the writing of this book). The extravagant fantasy that describes the genealogical background of the hero reflects a highly imaginative mind (the descriptions are often fantastic) but the irony lacks subtlety and mainly the writing is crude and lazy. When Martyn has difficulty in explaining something unimaginable, he writes: 'I have no wish or intention to describe to you what happened'! There are, however, some highlights. On page 183, while the *Enterists* are 'peregrinating', a great storm comes up. They are blown through rough seas, fetching up on a shore that they soon discover to be Hell.

In his untitled short story, previously described, Martyn has his hero, Crofton/Martyn declare: 'To me Dante is incomprehensible.' This is not entirely true because his chapter on Hell owes a little to Dante, the great poet who used another great poet, Virgil, as his guide to Hell. Dante loved Virgil. The poet was, for him, the image of Human Wisdom – the best that man can become without the special Grace of God. For Dante, art and philosophy could not be made into a substitute for religion.[27] Could they for Edward Martyn?

In Martyn's Hell, Morgante's guide was 'Boltaire'/Voltaire, whom the author hated but Morgante supposedly loved. The *Enterists* had arrived in that part of Hell that was reserved for Great Wits. On earth Voltaire had been 'ever bravely inflated'. He had paved the way for the Enterists. Now he was here where all the inhabitants had feathers for hair.[28] With Voltaire they walked the streets of Hell where there were great iron houses and factories manufacturing customs, manners and fashions. Utilitarianism was being pushed to its utmost. Everything that Martyn believed he had seen and heard in drawing rooms was in abundance in Hell. They meet many 'addlepated' scholars and there is a 'gossip club' to which only women are admitted.[29] This chapter is well imagined and reasonably well written. Unfortunately it tails off with his usual extravagant prejudices about women. In the end the reader feels that Hell is only really 'Hellish' because women have the upper hand. The chapter on Agathopolis, too, is also spoiled by vicious misogyny.

After their sojourn in Hell, Morgante and his friends continue their peregrinations but they begin to have some doubts about the greatness of materialism. This is brought on partly by their meeting with Theophilus, a devout Catholic, who agrees to tell them about another life: life on his island of Agathopolis. They went to meet him. As they waited for Theophilus to come, 'they had just entered the tropics: the sun burned in the hazy blue sky with a white heat: a deadly calm made rigid the glassy ocean: and no sound broke the elemental silence, save the regular beating of the ship's engine, like the pulse of a sleeping leviathan. When Theophilus appeared he was greeted with ironical cheers'.[30]

Lewis Mumford, who wrote *The Story of Utopia*, tells us that the 'Ideal Commonwealth' gets its form and colour from the time in which it was written.[31] It is the 'House of Refuge' to which we flee when our contacts with the hard facts become too rough to face. Agathopolis was, Edward Martyn believed at this point, his 'House of Refuge'. It was a dream, but it was not a generous dream. The writing of this chapter owes much to his reading and understanding of the work of Walter Pater. On the island, Theophilus tells them, 'that none may enter with corrupt mind', there is 'an ideal commonwealth of men in the world, though not of it … some in boyhood, some in manhood. Their bearing for the most part is exceedingly noble … and the moral beauty of youth endures untarnished through the seasons of manhood and old age'[32] (there are no women). Their language is Greek and everyone is a member of the beautiful old Greek Church 'in full communion with the one and indivisible Catholic Creed'.[33] The schism between the Greek Orthodox Church and the Church of Rome did not occur on Edward Martyn's island. And, anyway, he had never had a lot of time for the Vatican where, he believed, the Jesuits had the power.

On Agathopolis, politics are run by a benevolent dictator and a legislative commission. Democracy had been tried but it had fallen into 'the worst species of tyranny, in that it crushed down all pre-eminent talent to the common deal level of human mediocrity'.[34] The commissioners are now modelled on Plato's Guardians and the system of education is also taken from Plato's *Republic*. It is an *Ideal* education and the boys learn much besides learning that 'the world is indeed vanity and that the flesh is a horrid livid corruption'. When they are old enough, they come to understand that their bodies, after death, will be 'first dissected in the medical school attached to the hospital, and afterwards buried in consecrated ground according to the Christian rite. This compulsory dissection of the body is esteemed by us as most just and salutary in that it mortifies carnal vainness.'[35] This is precisely what was done with Edward Martyn's own body in 1923.

Martyn's early thinking about drama is well documented. On Agathopolis, 'drama maintains its literary vigour unimpaired, owing no doubt to the fact that the actor is still the servant of the dramatist, instead of, as elsewhere, his master. Drama has more or less a sacred character after the manner of the Greek tragedy, and deals with those old, but ever new springs of emotion in human nature, from which all great art alone derives its glory.' At the time of writing (1889) his 'affair' with Richard Wagner was at its height. He was attending the Bayreuth Festival annually, and preparing to write about it. In the paragraphs on sculpture and art, the influence of Walter Pater is strong, especially Pater's essay on Johann Joachim Winckelmann[36] and the connection between the Greek Palaestra and art. The early days of Greek art, when it was so influenced by Greek religion, was especially attractive to Edward and never left him. He envied the privilege of Greek religion to be able to transform itself into an artistic ideal. On Agathopolis, ancient sculpture is still a living art, for 'my countrymen combine an enthusiastic love of beauty with an absolute freedom from sensuality'.[37] There is no music on the island other than that of the Church; no opera because that would involve women singers (this is especially silly on the writer's part since he had already been to Bayreuth for a whole festival of *Parsifal* in which he considers Wagner, in his opera, to reach 'the highest point of ecclesiastical aestheticism'). The boy choristers provided 'plaintive old harmonies of our Greek hymns and responses, which linger among the mosaics in the cupola'.

In truth we are in a land where nature is no longer human. There is no passion, only cold form. No person would really want to live there, especially Edward Martyn, who would have been particularly bored. The book is meant as a defence of Christianity and it is clear that Agathopolis is some kind of Garden of Eden where there is no original sin. But if there is no original sin, can there be a crucifixion and resurrection? What is there to defend? It is confused; maybe it is even heresy. Clarity occurs only when the writer is defending the *Idealism* of ancient Greece. The pull of the pagan world is immense. If he was looking for a model for his Utopia, he almost certainly used Johan Valentine Andrea's *Christianopolis*, a description of which can be found in Mumford's book on Utopias. But Andrea 'who long tiraded about the wickedness of the world turns his head piously towards heaven'. Edward Martyn turned his to art.

In the last chapter of the book Morgante simply explodes while addressing the *Enterists* in Trafalgar Square. The reader is grateful. What did the friends and neighbours in south Galway make of this new young author in their midst?

5 • The Best of Times

THERE WAS SOME SURPRISE, but book-writing was not so unusual in rural Ireland in the nineteenth century, even by Catholic landlords. George Moore's first novel, *A Modern Lover*, had been published in 1883 and, while it had been banned by circulating libraries, the literati in south Galway would have been aware of it. They were also aware that Moore was, to an extent, Edward Martyn's mentor. His nearest neighbour, Sir William Gregory, wrote to Martyn: 'You have written a very clever book which not one in a thousand will read and not one in a hundred who do read it will understand. Still it is a very clever book, and has surprised me. I did not know you had inhaled so much of Rabelais.'[1] But Florimonde de Basterot's congratulations were tempered with criticism. 'I was struck with the good vigorous English', he wrote, 'and a strong vein of humour, and now I think I can affirm that the book is a good one, far above mere cleverness. I have reflected on this judgement and do not think I am biased by my affection for you.' He did not find it fully convincing and in the case of the chapter on Agathopolis he wrote: 'There is an exaggeration in your treatment of women, and something lame, for Agathopolis is not a convent and people must breed in the island. Your treatment of women-kind wants moderation.' He wondered what would be the fate of the book. 'A whole volume of satire is a *tour de force*. I think you have succeeded in keeping up the interest, but of course it cannot be called easy reading and you trample on the pet corns of the crowd, and you will have the women against you. What I can say is that *Morgante* ought to be read and discussed.'[2]

Florimonde wrote this from Paris where he had been spending the winter months with his friends Maurice Barrès and Guy de

Maupassant. The few critics who read the book were conditional in their praise – referring to it as 'a curious book'[3] and 'a most excellent piece of fooling'.[4] Edward was happy. It was a book after all. It had a beginning, a middle and an end. It had taken a certain amount of discipline to complete it within a year and a reputable publisher, Swan Sonnenschein, had published it. And although there was not a lot made of the publication of his first book, people did begin to take Martyn's literary pretensions seriously.

There was silence from George Moore, whose own novel *Mike Fletcher* was unsuccessful in 1889. This book[5] included a continuation of the adventures of John Norton (Edward Martyn) the hero of Moore's *A Mere Accident*, although the thrust of the story is an examination of the lives of Augustus Moore and the writer and critic Frank Harris (Mike Fletcher). Frank Harris had been born in Galway in 1856, three years before Edward Martyn, of poor parentage. In the narrative, Mike Fletcher becomes very famous in the literary world (as Harris did) but never develops any strength of character. He has a genuine affection for his friend John Norton. They are both misogynists, but Fletcher chases women and craves their affection, only to destroy it when his ends are achieved. The friends console themselves with the thought that it was always the same story, 'the charm and ideality of man's life was always soiled by women's influence'.[6] They 'strolled through the cloisters talking of art or literature', where 'the absence of women is refreshment to the eye'.[7] So Moore has his hero, Fletcher, commit suicide, while John Norton continues in the world which he has made his monastery.

No one liked Moore's book, least of all Frank Harris and Augustus Moore. It is a measure of Moore's guilelessness if he thought they might. In 1890 he was in a depressed state and would not have been cheered by reading *Morgante*. Edward didn't mind. He took himself off to Egypt and Rome to celebrate. During this holiday he read Leo Tolstoy's *The Kreutzer Sonata*, which had been given to him by Sir William Gregory. Gregory had found the book 'incomprehensible', which surprised Edward Martyn, on whom it made 'a deep impression'.[8] He did not think it was an attack on Christian marriage (which it is) but that it contained 'a lofty morality; viz. that he who married only for carnal lust shall suffer'. Gregory believed the book advocated the abolition of marriage, but Martyn assured him that 'far from advocating the abolition of marriage and promiscuous intercourse it seems to me to advocate marriage between persons of kindred sympathies who enter the state like rational beings and not like yahoos'.[9] This comment would indicate that, by this time, Edward had absorbed some of Henrik Ibsen's later ideas on the notion of freedom and responsibility within a marriage that was not based only (if at all) on carnal lust. But there is no indication that he understood the bleakness of a marriage that was built only on such notions rather than on total love.

This book created a sensation when it was published in 1889. In the immediate years before its publication, Tolstoy had had a spiritual crisis which had brought him to the edge of suicide. He became obsessed with the notion of carnal love as 'a condition of animality that is degrading to human beings'. And he believed that this was what marriage was based on. He cited the philosophy of the American Shaker Community, which believed that the sex instinct was an evil instinct. They were 'not against marriage *per se*, but in favour of an ideal of purity that is superior to marriage'.[10] This hardly varies from the Catholic Church's notion that celibacy is the superior state of being. Tolstoy was aiming at absolute chastity. He opens his story with the common quotation from Matthew v. 28: 'But I say unto you, That whosoever looketh on a woman to lust after her hath committed adultery with her already in his heart.' Edward Martyn too, liked this quotation. In the next few years we have him telling George Moore how and how not to look at women in the various squares of Europe. In the meantime he must have felt quite pleased with himself, for it looked as if one of the greatest world writers was seeking an *Agathopolis*. Tolstoy, however, does not necessarily condemn women but he does condemn the social institutions that compelled them to play a degrading role in the pursuit of a husband.

Another book published in 1889 which Edward Martyn had reason to write about in 1890 was William Samuel Lilly's *A Century of Revolution*.[11] Michael Morris of Spiddal, later Lord Killanin, wrote to him on 28 March enclosing a copy of an essay he had entered for a university prize, at Balliol. Martyn was very pleased with the essay and delighted that the young man had sent it to him. He was full of praise, although he found it necessary to point out that 'the idea of an anthem associated with the idea of anger is not quite satisfactory'.[12] 'I can see you are deeply influenced by Lilly's *Century of Revolution*,' he wrote, 'and if after reading that luminous book with which I much agree in almost all matters except in his courtesy and patience in dealing with that blasphemous prig John Morley, I find it the source of many of your thoughts, still that does not make me any less admire your essay.'[13]

It is difficult to believe that Martyn did not read Lilly's book before he wrote *Morgante*. But the publication date of 1889 does not allow for any confidence that he did. *Morgante* was completed in 1889. He may well have met the writer, however, at the Gregory dinner table in London.

There was much for him to like in the book. It was extremely anti-liberal, its thesis being that the Liberalism of the nineteenth century had been almost entirely generated by the French Revolution. For Lilly 'the great fosterer of liberty in the modern world had been the Christian religion. The cause of religious liberty in the Middle Ages was bound up with the struggle of the church against secular sovereignty.' All men were not equal and the revolutionary dogma that liberty resides in political equality was nonsense. He regarded John Morley as the professed apologist for the French Revolution. Morley believed that the Revolution, with all its flaws, belonged in the class of great religious and moral movements. Lilly was aghast. His book was an attack on all progressive movements, including Emile Zola's 'naturalism' and his 'unimaginative realism'. He regarded Denis Diderot as a 'filthy' writer. Perhaps this was because Diderot explored the relationship between psychology and morality; his materialistic interpretation of nature and his examination of the influence of the senses on ideas were abhorrent to Lilly. But it is interesting with reference to Edward Martyn for Diderot as a playwright was preoccupied with the dramatic viability of bourgeois domestic subjects. So too was Martyn and, as we know, he was also interested in the 'influence of the senses'. It is unlikely that he was being entirely truthful when he wrote Michael Morris to say that he so heartily agreed with all Lilly's sentiments. This book was written, however, against a backdrop of the extreme materialism and encroaching atheism of the age and, as such, gained quite a lot of positive criticism.

In July 1891, while J.D. Crace continued his decoration of the Great Hall at Tillyra, Edward went to Bayreuth for the annual Wagner Festival. It is unlikely he travelled alone, but there is no mention of companions on this occasion. In August he published an article in the journal *Black and White* that reflected his love of Richard Wagner and of his music. As already noted, the trip was becoming for him almost an annual event and he watched the small insignificant town grow so much that even by 1891 it could hardly contain the influx of visitors. In his article Martyn gives us an excellent description of Wagner's last home, Villa Wahnfried, which is approached by 'a short avenue of shady trees'. Here Wagner composed *Parsifal*, 'which breeds love and forgiveness'. And here the great artist is buried 'where the woodbird of his Siegfried may lament over his ashes from the leafy shelter of the green embowering boughs'.[14]

In this highly detailed, atmospheric piece, Martyn reveals to us the extent to which he understands and appreciates the visceral nature of Wagner's work. The *Gesamtkunst*: the complete uniting of poetry, music and theatre is, for him, hypnotic. While in his study of Greek art he is attracted to 'form', with Wagner it is the 'dissolution of form' that appeals to him. *Parsifal* was his favourite opera. Based on Schopenhauer's philosophy, it is the 'annihilation of the Will achieved through a denial of Eros'. Dealing with the problem of carnality and the pain it inflicts, *Parsifal* is fundamentally a cathartic ritual. Martyn wrote of it: 'Parsifal abounds in motifs of intense religious sentiment and meaning ... in the beautiful hall of the Holy Grail Wagner touches the highest point of ecclesiastical aestheticism. How transporting are the harmonies of those unseen choirs ... the voices of youth from the mid height and the pas-sionless note of boys chaunting [*sic*] from the cupola's extreme height ... like silver throated cherubins that herald the holiest mysteries.'[15]

Later Moore will tell us that Edward Martyn saw himself as Parsifal. We get some notion of why he might. In the third act, Martyn tells us: 'Wagner achieves his greatest triumph of orchestration in illustrating the pure passionless joy which the lover of nature experiences at the awakening of the year. Many a magic flower has Parsifal seen, but none so sweet as those whose scent recalls the *painless day of childhood*; and the culminating beauty is reached when Gournemanz exclaims "This is Good Friday's spell, my Liege".' In return Edward asks: 'who has not felt the spell of Eastertide, the glorious feast arrayed in the freshness of spring'. The essential humanity of Richard Wagner reached out to Edward Martyn. But he was also attracted to Wagner's anti-reason and anti-Enlightenment tendencies. Wagner was passionate in his belief of the power of the imagination and the depth of the subconscious. He wanted people to understand that it was a good thing to love art for its own sake. Many disagreed, but not Edward Martyn. Rushing through the sunny cornfield to the *Festspielhaus* on the hill on those bright July days, the bulky young man from Galway was enjoying the best of life. He knew what the purpose of great art was and he knew he would be all right.

It was on this trip too that he heard, for the first time, the Cologne Choir and their wonderful renditions of the music of Palestrina and Vittoria. In his *Paragraphs for the Perverse* he writes about his interest in liturgical music. It arose from 'an early instinctive and indeed medieval love for the liturgy of the Catholic Church. The red letters of the Rubric are to me what the stars are to the astronomer'.[16]

Back home the dramatic scenario that made up the last months of Charles Stewart Parnell's life was being played out. The 'uncrowned King of Ireland' had been brought to his knees by the dispossessed, but never deceived, Captain William O'Shea. With Parnell's death on 6 October 1891 the political assassins behind Katharine O'Shea's ex-husband had achieved their goals beyond their wildest dreams. The 'King' was dead; the Irish Parliamentary Party was irrevocably split, and Gladstone's plans for Ireland were wrecked. There is no record of how the gentry of south Galway felt. In the summer of 1892 Martyn went again to Bayreuth, this time in the company of his 22-year-old cousin Anthony Nugent, later Earl of Westmeath, who in 1897 became the private secretary of the Right Hon. Joseph Chamberlain, in the end the arch-enemy of Parnell.

On 6 March 1892 William Gregory died at his house at Hyde Park Corner in London. His wife was heartbroken. She had learned to love this vital and intelligent man. He had taken her from the drab life of a rural spinster and had introduced her to a world of culture and grace. A trip to Algeria had been planned in the hope that the sun would restore him to health, but he passed on while the arrangements were being made. At the house he was laid out beneath Velazquez's *Christ at the house of Martha and Mary* and opposite Giovanni Savoldo's *Adoration of the Shepherds*.[17] Then they took the body home to south Galway for burial where 'the people met him at the train & carried him to the Church & went into the service.'[18] Augusta Gregory was approaching her fortieth birthday and their son, Robert, was almost eleven. Years later, when Edward Martyn was immersed in his own troubles and suffering the slings and arrows of his own bad fortune, he wrote to Gregory to tell her how much he missed William and what their friendship had meant to him. In

9 Portrait of Eric Stenbock: 'he had a vain desire to penetrate the
core of evil', according to Arthur Symons.

1892, however, he was a slightly arrogant young man and he had lots of
other friends. And some of them liked his *Agathopolis*.

Before he went to Bayreuth that summer, Martyn had entertained
his old friend Count Eric Stenbock. By this time the Great Hall at

Tillyra was completed with its stained-glass windows featuring the Martyn armorial bearings. The organ was installed in the stairwell and the helmet of the crusading ancestor, Oliver Martyn, decorated the tiles. Stenbock was just back from Estonia where he had been sorting out his family fortunes. He was writing for *The Spirit Lamp*, an Oxford journal that was edited by Lord Alfred Douglas,[19] lover of Oscar Wilde. It was a journal whose *raison d'être*, many believed, was the legitimisation of masculine love through discourse. The atmosphere in Tillyra that summer was well disposed to his endeavours. In reply to a letter from Terence Woulfe Flanagan, who wished to orchestrate an invitation to Tillyra for a young woman he was interested in, Edward penned the following:

My dear T,

I received your letter of the 26th inst. in which you ask me to invite Mrs. L and Miss L. to meet you at Tillyra for some unexplained reason. I was upon the point of asking you when you could come to see me over there and hope that you will do so as soon as I return myself. Nothing would give me greater pleasure than if the L's would pay me a visit if they should happen to go to Ireland: but do you not yourself see that it would be a most marked thing if I were not also to mention in the invitation Mr. L. whom I have always found interesting and civil to me.

However, there is one thing which I clearly see would be most unwise, as it might possibly lead to misunderstandings, and would certainly make me ridiculous, and that is, that I should ask you and the L's. to meet each other. Never having had a love affair myself, and not being a marrying man, it would be affectation on my part, if I were to say that I took a very lively interest in the love affairs of others. My enemies, if I have any, will even allow that I have a certain sense of the absurdity of certain things; and that a person of my mode of life or oddities, whichever people may please to term them, should turn his philosophic abode into a temple of Hymen, would be an absurdity, seems to me to admit of no doubt. I hope you do not mind my writing frankly to you. You are a near relation and a dear old friend, and you will prove that you are the latter by coming over to meet Stenbock and Bond in the course of a fortnight or so.

Ever yours affectionately, Edward Martyn

In 1892 Eric Stenbock, an opium smoker and an alcoholic, was a pathetic, degenerate man. It is unlikely that while he was in Tillyra Annie Martyn entertained many of the young ladies of south Galway in the rose and gold drawing room. When W.B. Yeats described him to his father, John B. Yeats, he saw Stenbock as one of those men who was a 'scholar, connoisseur, drunkard, poet, pervert and most charming of men; his father replied 'they are the Hamlets of our age'.[20] He died a few short years later and he left some of his fortune to his old Oxford companions Con Costelloe and Terence Woulfe Flanagan. But they, too, saw early deaths. The loss of his friends so young narrowed the margins of Edward Martyn's own life. That was not clear in 1892 and it was in the course of this busy summer that he introduced George Moore to the operas of Richard Wagner. He took him to Drury Lane first to hear *Das Rheingold* and then to *Tristan and Isolde*. 'Words cannot tell my delirium, my madness,' Moore later wrote of his reaction to the performances.[21]

In 1893 Gladstone, at the age of 84, introduced his second Home Rule Bill for Ireland, while John Morley was Chief Secretary. It was rejected in the House of Lords on 8 September. The gentry of south Galway were almost indifferent, although Luke Dillon (later Lord Clonbrock) was circulating an anti-Home Rule petition, of which Martyn wrote to him he would be 'very pleased to obtain what signatures he could'. Although he pointed out to Dillon that 'you are aware of the difficulty I shall encounter from your knowledge of popular feeling. Indeed with the exception of my mother and myself and possibly the steward, I hardly know anyone about here who can be induced to sign.'[22] But they won the argument and the tenant farmers were not as disappointed as they might have been. Home Rule for many of them meant exchanging their English landlords for Irish ones, whose reputation had little to commend them. By 1893, anyway, they were beginning to see how the Land Acts, of which by now five had been passed, to the benefit of tenant farmers, might ultimately give them what was most dear to their heart, i.e. the land. Certainly Edward Martyn would soon be ready to sell out to them. While he continued to be a magistrate and a Deputy Lieutenant, he often acted in a way that showed how little interest he really had in what it entailed. As a squire he was especially negligent when it came to such country pursuits as shooting. To the chagrin of his neighbours, he was simply not interested in his shooting rights. He was regarded as a harsh landlord but it was fear of his tenants, and the way in which he had been brought up to fear them, that made it impossible for him ever to confront them. Nevertheless, when he gave them permission to shoot on his land, it was out of indifference and not from any wish to ingratiate himself with them. In 1899 his neighbour Lord Gough of Lough Cutra almost had apoplexy when Edward handed over the shooting rights entirely to them. 'Whether you or I individually shoot is of no importance,' Gough wrote him from Berlin, 'but I would have suggested you keeping all your shooting rights and not giving them up gratis.'[23]

The lull in Irish politics in these years (it was a lull and not a vacuum), when the Conservative government practised 'constructive unionism', was offset by the beginnings of a cultural revival that would become, many later believed, the principal driving force for the liberation of the nation. Douglas Hyde, the son of a Protestant clergyman from County Roscommon, had founded the Gaelic League in 1893 and published his *Love Songs of Connacht* the same year. Edward Martyn began to question his unionist heritage. 'I wish', he said to George Moore in 1894, 'I knew enough Irish to write my plays in Irish.' Moore was astounded. They were both still living in the Temple and while the novelist's description of his friend 'seated in his high canonical chair, sheltered by a screen reading his book, his glass of grog beside him, his long clay pipe in his hand'[24] is taken from a later image, when Edward was more mature and living in South Leinster Street, Dublin, it is, nevertheless, arresting.

Was Edward Martyn's statement so astounding? On the face of it, yes. To date he had shown no interest in the political struggle except to denigrate it. However, to anticipate, he did write to Lord Clonbrock in 1900, with regard to his resignation as J.P. and Deputy Lieutenant, that he had felt 'vaguely conscious that there was something unsatisfactory in my position' for some time.[25] The sands were shifting and Edward Martyn became aware of it quicker than George Moore. Cultural nationalism was set to become the new idealism. There is a degree of spiritual sustenance in cultural nationalism, perhaps the sustenance that Edward was still seeking in Hellenised aestheticism. Late Victorian materialism was rife. Political nationalism, an arid creed, attracted many but it could never be enough. Irish people had religion in abundance, but it did not necessarily represent the essential spiritual life of a people.

To a greater extent that spirit manifested itself in language, literature, myths, songs and stories. This was not obvious to many who felt the gap in their lives that involvement in a rich culture fills.

At its outset, the new crusade mainly involved Protestants and almost all Edward Martyn's friends were Protestant. He was looking for subjects to write about and they presented themselves. In his fourth play, *The Enchanted Sea*, he has his hero being told in a dream to leave the land of Greece and all its beauties and 'go where their genius had fled and was sleeping'.[26] A chord had been struck. The 'degeneracy' of Greece was to be replaced by the freshness of the Irish renaissance, the renaissance based on the 'purity' of Ireland's mythical past, the new 'Ideal'.

To spread the word, many turned to drama. Perhaps the surprising thing about Edward Martyn is that he came to this through the work of Henrik Ibsen. Not Ibsen, the social philosopher, but Ibsen the poet, whose later work is deeply concerned with the forces of the unconscious. Ibsen, for Martyn, was 'the most original of dramatists' but he was also, and this is most important, 'primarily intensely Norwegian'.[27] And he had 'invented the drama of the mind, where outer action is all subordinate to the tremendous strife of wills and emotions, which work out to their inevitable conclusions with a mastery of art that intellectually delights a thinking audience'. Martyn was not so interested in the Ibsen plays that dealt with man's relationship to society, but with those dealing with man alone with his mind. The 'dramatic situation of psychology' motivated Ibsen's characters and Edward Martyn identified with them. It is likely that he first came across the Norwegian while travelling in Germany in the mid-1880s, where Ibsen became a superstar in Berlin in January 1886 after a production of *Ghosts*. Thomas MacGreevy, poet and critic, who later wrote about Martyn's interest, was sceptical. 'Ibsen was', MacGreevy tells us, 'a Norwegian Lutheran who used the technique of the Parisian well-made play to state the dubiously interesting problems of small town egoists.'[28] The dramatist was certainly caught up in the psychology of bourgeois domestic subjects. And this was grist to Edward Martyn's mill. He wanted to examine the minds of educated people. He was never interested in the 'peasant play'. He didn't like peasants and while his attachment to Ibsen, whose work W.B. Yeats did not like, would ultimately leave him with a lonely furrow to plough, it was, in those early days, pure poetry and sheer excitement.

The excitement is best reflected in an essay he wrote on the first performance he had seen of *Little Eyolf*:

> After the performance of this play in the Little Theatre I went away with its exquisite music still trembling in my heart; I wished to be alone so that the exaltation should not be interrupted. For the way with these wonderful plays, where subtle mental poetry finds expression in the most realism of speech, as here and in *Rosmersholm* and above all in *The Master Builder*, is to give the sensation of rare harmonies, to produce with their triumphant construction the effect of a symphony where idea grows naturally from idea, where dramatic effects are but the natural outcome of logical combinations of circumstances, where profound knowledge of the human heart and character is set down with such certainty of intellect as may be seen in the lines of a drawing by some great master. As in *The Master Builder ... Little Eyolf*, in those scenes between husband and wife, there is the same symphonic beauty with an exaltation of beauty that lingers haunting our souls. When, out of the psychological subtleties of the characters of Alfred and Rita Allwers, the respective mental tragedies of husband and wife rise to a climax of conflict, there is brought home to an audience with tremendous impressiveness how greater far is the dramatic situation of psychology than that of mere exteriority expressed only in bodily action. It is this very dramatic psychology coming in logical sequence that is just the quality which makes the work of Ibsen repellent to average playgoers who, in the miserable decadence of serious drama throughout England and America, and of course, worst of all, throughout Ireland, abhor above all dramatic requirements, the requirements of having to think consecutively in the theatre.[29]

Martyn was not the only one with these feelings about *Little Eyolf*. George Moore's friends Edmund Gosse and William Archer were translating Ibsen for the London stage in the early 1890s and worrying that the soul-searching 'might be too terrible for human endurance in the theatre'.[30] Conversation is more important than plot in *Little Eyolf*. This was very appealing to Martyn. Gosse and Archer were also reading Moore's plays and were not impressed. His *Strike at Arlingford* had been rejected for the stage by Herbert Beerbohm Tree in 1890 but was published in 1893. Moore was trying to develop an independent Theatre Society that would perform 'unconventional', 'original' and 'literary' plays.[31] He wasn't being very successful and it is in this period that his latest biographer, Adrian Frazier, claims that he wrote a synopsis for Edward Martyn's first play, *The Heather Field*.[32] This is quite likely but it doesn't make Moore the author of the play. The subject and central theme were certainly Martyn's and the two main male protagonists, Carden Tyrell and Barry Ussher, represent the two sides of his nature: the practical man and the dreamer. The central theme is the fatal clash of dream and reality, revealing a soul in crisis. And the 'soul in crisis' continues to be a central theme in all Martyn's serious attempts at creative drama.

Carden Tyrell, the chief protagonist in *The Heather Field*, is to some an idealist and to others an uncompromising fanatic and moralist. He is a landowner in the west of Ireland where his estate is in financial trouble. He is married to Grace Desmond and they have a son, Kit, whose characterisation owes much to Eyolf in *Little Eyolf*. The marriage is in trouble and it becomes clear, very early on, that Carden should not have married Grace or anyone else. Grace is reasonable and practical and could never understand the idealism that Carden aspires to. Furthermore, Carden's sexuality is problematic, as is that of his alter ego Barry Ussher. 'There is always the original pain,' Ussher tells Miles Tyrell (Carden's younger brother) when he assures him that having money and position does not necessarily make for happiness.[33] This is a play where all the men prefer the company of men and Ussher tells Miles how, in the early days when he and Carden had been intimate, he had tried to prevent the marriage to Grace, for whom Carden had no respect or affection. 'The sudden overturning of all his ideas at that time seem to me strange and unnatural,' says Ussher. Carden Tyrell did what Edward Martyn refused to do: he married against his nature and the consequences were disastrous.

In the first act of the play Grace is trying to prevent her husband from borrowing yet more money to plough into his pet project, the heather field. The heather field is being changed from scrubland into a field that will produce the most beautiful grass imaginable and will save the Tyrell estate from bankruptcy. For Carden the task is an obsession and he is willing to sacrifice everyone and everything to it. This is similar to many of Ibsen's characters, whose desire is often to carry out the impossible. Barry Ussher is the practical man whose estate is in good shape, but he understands Carden's idealism and sympathises with him over his marital unhappiness. But even though he had tried to prevent Carden from marrying Grace, he now knows that she is within her rights in trying to prevent him from squandering any more money on the heather field.

In the second act, however, Grace goes too far when she tries to have Carden committed to a mental asylum. Ussher manages to prevent this but everything goes from bad to worse. The bank is about to foreclose on the mortgages. The tenants, stepping out from the shadows of Carden's consciousness, are causing trouble. They are literally on the doorstep demanding a reduction in rents. The police are obliged to protect both him and his family and he is confined to the house. There is an atmosphere of depression and foreboding. Then, in the third act, the gorse breaks through in the heather field and all is lost. Carden Tyrell loses his mind. The materialism of the modern world has overcome him. We are left with the notion that the sanity of the average man is dependent on his being allowed to preserve his illusions.

How much of Edward Martyn's philosophy on life is in this play? Carden Tyrell and Grace Desmond had married for the wrong reasons. He thought she was pretty and graceful and she thought he was malleable enough to be changed into a practical man. As we have already seen, Martyn regarded such people as behaving 'like yahoos'; it could end only in failure. Martyn does not place any of the blame on Carden, whom he sees as an idealist, perfectly entitled to his dreams, and he is also sympathetic to Barry Ussher, the practical man. But poor Grace is the epitome of all the young ladies that Annie Martyn had brought into the drawing room at Tillrya in the previous ten years. Grace tried to tame Carden and is not forgiven. Carden tried to tame nature and this is 'idealism'. The real message of the play remains, nevertheless, that a man should not marry against his nature and, if he does, there would need to be a great deal of Ibsen's notion of 'freedom and responsibility' to make the marriage work. 'The old wild nature had to break out again,' Barry Ussher tells Miles, just as the heather did in the manicured field. Depression and disillusion stalk the action. The dialogue is stilted and the style is uneven. But the 'décor parle' is good; the landscape is well represented in dialogue. It is very easy to conjure up an image of the heather field. The house is old and crumbling and the sea is never very far away. There is, however, an overwhelming sense of a drift towards madness. When it played in London in 1900, the critic William Archer referred it as 'morbid psychology' which, in fact, is a very fair critique. Edward Martyn wanted to imitate Henrik Ibsen, but his focus is entirely psychological, never sociological. We never really know what his characters are like. They lack both animation and emotion and are, in the end, utterly banal.

There are, however, compelling arguments for accepting that George Moore played a role in bringing this play to fruition. On 28 September 1900 Martyn wrote a long letter to Moore, mainly about the former's third play, *The Tale of a Town*, but it also includes the following passage:

> As regards the help you gave me in *The Heather Field*, much of it was valuable and I am sure I always told you how obliged I was for it. At the same time I accepted some things which I did not like. But then I would have accepted anything no matter how my literary judgement disliked it. You suggested I should do the second act with the theme of the wife trying to shut her husband up in the madhouse ... the critics would probably say I was cribbing from Strindberg's *Father*, a play I have never read. After the play was published I was told by another it resembled *The Father* on account of this incident. In all you did for *The Heather Field* you appear not to have acted solely with a wish to help me ... you always stipulated you should get some of the receipts. When the play appeared to be a commercial success in Dublin you again reminded me of your claim.[34]

In his *Autobiographies* W.B. Yeats writes that George Moore told him that it was he, Moore, who had constructed *The Heather Field*. They were walking by the lakeside at Coole during the time when there was trouble over Edward Martyn's third play. He told the poet that he had instructed Martyn on 'what was to go into every speech', although he himself had never written a word. He also said that he had 'partly constructed *Maeve*', Martyn's second play.[35] He claimed that while Martyn was very good at finding subjects, which Moore was not, 'he will never write a play alone'. There is extant evidence of Moore and Martyn collaborating in literary matters, but mainly they concern Moore's demands on Martyn to assist him with a choir scene in his novel *Evelyn Innes*.[36] *Evelyn Innes* is a novel about a Wagnerian diva, with two lovers, one of whom is loosely based on the character of W.B. Yeats. When Yeats revealed all this to Augusta Gregory, she thought of it as 'a new story'. She felt that the poet was selective in what he chose to believe in Moore's 'stories'. But then Augusta Gregory never liked, or trusted, George Moore, and the feeling was mutual.

One of Wagner's great themes was the complex middle-aged man and his redemption, in most cases, by the love of a good woman. Carden Tyrell is Edward Martyn's 'complex man'. He could not, for Martyn's purposes, be redeemed by a woman but he could by idealism. In these early days, this notion was something Martyn was grappling with and which Moore did not fully comprehend. In 1900 when discussing *The Heather Field* in correspondence with Yeats, Moore wrote: 'I should not have attempted to add a word to the character of Carden Tyrell',[37] which, fairly convincingly, contradicts Yeats's memory of the lakeside confidence. A letter from Moore to Martyn, dated 14 July 1897, also reflects the extent to which this was, in fact, the latter's play:

> My Dear Edward,
>
> Could you be here before the 22nd? That will not leave us much time to get to Bayreuth, only four days. I have got the rooms and am assured that they will be clean. I have read with great interest your play; it seems to me very good indeed. I strongly advise you to publish it; you will have a better chance of getting it acted when it is published; it will act very well; but of course it will not attract popular audiences any more than Ibsen. But we'll talk about that when we meet ... .[38]

It is also interesting to note that, for all its shortcomings, this play is the first of its kind written in Ireland. It breaks the mould of the 'stage Irishman' and the ultra-patriotic 'true man and traitor' of Dion Boucicault.[39] The most convincing evidence, however, that Martyn is, essentially, the author of *The Heather Field* comes in a codicil he made to his will in 1919 when he bequethed to George Moore 'any right title or interest which I may have at my death in the two plays of which I am the author and which are respectively entitled *The Heather Field* and *Maeve*'.

6 • All Things Irish

IT HAS BEEN GENERALLY accepted that *The Heather Field* was completed by 1894. The scene, however, where Carden Tyrell is under the protection of the police is so similar to Edward Martyn's own experience in the summer of 1895 that it is more reasonable to assume it was finished after this date (it was first published in 1899). That summer had seen a high degree of restlessness in south Galway, mainly as a result of land agitation. The tenants on the Martyn estate went to the Land Commission to have 'fair rents' established and they were refused. In July, returning home from the court, the Tillyra agent James Acton was shot outside the gate lodge at Coole. He was injured, not killed,[1] but it was, the judge said, 'a most cold-blooded and daring outrage'. Afterwards the Martyns were afforded police protection for some time. In March Edward had been sworn in on the County Grand Jury for the Spring Assizes but there is no evidence of him sitting. Work and unrest made it a quiet year for travelling. He had been to Paris for Easter but after that the diary merely records 'autumn at home – troubles'. It is safe to assume that Annie, who was getting old and frail, did not want to be left alone in Tillyra.

The previous year had been quite different. A large part of the spring was spent in London and much of it in the company of Augusta Gregory. She had set up in some 'nice rooms in Queen Anne's Mansions', close to Saint James's Park and Parliament buildings. Coole was let to Sir Charles Hunter because Gregory was not yet ready to live in it alone so soon after the death of William. In this period she was close to Edward Martyn and especially close to his best friend, Nevill Geary. The Gearys, mother and son, were living in fairly straitened circumstances in Warwick Square and Gregory was working hard to get

10 Nevill Geary. The silver spoon with which he had been born became silver-plated, so he went to Africa; Augusta Gregory gave a little dinner for Edward to console him in his loss.

Nevill some form of colonial post. They had property in Kent, but Nevill later wrote that the lack of rents and agricultural depression had turned the silver spoon with which he was born into 'silver plated'. He was a 'briefless barrister'.[2] When he wasn't living in Warwick Square, he still shared rooms with Edward in the Temple and, in this period, they brought Augusta Gregory there to meet George Moore.[3] Moore had just published *Esther Waters*. She also met 'Yates', who had brought out the *Celtic Twilight* in 1893. He was 'every inch the poet', she told her diary. Edward also attended to family matters in having his cousin Richard Corballis initiated into the Reform Club.

The highlight of the summer was the trip to Bayreuth with George Moore. It was Moore's first visit to the Festspielhaus and he met his friend Edward Dujardin, the great Wagnerian, there. George Bernard Shaw was also a visitor in 1894. Before they reached Bayreuth, they visited many German cities, especially to listen to the Cologne Choir on tour. But, with the exception of Bayreuth, Moore found Germany 'dreary'[4] and, defying Martyn's dictum that he 'not make up to English and American women that congregate in Continental hotels', took off for Aix-les-Bains via Dresden where he met with Maud Burke, later Lady Cunard.[5] There would be many more trips for the friends to Bayreuth and a close reading of Moore's work reveals a clear influence of the master composer. Moore learned from Wagner how to reveal a man's inner consciousness through a narrative of memory.

In October Nevill Geary left London for Sierra Leone. He had been awarded some form of colonial post, but it is not clear what exactly it was. His friends were worried about him. 'I have not yet heard a word from Geary,' Edward wrote to Augusta Gregory in November, 'it is very strange. I only hope he is not ill.' He may have been but he was back in London in the spring of 1895 and Gregory renewed her exertions to get him a job. The friendship between the three remained warm and close. In July the Gearys, mother and son, were in Tillyra, and this must have been a great support for Edward and Annie in the midst of their 'land troubles'. In April, Stenbock had died. He was buried in the Catholic cemetery in Brighton, but his heart was extracted and sent to Estonia. For Arthur Symons, who was about to become Edward's neighbour in the Temple, Stenbock was 'one of the most inhuman beings he had ever encountered'.

The Oscar Wilde trial started in London. There are no voices from south Galway on this subject. They didn't like Wilde but there is certainly no evidence that they wished him ill. W.B. Yeats went to see him after the first trial and told him he had the sympathy of many of the 'Dublin literary men' but, of course, with some of them he didn't. That month Martyn was at Tillyra organising some restoration work on Dunguaire Castle, his property at Kinvara. Augusta Gregory was back in Coole and afternoon tea parties included Mrs Martyn and Father Fahy, author of *The History and Antiquities of the Diocese of Kilmacduagh*. Gregory and Martyn were both reading Arthur Balfour's *The Foundations of Belief: Being Notes Introductory to the Study of Theology*. Martyn loved it because it questioned the flaws in science as a replacement for religion, while Gregory didn't like it because she felt it might drive readers 'to the Pope or General Booth or anyone who holds conviction'.[6]

In December Geary left again for Africa. This time he was appointed Attorney General for the Gold Coast. Sir William Maxwell, a close friend of Augusta Gregory, was the Governor. She gave 'a little dinner' for Edward to console him in his loss. Geary did not like his posting and wrote very homesick letters to Gregory expressing, in at least one, his wish that Edward was out there with him. His superiors were not happy with him and Maxwell warned Gregory that he would not be given another job. Geary was, Maxwell said, 'too much of a dilettante'. Later Geary wrote that he had gone to Africa because it was 'the line of least resistance, the cheapest passage'.[7] Long after Martyn was dead, Geary again wrote to Augusta Gregory reiterating his feeling that had their friend been forced to 'take the boat' with him he might have had a much happier life. Given the chance, Edward Martyn might well have cut and run. In November he had tried to compromise with his tenants and had failed. 'He is very low at the prospect of having to stock the land and begin farming', Gregory noted in her diary on the tenth.[8]

Things were changing in the Temple. Moore moved out in March and went to live in a flat in Victoria Street. W.B. Yeats finally left home (he was 30) in Bedford Park and went to live, temporarily, with Arthur Symons in Fountain Court. Arthur Symons is largely remembered as a leading light in the Decadent movement of the nineties. He was a great defender of 'Art for Art's Sake'. In the summer of 1896 he was working on his great work, *The Symbolist Movement in Literature*, which he dedicated to Yeats. He was also editor of *Savoy*, an experimental literary magazine. He and Yeats paid a visit to Martyn in Tillyra and they stayed from 27 July until late August. Edward had been introduced to Symons by George Moore and may have met Yeats through Symons. It is also likely, however, that he met him when he was a visitor to the Yeats's

11 Dunguaire Castle, Kinvara, Co. Galway. Ownership went
back to the Martyn's time as a leading 'tribe'.

family home in Bedford Park where the Irish Literary Society, reconstituted from the Southwark Irish Literary Club by Yeats in 1891, often met. Also it is possible that he was introduced to him by Douglas Hyde. Both Yeats and Symons loved their summer at Tillyra and each has left us a vivid and compelling narrative of the visit.

Yeats's relationship with Martyn was complex, interesting and often spiteful and this will be explored in the coming chapters. But in the summer of 1896 they were just good friends with wide mutual enthusiasms. Edward's attraction to all things Irish had quickened, and the early summer had been taken up with organising the first Feis Ceoil and the Galway Feis. By July, however, he was in Tillyra to greet his friends on their arrival. Symons describes Tillyra at this time as: 'a mysterious castle lost among trees that start up suddenly around it, out of a land of green meadows and gray stones'.[9] It was exactly what he wanted. Symons had gone to the west of Ireland looking to be enchanted. It is, he wrote: 'a castle of dreams, where, in the morning I climb the winding staircase in the tower, creep through the secret passage, and find myself

12 (a) Arthur Symons, 1895. In Tillyra he found a castle 'at once so
ancient a reality and so essential a dream' that he worried about
'losing his grip upon external things' and left.

in the deserted room above the chapel, which is my retiring-room for
meditation. In the evening my host plays Vittoria and Palestrina on the
organ, in the half-darkness of the hall, and I wander between the pillars
of black marble hearing the many voices rising into the dome.'[10]

12 (b) W.B. Yeats *c*.1895. As they sailed out of Cashla Bay on
Tom Joyce's hooker, he read 'The Washer of the Ford', by
Fiona MacLeod, to the Aran fisherman.

Yeats, too, was much taken with Tillyra. He had not expected to be
and he had told Symons before they arrived there that they might
expect to be 'waited on by a barefoot servant'. Edward Martyn, he
pointed out, 'had seemed so heavy, uncouth and countrified' in London.[11]

But Yeats was seduced by the modern comforts and impressed by the art on the walls, which included Degas, Monet and Corot, although he hated the mock Gothic architecture. In the *Autobiographies*, the total veracity of which is suspect, he describes it as 'among the worst inventions of the Gothic revival'. It is from Yeats, however, that we discover that the old house at Tillyra had been gutted by fire. He was struck by the fact that there was no old furniture or family portraits and thought that this lack of material heritage had a lot to do with what he considered Martyn's 'abstract mind'. He remembered Annie Martyn as a 'pale pinched figure'. No doubt she was. Even Maud Gonne, in the end, grew to be a 'pinched figure'.

Yeats's description of evening entertainment is much the same as that of Symons's: 'We asked Edward Martyn to extinguish all light except that of a little Roman lamp, as though upon a stage set for *Parsifal*. Edward Martyn sat at this harmonium, so placed among the pillars that it seemed some ancient instrument, and played Palestrina.'[12] On the warm summer evenings, out on the lawn and in the large room above the chapel where Symons meditated, Yeats 'threw himself into cabbalistic experiments and shared visions'.[13] This period, when Yeats was in Tillyra, coincided with a mild crisis, for him, of artistic identity. He decided 'to evoke the lunar power which was, I believe, the chief source of my inspiration. ... On the ninth night as I was going to sleep I saw first a centaur and then a marvellous naked woman shooting an arrow at a star. She stood like a statue on a stone pedestal, and the flesh tints of her body seemed to make all human flesh in the contrast seem unhealthy.' Like the centaur, she moved among brilliant light.[14] Arthur Symons and Florimonde de Basterot also shared in these visions. De Basterot believed Yeats was a 'Finnish sorceror' and 'locked his door to try and keep it [the centaur?] out'. Edward worried that these activities might 'obstruct the passage of prayer'.[15]

In a retrospective diary entry for this period, Augusta Gregory refers to her meeting at Tillyra with 'Symonds [*sic*] and Yeats – the latter full of charm and interest & the Celtic revival – I have been collecting fairy lore since his visit'.[16] George Moore gives us a much more insightful description of the meeting which Martyn relayed to him: 'She seems to have recognised her need in Yeats at once', he wrote, 'foreseeing ... that he would help her out of conventions and prejudice, and give her wings to soar in the free air of ideas and instincts'.[17] For our purposes it is interesting to note, at this point, how Edward Martyn brought all these people together, helping them, from the outset, to make a mark on the world that he so singularly failed to make himself.

On 5 August 1896 they set out to visit the Aran Islands. Martyn's cousin Michael Morris of Spiddal joined them. Symons was in his element. 'As we drive seaward', he wrote, 'the stone walls closing in the woods dwindle into low roughly heaped hedges of unmortared stones over which only an occasional cluster of trees lifts itself; and the trees strain wildly in the air, writhing away from the side of the sea, where the winds from the Atlantic have blown upon them and transfixed them in an eternity of flight from an eternal flagellation.'[18] He was getting 'all kinds of literary material' which he would soon use in his essay 'The Isles of Aran', published in *Savoy* later that year.[19] So was Yeats. When they sailed out of Cashla Bay on Tom Joyce's Galway hooker, he read Fiona Macleod's *The Washer of the Ford* and talked to the Aran fishermen about the myths and legends of the islands.[20] Later he wrote to William Sharp (Fiona Macleod) that he was sure there were 'fairy manifestations' on the islands.[21] They put up in the Atlantic Hotel in Kilronan village and also managed to visit Inishmaan, but poor weather conditions stopped them landing on the smallest island, Inisheer. Martyn had already visited the islands with Augusta Gregory. He would have proved a good guide and was obviously happy in their company. Unlike his cousin, he would not have speculated on whether or not they were 'true gentlemen'.[22]

They were delighted when he took them to visit de Basterot at Durus. Paul Bourget, the French novelist, critic, psychologist and friend of Henry James, was there. Yeats gives us what is probably a true picture of Florimonde de Basterot at the time, describing him as an old man 'crippled by the sins of his youth, much devoted to his prayers'. An accomplished man of the world all the same. He was impressed with the notion that de Basterot kept flats in Paris and in Rome despite the straitened circumstances of the family which was reflected in the very small residence at Durus. It seemed that Symons continued to enjoy everything. He found 'all this bareness, greyness, monotony, solitude at once primitive and fantastical, curiously attractive'. But as the month wore on, it was all too much and he became disturbed. 'Among these solid and shifting things', he wrote, 'in this castle which is at once so ancient a reality and so essential a dream I feel myself to be in some danger of loosening the tightness of my hold upon external things. No, decidedly I have no part among those remote idealists. I have perceived the insidious danger of idealism ever since I came into these ascetic regions.'[23] Within ten years of this vivid period of his life, Arthur Symons suffered a major nervous breakdown from which he never fully recovered.

How much did this 'dreaming' have to do with Edward Martyn's dream-drama, *Maeve*? How much help did he get from Symons with the writing of it? It has been accepted that he got quite a lot. The central theme of *Maeve*, as in *The Heather Field*, is 'the soul in crisis', Martyn's own theme. The whole play is a product of nineteenth-century literary aestheticism and Martyn's attachment to Greek thought and art. The west coast of Ireland, Tír na nÓg and the Greek classical past are skilfully linked and the play pays homage to the Celtic nature poet. Many felt it was Martyn's best work, although, as an actable play, it left a lot to be desired. This is not to say, however, that it was not successful on its first night. It was and the reasons for this success will be explored later.

Maeve was published in 1899, in tandem with *The Heather Field*. Moore wrote a highly flattering introduction to both plays, claiming the playwright as the new Shakespeare. This hyperbole, however, has to be seen in the light of the publication date which was just before the inaugural performance of the Irish Literary Theatre. Of course, he also felt some proprietorial rights. As we know, he told Yeats he had partly constructed both plays. Yeats claimed with reference to *Maeve* that he had been told that Arthur Symons 'had revised the style for a fee, setting it high above Martyn's level'.[24] Symons did help Edward with the style and structure of *Maeve*, but it is highly unlikely that he was paid for it. Edward Martyn was a very generous host, and about to become an equally generous patron, but he was very careful about what he paid for.

He was working on *Maeve* during the summer of 1896 when Symons was at hand. They were both interested in nineteenth-century literary aestheticism and Arthur Symons was a great stylist. But 'this play', wrote William Archer who, at the time of its production, was the chief critic of the *Daily Chronicle*, 'is a piece of frigid self-conscious Celticism totally lacking in inspiration and charm of style. It is Mr. Yeats without his poetry and without his exquisite naivete.' Archer believed that 'Mr. Martyn, in a word, is a clever and thoughtful man who has not the gift of animating his creations with the breath of dramatic life.'[25] He did concede, however, that if the writer approaches real power anywhere, it is in the last scene of *Maeve*.

Is it a piece of 'frigid self-conscious Celticism'? For the most part it
is. In modern parlance, one is inclined to think of the subject of the
play, Maeve, daughter of the great O'Heynes, Prince of Burren, as
someone who needs to 'get a life'. In fact she chooses death. She is in
love with death almost as Carden Tyrell is in love with madness. Once
again we are in the throes of idealism versus materialism. The portrayal
of Maeve as the truly self-absorbed dreamer (although character
drawing was not Martyn's strong point, he was very good at portraits of
self-absorption) reflects Ibsen, but the 'Celtic Twilight', and all that
meant at the time, is highly significant too.

The play is about a young woman who spends her life pining for a
lover who has no existence. It is set in a realistic framework in a shabby
castle, surrounded by an abundance of ruined abbeys and cairns, in the
west of Ireland. It is the home of Coleman O'Heynes. He has lost his
land and his wealth, but is about to get it back through the expedient
marriage of his elder daughter, Maeve, to Hugh FitzWalter, a young
Englishman. Maeve is described by the author as 'a girl of about three
and twenty with a fair complexion, golden hair and a certain boyish
beauty in the lines and movement of her slim figure'.[26] She is not real,
however. She represents the beauty of form. It is easy to imagine Arthur
Symons and Edward Martyn having a good time collaborating on this
play. Maeve has agreed to the marriage but, in the dream sequence at
the end of the play, she forsakes her earthly lover and goes with
Queen Maeve, who is still young and beautiful after two thousand years,
to Tír-na-Óg. 'Your Prince of the hoar dew, when he comes, will bring
you rest', the queen promises young Maeve.[27]

This dream sequence, when Maeve goes off into the Celtic twilight,
is probably Martyn's best work, but hardly all his own work. When the
play was completed, Symons read and rewrote many of the passages.
'The vision I have given particular care to,' he wrote. 'I have tried to get
a sort of exalted chant into the rhymes, and to distinguish between the
mortal ecstasy of Maeve and the immortal peace of Queen Maeve.'[28]
While William Archer is correct in his assertion that the writer cannot
animate his creations with the breath of dramatic life, to any great
extent, there is an exception here. When Maeve is about to die, she is
most alive. Symons, no doubt, polished the dialogue but the atmosphere
created is certainly Martyn's. It is the 'chorus of boy pages' who accompany Queen Maeve when she comes to claim our young protagonist

13 (a) Edward Martyn as Gaelic Leaguer, 1899

which creates this atmosphere. In this period Edward was spending a great deal of time listening to boy choirs all over Europe and his beautiful protagonist in this play conjures up an image of an innocent choirboy. It is a play, however, which draws fairly sympathetic women characters and we begin to see fractures in the playwright's more deep-rooted misogyny. This can hardly have been all the influence of

Edward Martyn

13 (b) Edward Martyn and Susan Mitchell by John B. Yeats, 1899

Symons, who, despite many amorous affairs with women, was highly ambiguous in his attitude towards them.

Finola O'Heynes is the sister of Maeve. She is in love with FitzWalter, but accepts his preference for her older sister and does her best for him when she sees her wavering. Finola is a strong, likeable woman, who reflects the world as it is. Peg Inerny, the vagrant old woman who brings the ancient Queen Maeve and the young Maeve together, is very well drawn. Coleman O'Heynes, whinging about the loss of his land, his willingness to sacrifice the happiness of his daughter and the blatant use of an innocent young Englishman to achieve his goal, is highly authentic. The fact that Maeve resisted marriage to an Englishman by choosing death is, not surprisingly, what attracted Irish audiences to the play four years hence. How a work of literary aestheticism was turned into a 'nationalist play', we shall come to later.

Edward Martyn dedicated *The Heather Field* and *Maeve* to W.B. Yeats, Arthur Symons and George Moore. While we know that he was confident it was he who was the author of these plays, it is clear that he also accepted there was collaboration. But John Millington Synge, in his preface to *The Playboy of the Western World*, tells us that 'all art is collaboration'. The ideas for the plays were certainly Martyn's and the ideas were usually good. Years later he told John MacDonagh, playwright and patriot, 'if we stick together we will achieve something'. There was a lot of 'sticking' done in the next five years and much was achieved. Things became 'unstuck', however, and these golden years did not last, but they were beautiful while they did.

Life at Tillyra remained tranquil, although what Annie thought of Edward's artistic friends we shall never know. By now some distance had been created between him and his Smyth relations, but they would soon be together again at the laying of the foundation stone for the cathedral at Loughrea. On the Martyn side, too, there was a slight rift. One relative claimed that Edward lived two lives: a bohemian life in London and Dublin and that of a proper Catholic landlord in Galway.[29] It was hardly the truth. He carried with him all his interests wherever he went. It was about this time, though, that he gave up his lodgings in Pump Court. On trips to London now, he tended to stay at the Reform Club. England was beginning to be, for him, a 'half-civilised country'. And this feeling was enhanced by his growing interest in the theatre. On his numerous trips to Europe he did not spend all his time in the great cathedrals listening to polyphonic music or at the opera in his beloved Bayreuth. He also haunted small independent theatres, absorbing what they had to offer.

'Almost every town in Germany has its theatre subsidised by the state,' he wrote, in the *Dublin Daily Express* in February 1899. In 1897 he had become aware of this because he had been looking for a small experimental theatre to stage *The Heather Field*. 'After the wonderful modern drama in Scandinavia the modern drama of Germany is the finest and most intellectual in Europe,' he wrote, 'and this drama, strange to say, is popular and what is stranger, perhaps, is that there is a very inferior drama popular also ... the good and the bad being popular at the same time. The theatre is held in high honour as the home of great thought and great art. They understand its fascination when it becomes truly elevated and if, at the same time, they can be interested in its degradation, through either silliness or sensuality ... there must, after all, be two publics – one for the good and one for the bad.'[30] In England, he felt, 'the public is wholly for bad modern drama and for

14 Tillyra Castle, 1907, as Yeats and Symons saw it; Daisy Fingall recalled 'plain living, good wine and brilliant talk and thinking'.

bad art in general, for the most part. That is why, I suppose, when returning to England from the Continent, it always seems to me like entering a comparatively half civilised country.' (This was written within a month of William Archer turning down *The Heather Field* for production in London because he said 'it simply is not good enough'.) 'English theatres', Edward Martyn wrote, 'are commercial institutions by the manner alone in which they pander to the mere creature comforts of the audience. And, after all, what else can they do? If they will not pamper the multitude with the food that the multitude desires, they are speedily neglected and fall into ruin. Nothing short of a state subsidy or a subsidy from private individuals, whereby a theatre might be made independent of public favour, and so might become a public instructor, can rescue the drama from the slough in which it is wallowing.'[31]

So what of theatre in Ireland? Was it in this 'slough'? Not really, but in the eyes of the new movement for a Celtic renaissance, it couldn't have been worse. For nothing being shown in the theatres could claim to be 'Irish'. That was about to change and with it Edward Martyn's life. The theatre would become, for him, 'the most significant thing in my life' and he would live to greatly regret not owning his own theatre venue. But, for the start of the story, we have to go back to 1897.

It was an exciting year. On 6 February the *Galway Observer* reported that a movement had been set in train for the building of Loughrea Cathedral. Doctor John Healy, Bishop of Clonfert, was at the head of it. Captain Smyth of Masonbrook initially donated £2,000 but this was quickly increased to £5,000. Both he and the local curate, Father Maher, were appointed treasurers. In April Smyth was also appointed to the new Board of Guardians, reminding us that the Smyth family was still very conscious of its civic and religious duties in the town of Loughrea. Edward Martyn donated hugely to the building of the cathedral, but it would be three years before he would take a real interest. Then the artistic decoration was put mainly in his, and Father Gerald O'Donovan's, hands. They were given an opportunity to fill an Irish church entirely with Irish art. It would spearhead Edward's campaign to root out 'the foreign art commercial traveller', the mere existence of whom, in years to come, often brought him to the point of apoplexy.

In the meantime there was the Feis Ceoil to be prepared. The idea of Irish Art Music was first mooted in the pages of the *Evening Telegraph* on 8 September 1894 in the form of a letter from Mr O'Neill Russell. It was taken up by Annie Patterson, who lectured on Irish music to Gaelic Leaguers. They began to plan an Irish Musical and Literary Festival. Everyone basically agreed with the general idea, but there was an immediate split between those who wanted purely Irish music and those who wanted a wider brief. Given Edward Martyn's attachment to all things European, it is not surprising that he sided with the latter. So in 1897 there were two festivals, the Oireachtas and the Feis. The Oireachtas had a programme for competing essays, songs, poems and stories in the Irish language and, after a while, music lagged behind.[32] (In the immediate years following, nevertheless, all the leading actors in the renaissance were to be found enjoying the Oireachtas, which was considered to be the annual festival of the Gaelic League.) But the Feis put forward a much stronger and focused idea of Irish music 'as an independent mode of artistic endeavour'; it was to be nationalistic but not a narrow cultural nationalism.[33]

In an article at the front of the programme for the 1899 Feis, entitled 'The possibilities of the Feis Ceoil', Martyn claimed that: 'The grand central aim of the institution is to call into being a modern school of Irish musicians taking their inspiration from the ancient music of our race'. But as well as that, what he wanted to see was that 'choirs in future be directed to the singing of the madrigals and motets of the sixteenth century'. There is no Gaelic League voice from the period to tell us what they thought of this idea but, if they thought it preposterous, they may well have forgiven him for he went on to say that the roots of ancient Irish song and dance 'are in no foreign lands or systems but in the ancient civilisation and ancient art of Ireland. This is the secret of its true nationality. This will be the pledge of its lasting success.'

'The Feis was by all accounts a great affair,' Yeats wrote to Lady Gregory in May. It had been held from 17 to 22 May in the Royal University buildings in Dublin and it had included Michele Esposito's cantata *Deirdre*, a romantic cantata for soprano, tenor, baritone, chorus and orchestra, set to a poem by T.W. Rolleston. Original composition was one of the competitions and, in the early days, the festival encouraged works based on traditional Irish airs. This was a deliberate attempt to encourage cultural nationalism in Irish music while, at the same time, seeing if it was possible to reconcile an Irish repertory to a European aesthetic. The Feis was Edward Martyn's first encounter with Michele Esposito, an Italian national who had brought his family to settle in Dublin. In the following years they were to go on together creating spaces for the cultivation of music in Ireland, including the foundation of the Dublin Symphony Orchestra.

No doubt Edward was excited by the foundation of the Feis Ceoil but, of course, his first great musical love was sixteenth-century polyphonic music and he had been writing about it regularly in *The Speaker* since 1895. He was very familiar with its revival in the great cathedrals of Europe and, ambitious to spread the word, had written: 'I have often wondered whether the countless pilgrims to Bayreuth, who are wont to pass through Cologne, know that in its famous cathedral any Sunday morning at High Mass they may hear rendered on a scale of rare magnificence the masterpieces of another art reformer mighty in his day as Wagner is in our time, Giovanni Pierluigi da Palestrina.'[34] In 1896 his article had concentrated on Vittoria, Palestrina's contemporary. But it was also a rant at the Irish clergy, who were, for the most part, utterly indifferent to this music or any other. A crusade to change music in Irish churches forever had begun, but before we come to that we must go back to the drama.

7 • A 'Celtic' Theatre

IN JUNE 1897 W.B. Yeats was back at Tillyra. There had been a lot of coming and going in London throughout the spring, with George Moore, Yeats and Martyn often meeting at Augusta Gregory's dinner or tea table in Queen Anne's Mansions. On 23 February Gregory reports in her diary that Yeats 'is very full of play writing. He is delighted with E. Martyn's new Celtic one – "Splendid and stirring" – He, with the aid of Miss Florence Farr … is very keen about taking or building a little theatre somewhere in the suburbs to produce a romantic drama, his own plays (and) E.M's.'[1] But nothing came of this and it is notable that in these early months of the year they were discussing not only plays but also protest. There was to be a protest against the coming celebrations to mark Queen Victoria's Diamond Jubilee and, at the same time, a committee was being set up to arrange the celebration of the centenary of the 1798 uprising the following year. The first meeting was held in March. Both these actions reflected how far these people had come in their nationalist aspirations for some form of separation from Britain.

Nevill Geary was left out of it all. In April he returned home on extended leave from Africa, looking, Augusta Gregory wrote, 'very well and bright'. It was, perhaps, in this period that he met his future wife, Florence Burke of Danesfield, County Galway, who was the sister of Daisy Fingall. Lady Fingall figured regularly in Gregory's diary in this period. She was in London helping Horace Plunkett, a Unionist MP at the time, with his work for Irish agriculture and industry.[2] Gregory was also helping him with his speeches on Irish grievances in the House of Commons. There is no documented evidence of Geary meeting Edward Martyn on this holiday and the latter is missing from Augusta's frenetic socialising and theatre-going in April. That may well have been only because he was travelling. The diary records that he was in Rome for Holy Week.

But the summer was for Tillyra and Coole and both Martyn and Gregory stayed well away from Dublin and the demonstrations that were organised against the Jubilee celebrations on 21 June. These celebrations provoked much anger and rioting quickly ensued. The friends in south Galway, however, marked their disapproval in their own way. George Gough of Lough Cutra had written to all his neighbours requesting that they light bonfires as a mark of celebratory respect. Gregory blankly refused, saying that 'after long and marked neglect shown by the Queen to Ireland I thought it right to preserve an attitude of respectful disapproval'. W. Shawe Taylor, Gregory's cousin, said he couldn't afford the turf and Martyn said 'he had no turf himself, but he hoped that those of his tenants who had bogs might see their way to lighting bonfires'.[3] A rather unlikely prospect, as he well knew.

On 25 June Gregory drove over to Tillyra to give Annie Martyn some fresh trout she had received from the local RIC Sergeant Hanlon. Yeats had just arrived from Dublin. He was 'white, haggard, and voiceless fresh from the Jubilee riots which he had been in the thick of'.[4] He was involved in the violence, he explained, only to protect Maud Gonne, who was the chief organiser of the demonstration. He had locked her in a room in the National Club in Parnell Square for protection. She was furious but forgave him, realising that she should not have encouraged him in what she called 'the outer side of politics … you have higher work to do'.[5] One woman was killed in the riot, so it was hardly surprising that Yeats was 'white' and 'haggard'.

Yeats stayed at Tillrya for almost a month, leaving on 17 July to visit Sligo. He and Edward both worked and Yeats gave his host a copy of Fiona MacLeod's *The Three Marvels of Iona* to read. These stories deal with the supernatural manifestations in the life of St Columba. Edward was delighted with the third and final one entitled 'The Moon Child', which deals with a seal-man who fathers a child by a mortal woman. Columba orders his crucifixion. The child, when born, is supernaturally radiant and wanders the earth singing of her ancestry. When she meets Columba, she forgives him the death of her father. Then she is transfigured into Christ and she blesses the saint as he dies. In a letter to William Sharp (Fiona MacLeod) telling him of Edward's delight, Yeats also remarks that 'he [Edward] has rewritten much of his Celtic play "Maeve" and it is now very fine'. (Yeats, who claimed to be surprised when George Moore later told him how much help Martyn had got with his first two plays, had written to the latter in this period regarding Queen Maeve … 'I have found an old woman who has seen her … . Maeve, as she describes her, is a tall beautiful amazon kind of woman in a white tunic that leaves her arms and legs bare. She has both sword and dagger. This woman saw her coming from the place of her tomb on Knocknarea).'[6]

He also writes that 'Martyn is starting a new Irish play about political life'.[7] This would become *The Tale of a Town*, Martyn's first attempt at satire since the publication of *Morgante the Lesser*, the existence of which his new friends seemed to be completely unaware. At this point it is interesting to note the facility and speed with which Edward Martyn hops from 'supernatural manifestations' to 'literary aestheticism' to 'political satire'. It causes some pangs of apprehension. What is emerging is the oeuvre of a talented amateur rather than that of a potentially serious artist. Frustration and heartache cloud the horizon.

On a drenching wet day in July 1897, Yeats and Martyn went to visit Florimonde de Basterot at Durus. Martyn had given the Comte the script of *Maeve*. When they got there, they found him with Augusta Gregory reading the play while the rain fogged up the small cottage-style windows of the modest house. They all loved the work, and the conversation for the afternoon turned on drama and the necessity for an Irish theatre to accommodate Irish plays. This day was crucial to the future of the Irish National Theatre. Augusta Gregory wrote of it: 'we had a general conversation for a long time. I divided the party by taking Yeats into "Mr. Quin's office" – and there we had tea and talked & the idea came to us that if "Maeve" could be acted in Dublin, instead of London as E.M. thought of, with Yeats ['s] "Countess Cathleen" it would be a development of the literary movement, & help to restore dignity to Ireland, so long vulgarised on the stage as well as in romance – and we talked until we saw Dublin as the Mecca of the Celt – This was the beginning of our movement.'[8] It was somehow fitting that this little bastion of European civilisation in south Galway should house the genesis of the Irish National Theatre. For Martyn, especially, there was the aspiration that an Irish theatre would develop a repertory that could

15 Florimonde de Basterot's modest house at Durus where, on a
drenching wet day in July 1897, Yeats, Martyn and
Augusta Gregory decided to found a theatre.

be reconciled to a European aesthetic. It was part of the same
aspiration he held for traditional Irish music and part of his European
dream.

At first they called it 'The Celtic Theatre' and in the week following
their trip to Durus, Yeats and Martyn were in and out of Coole every
day. (By the end of the month, however, Martyn was on his way to
Bayreuth with Moore.)[9] They hoped to have their inaugural performance in the spring of 1898. They needed money and Augusta Gregory
typed out, on one of the first ever Remington typewriters, given to her
by Enid Layard,[10] a list of people who could be approached as
guarantors. From Galway they sent, with their appeal for money, a copy
of their aims:

To the Guarantors for a 'Celtic' Theatre.

We propose to have performed in Dublin in the spring of every year certain Celtic and Irish plays, which whatever be their degree of excellence, will be written with a high ambition; and to make a beginning next spring with two plays, a play of modern Ireland and in prose by Mr Edward Martyn and a play of legendary Ireland and in verse by Mr W.B. Yeats. We expect to follow these plays by Mr George Moore, Mr Standish O'Grady, Miss Fiona McCleod [*sic*] and others, in other years; so to build up a Celtic and Irish dramatic school. Dramatic journalism has had full possession of the stage in England for a century and it perhaps impossible for audiences, who are delighted by dramatic journalism, however brilliant, to delight in the simplicity and naivety of literature unless it is old enough to be a superstition. We hope to find in Ireland an uncorrupted audience trained to listen by its passion for oratory and believe that our desire to bring upon the stage the deeper thoughts and emotions of Ireland will ensure for us a tolerant welcome and that freedom to experiment which is not found in the theatres of England and without which no new movement of art or literature can succeed. We will show that Ireland is not the home of buffoonery and of easy sentiment, as it has been represented, but the home of an ancient idealism and we are confident of the support of all Irish people, who are weary of misrepresentation, in carrying out a work that is outside all the political questions that divide us.

We have asked for a guarantee fund of £300 for our first attempt and almost half of this has been guaranteed already. The profits if any will go to a fund for the production of plays in the succeeding years.

Signed for provisional committee by WBY

The 'provisional committee' was Edward Martyn, Augusta Gregory and W.B. Yeats. The original patrons were Gregory, Martyn and Annie Martyn. Martyn also agreed to underwrite any overrun that might occur and this was all formalised at a later date.

But who cared about the money? That wet summer in south Galway was bliss. They were ambitious to use drama to develop an Irish cultural psyche. In the early days there was a lot of fun, but it quickly became stressful. They had the plays; they had some money. Now the most pressing need was for a theatre. It was Martyn's idea to put on a play in 1898 in tandem with the Feis Ceoil. Having the plays run alongside the Feis would guarantee an audience and a venue. But it had already been decided that in 1898 the music festival would be held in Belfast and the founders of the theatre definitely wanted to put on their plays in Dublin. Then Martyn suggested that they amalgamate with the Oireachtas and Yeats approached Douglas Hyde for permission to do this, but he was not successful. What they needed was a theatre. Those available in Dublin proved grossly expensive, so they turned their attention to halls and concert rooms. The problem with the latter was the necessity of having a special license to perform plays for money. An appeal for a license had got to be pleaded for before the Privy Council and that could cost as much as £80.[11] For the moment they were stuck and it was increasingly unlikely that they would get off the ground in 1898.

While Martyn was in Bayreuth, Yeats came back to Coole Park in the company of George Russell, rural economist as well as poet, mystic and painter, who had assisted Horace Plunkett in the foundation of the Irish Agricultural Organisation Society. He stayed there on and off for almost two months. He was not finished visiting Tillyra but he had found a niche in south Galway. This was the beginning of his great friendship with Augusta Gregory and, in many ways, it changed the nature of her relationship with Edward Martyn; a change that she came to regret and for which she spitefully, and unjustly, blamed George Moore.

While he was in Coole, Yeats wrote to Alice Milligan, a playwright and a leading member of the Gaelic League, urging her to use her influence to have the 1898 Feis put on in Dublin. He explained to her that 'we cannot go to Belfast for we must begin where the Literary Movement has done most to prepare the ground'. In an effort to persuade her, he said: 'The chief play will be a prose play by Edward Martyn – a celtic play of a strongly propagandist kind but of course without politics.'[12] But Alice Milligan was a Belfast nationalist who strongly objected to Dublin being the Mecca for all political and cultural activities. She actively wanted the Feis to be held in Belfast. Yeats and Martyn took themselves back to Dublin to look at halls but not before Augusta Gregory and the poet moved over to Tillyra to help Edward with his 'Celtic Party'. This is vividly described by Lady

Gregory in her retrospective September diary entry: 'William Sharp was there, an absurd object, in velvet coat, curled hair, wonderful ties – a good-natured creature – a sort of professional patron of poets – but making himself ridiculous by stories to the men of his love affairs and entanglements, & seeing visions (instigated by Yeats) – one apparition clasped him to an elm tree from which he had to be released – Martin Morris was also there & Doctor Moritz Bonn, an odious little German sent to me by Horace Plunkett, studying political economy & "not seeing what relation the Celtic movement had to it" – and Doctor Douglas Hyde came full of enthusiasm and Irish.' Shortly after that, she went to Spiddal to visit the Morrises 'for the fine weather had come at last, a sort of Indian summer and the Atlantic was beautiful'. Lord Morris, who did not want his son becoming involved in the Literary Theatre, was 'very cross, very violent against literature & writers', so she was glad to see Martyn and Yeats, who soon joined her there. She had arranged an interview with a witch doctor for Yeats.[13]

By November they had a large number of guarantors for the theatre and they were hopeful of getting a venue. But on 20 November Yeats wrote to William Sharp that: 'Martyn and myself have had a rather discouraging time in Dublin. Everybody is enthusiastic about the Celtic Theatre, more than enough of money is ready, and all the great names in Ireland are on our list but the law is apparently against us, unless we perform under impossible conditions. It may be necessary to begin in London & Martyn is depressed at the prospect.'[14] Yeats was anxious to keep Martyn's enthusiasm bubbling. He was about to give a lecture to the Literary Society in London, at which Sharp was to take the chair. 'I want you to give way to Martyn considering all the circum- stances,' he wrote to Sharp. 'I want him to be made much of by our people and to be encouraged to throw himself wholly upon our movement. Little things like taking the chair & so which mean nothing to you and me mean something to a man like him, a man who is not very young and not at all successful. ... If we can make Martyn a kind of Center [sic] it will be a great thing.' Yeats then went on to show how overbearing and controlling he could, at times, be. Referring to Martyn he wrote: 'Get men so much attention that they will feal [sic] that their words are effective and they will go in the path you have shown them.'[15] But having the chair was very important to Sharp and he refused to yield.

Augusta Gregory thought the notion of Edward Martyn taking the chair at the Literary Society was ridiculous. When he told her, she said she was 'not very polite for I said "you chairman" in an incredulous tone – but it was really absurd – He grew uncomfortable then & said he wished to get out of it if anything else could be managed.'[16] Edward was not then, and never would become, a creditable public speaker, but that hardly excuses either Augusta Gregory or Yeats for their gross insensitivity. He was good-natured enough to rise above it on this occasion, but it would not always be so. Still, Yeats's instincts that it might be necessary to work on keeping him interested were right. Lady Gregory notes in her diary for December that she had 'a nice letter from poor Edward Martyn who is low about the theatre'.[17]

In the early months of 1898 plans slowed down. Yeats's time was taken up with his work for the '98 celebrations. Maud Gonne was a heady attraction and kept him involved, but the amount of conflict and infighting was exhausting. In the spring Martyn did some travelling in Europe with Moore and they spent Easter in Paris. He was closely following his love of polyphonic music. Ideas for the formation of an Irish Choir were gathering in his head. But in March he was back in London for the Literary Society meeting and they still had no venue to produce their plays. They decided to lobby for a change in the law that allowed a patent to a mere three theatres in Dublin to stage dramatic productions without incurring a fine of £300 per performance. 'Thus is higher culture and native talent nipped in the bud,' the *Irish Figaro* wrote in January. It certainly excluded the performance of any experimental theatre. Then, Timothy Charles Harrington, who was the MP for Dublin Harbour, offered to insert a clause in the coming Local Government Bill to have the law changed. Yeats wrote to many MPs, including John Redmond, leader of the Irish Parliamentary Party, explaining exactly what they were trying to achieve: 'Our wish is to be able to produce once a year for (say) four days at a time, certain plays, which shall be the very reverse of "popular" in kind or in ambition, but a permission to give our first performances in February of next year at the Ancent [sic] Concert Rooms is our only ambition for the moment.'[18]

While Yeats went about other business in Paris, Martyn stayed in London to monitor developments on the political front. It was proposed that there should be an Amendment to the Bill that would give control of theatrical licensing to the new Dublin County Council. Martyn got Yeats back and made him stay in London until the matter was sorted.

On 12 May 1898 Annie Martyn died. She had outlived John Martyn by 38 years but she was still only 67 years old. A frail but feisty woman, she might have been expected to live longer. She had long since given up any idea of her son marrying and starting a new Martyn dynasty. An early patron of the Irish Literary Theatre, it is likely that she accepted and was interested in his artistic life. On 4 July, Yeats wrote to William Sharp that Martyn was 'horribly miserable', but we have no way of knowing for sure. Edward Martyn rarely wrote of his feelings. However, a letter to him from Arthur Symons, who had so recently been at Tillyra and who obviously regarded himself as a close friend, would indicate an intimate relationship between mother and son. 'I heard yesterday of your irreparable loss,' Symons wrote, 'the one absolutely irreparable loss that one can have in a lifetime. There is no consolation for this; only, in some degree, the very slow medicine of time. I sorrow with you through my own memory of my own sorrow, and I beg you to believe me, now more than ever, always your friend.'[19]

Edward organised an elaborate funeral. There were two bishops and 'a host of priests' in attendance.[20] She was laid to rest in the Martyn family tomb in the ancient cemetery at Kilmacduagh; the tomb erected by the first Edward Martyn as the resting place for his beloved Mary Brown. In due course he had a beautiful stained-glass window (executed in Sarah Purser's studio) in the parish church at Labane dedicated to her memory; the saint depicted in this work of art is Saint Bridget but contemplating the figure and the features one is immediately reminded of George Moore's physical description of Annie Martyn.

Over a year after her death, he was still using black-edged stationery for his correspondence. Still, a new freedom came into his life. He was comfortable in Tillyra with Gantly, the butler, and Mary Anne, the housekeeper, to look after him. They were both devoted servants and the evidence indicates that they were very fond of him. There was a form of release. But he was lonely. In one of his many reflections on Edward Martyn's nature, George Moore concluded that 'he who avoids the wife and the mistress becomes his mother's bond slave'. This contradicts his own perception of Annie Martyn as a bright, articulate and sensible woman who, almost certainly, did not want a 'bond slave'. There had been no indication in recent years of her interfering in

Edward's life. He can only have been disappointed that she did not live to see him become a 'public man'.

In June Yeats brought John Millington Synge to Tillyra. On his journey back to Wicklow from the Aran Islands he had stopped to spend a few days at Coole. What did Edward Martyn think of Synge? Alas, there is nothing documented with regard to this meeting. When, in 1902, Martyn refused to become a member of the National Theatre Society, part of the reason was his disagreement with Yeats and Gregory over what came to be known as 'the peasant play'. In the minds of many people this was mainly associated with Synge. When he opened his own theatre in 1914, Martyn offered a prize of £10 for the best play that had nothing to do with peasants. It is inconceivable that he did not recognise in Synge a nature mystic and dramatic poet unequalled in the Irish canon. Some of his own work attempted to do what Synge had achieved. Synge, however, looked back on Ireland's mystical past with rigorous clarity and managed to get under the skin of the people, while Martyn descended into a slough of sentimentality. With the exception of a letter to John Horgan, a Cork solicitor and ardent Home-Ruler, in August 1910 when Edward wrote: 'I am afraid I do not understand your friend the student of modern drama in his depreciation of Ibsen any more than his appreciation of Synge',[21] there is only silence. All we can be sure of is that, given his own poor relationship with his tenants, he would have had no problem at all with the notion of a peasant killing his father, the plot of *The Playboy of the Western World*.

By 12 July the 'Celtic Theatre' was safe. With the help of W.E.H. Lecky, a clause had been included in the Local Government Bill allowing that in the case of dramatic productions Dublin County Council could 'grant an occasional licence for the performance of any stage play or other dramatic entertainment in any theatre, room or building where the profits arising therefrom are to be applied for some charitable purpose or in aid of the funds of any society instituted for the purpose of science, literature or the fine arts exclusively'. This was not the only good news at this time. There was also the takeover of the *Daily Express* by a syndicate with Horace Plunkett at its head. Plunkett appointed T.P. Gill editor. Gill had been the MP for South Louth from 1885 to 1892 and was now a nationalist and journalist. Later, when the paper failed, Plunkett was instrumental in ensuring his appointment as secretary of the Department of Agriculture and Technical Instruction and came under much criticism for it. Gill had not the experience for such a position and the appointment smacked of 'jobbery'. In 1898 he was close to Yeats and Martyn and was in a position to offer them a platform in what he hoped to turn into a relatively popular paper to promote their theatre.

Under Gill's editorship, the *Dublin Daily Express* did move from being an extremely conservative organ to a moderately nationalist one. It lasted in its reformed state only until December 1899 but, for that period, it had a Saturday literary page and this provided an outlet for a wide range of literature and drama and what Gill called 'new ideas'. In September Martyn used it to write about and praise the Galway Feis. The Feis allowed only Irish-speaking peasants to perform, thus revealing, he wrote, 'in the Celtic peasants of the uncontaminated West a complete lack of coarseness; a people who are naturally poetical and refined'.

At this time too Standish James O'Grady took over the *Kilkenny Moderator*, which was a Unionist and Protestant weekly. O'Grady, who had written the *Bardic History of Ireland*, was Augusta Gregory's cousin. He was a champion, but also a savage critic, of the landed gentry and, under his editorship, many Gaelic Leaguers wrote for the *Moderator*.

When *The Heather Field* was published John B. Yeats wrote to Edward: 'Do you know Standish O'Grady – Tyrell is he – the same sincerity, vehemence, gentleness and confiding simplicity and the same affection for his offspring!' Edward did know him.

Also in September Edward Martyn met Vincent O'Brien, who would go on to have a major influence on the foundation of the Palestrina Choir. His life was filling up. Music was on his mind. At the Feis he had been struck by the 'rich colour and ancient tonality that reminded him of Oriental folk music of the Arabs and the Liturgical music in Coptic and Greek churches'. He 'found Mr. Vincent O'Brien producing *Missa Papae Marcelli* by Palestrina at the Carmelite Church of St. Teresa in Clarendon Street Dublin with some admirably efficient boys'.[22] O'Brien was the music master at the Christian Brothers School in Saint Mary's Place and they had about forty choir boys who 'had been used to winning prizes for choral and solo singing'.[23] He was a member of the Irish Society of Saint Cecilia, whose special aims came directly from European sources. It invited 'all who are zealous for the decorum and splendour of Catholic worship' and all who were interested in 'ancient and modern polyphonic music' to join the society. Very much a

European reform movement, it did not exclude women. As a general movement it had been started by Cardinal Paul Cullen, the instigator of the 'Devotional Revolution' in Ireland in the second half of the nineteenth century.[24] Martyn had come upon an excellent choir that could provide the foundation for the choir he had in mind, and a choirmaster who was in tune with his ideas. Moving between south Galway and London, he had not been paying as much attention as he might to Dublin. It was not so completely barren of aspiration to high art as he had thought. Still, there was much work to be done.

Edward Martyn's love of ecclesiastical music, as we have seen, pre-dated his interest in Wagner's music. But the interest, nevertheless, was all of a piece. In his articles in 1895 and 1896 in *The Speaker*, he had told his readers that in the sixteenth century Giovanni Pierluigi Palestrina, who had been commissioned by the Pope to reform ecclesiastical music, had found it in much the same degenerate state that Wagner had found dramatic music during the 1850s. It was no longer beautiful, nor was it inspirational. Musicians, except perhaps the very greatest, had made the mistake of supposing that vocal music may seek to become absolute and to supersede the importance of the words to which it is wedded: 'Wagner has shown with irresistible argument in his *Oper und Drama*, where he defines music as a purely emotional art, capable of becoming absolute when in instrumental form, but when set to speech takes necessarily a second place as the interpreter to our feelings of the hidden sentiment in that speech, which mere words must fail to express. His fidelity in practice to this all-important law is the secret of the overwhelming interest awakened by the hearing of his vast music dramas. ... The fidelity of Palestrina also to the same law is the chief secret of His immortality. ... In the same spirit as the Bayreuth master treated the dramatic poem, the old Italian treated the Liturgy of the Catholic Church. I would relinquish all – even Bach, Beethoven, Wagner – for the incomparable Pierluigi.'[25] His early contempt for all things Italian had obviously left him.

Now he was very keen to become the instigator of what he considered to be a true reform in ecclesiastical music in Ireland. Why he did not join forces with the Cecilian Movement is not clear. The people involved in it seemed far more likely to achieve a great city choir because they were, already, a successful choir. Perhaps he eschewed them because the whole debate in this period became an academic quagmire.[26] And, anyway, he really just wanted his own choir and for it to become a dedicated *Schola Cantorum* (cathedral choir). A *Schola Cantorum* had already been established at Maynooth College by Professor Heinrich Bewerunge, who had the chair of Church, Chant and Organ, but Edward Martyn's choir was to be specifically for the city of Dublin. He was more than willing to pay for it. Being a timid man and knowing, as he did, the philistinism and indifference of most of the Irish clergy, the fulfilment of this ambition must have seemed, all the same, a daunting prospect. He had heard Palestrina's masterpieces reduced to 'little piping quartettes' even by 'good' choirs and he was passionate to do something about it. In his article in 1896, he was dealing with Palestrina's disciple Vittoria but he mainly wrote about the work of the choirmaster of Saint Gervais in Paris, M. Charles Bordes. Bordes had been given permission to revive the ecclesiastical music of Palestrina and Vittoria for the cathedral. Arising from this, Martyn painfully felt the neglect of church music by the Catholic clergy, in both England and Ireland. The article vigorously attacks this neglect. So, he concluded, 'the old polyphonic masters, as under the auspices of M. Charles Bordes, have found their way into the coffers of the old Parisian church of Saint-Gervais. I fear such a choirmaster as M. Bordes is not to be found often.'[27]

In December 1898 Martyn had reason to think differently. He had met Vincent O'Brien. He was two months short of his fortieth birthday and he was in Paris for Christmas. One of his tasks was to seek out book and music shops to find some of M. Bordes's sheet music. He was enjoying himself. 'Paris is very pleasant,' he wrote to Augusta Gregory from the Hotel Continental on Rue Castiglione. She was keeping him informed about theatre business. *Tableaux Vivants* of Yeats's *Countess Cathleen* (the play that opened the Irish Literary Theatre the following year) were to be held at the Chief Secretary's residence at the Phoenix Park in Dublin. 'I think it is a capital idea,' he wrote, 'more especially as we shall probably afterwards get the loan of the dresses for nothing.' The news from Durus had been bad, but 'I'm glad to hear that our dear friend, de Basterot, is better,' he wrote. 'I sent a message to Robert to the effect that he might go with his friend to shoot at Tillyra,' he concluded.[28] Robert Gregory was then seventeen years old. After Edward Martyn's death, the most salient thing Lady Gregory remembered of him was his kindness to her son.

8 • Controversies

YEATS WASN'T SO sure that he was pleased about the prospect of his play being staged at the Chief Secretary's Lodge in the Phoenix Park. But it was being produced by Betty Balfour, wife of the Chief Secretary. She was a popular woman, and while the Literary Theatre was a 'national' project, most of its guarantors were members of the establishment. Still, despite his misgivings, he managed to coach Daisy Fingall for her part as the Countess and when she complained that she had the 'flu and didn't look well', he rebuked her sharply, telling her that 'you cannot be too thin or too miserable for this part'.

The theatre project had been officially announced at a meeting of the National Literary Society in Dublin on 9 January 1899. It was to be launched under the auspices of the society, and the Antient Concert Rooms in Great Brunswick Street had been booked for the first performance on 8 May. Gill's *Daily Express* did justice to the announcement, giving Yeats lots of space to explain the aspirations of the founding members. They were, he told the readers 'endeavouring to found an "Irish Literary Theatre", to do for Irish dramatic literature, as was hoped, what the Théâtre Libre and the Théâtre l'Œuvre have done for French dramatic literature. ... We propose to give our first performance in May when *The Heather Field*, a play of modern Irish life by Mr. Edward Martyn, and *The Countess Cathleen*, a play of medieval life by myself, will, we hope, be produced under the management of Miss Florence Farr, late manageress of the Avenue Theatre, London.'[1] On 16 January it was recorded in the minutes of the National Literary Society that Edward Martyn would hold the society 'harmless and free from any financial liability in connection with the promotion of the Irish Literary Theatre'.[2]

Martyn's plays, *The Heather Field* and *Maeve*, with their introduction by George Moore, were published in mid-January. Yeats had planned the announcement of the theatre to come just after the publication, reflecting an attention to detail that boded well for success.[3] On the flyleaf Edward Martyn is referred to as the author of *Morgante the Lesser*. On 20 January William Archer's review appeared in the *Daily Chronicle*. With regard to *The Heather Field*, he felt that the idea was a good one and might make a strong play and that 'Mr Martyn handles it with a good deal of general ability but without a trace of specifically dramatic instinct or talent. He develops his story flatly and languidly and his dialogue is not only flaccid but written with a curious constraint as though it were a not very expert translation from some foreign tongue. He is like a man with a strong taste for music trying to perform on an instrument of which he knows neither the resources or the subtleties.'[4] As already noted, Archer said of *Maeve* that it was a piece of 'frigid celticism'. 'Put these plays on in an "Experimental Theatre". Let them prove their worth to an intelligent public as "aesthetic curiosity".' But he could see no reason why they should be produced by his own New Century Theatre.

It was George Moore's introduction to the plays, however, which led to the controversy that ensued in the pages of the *Daily Chronicle* in the days after this review. Moore had used the introduction to lambast William Archer and George Alexander for their handling of theatre matters in London. So much so that Archer's review of the plays had, in fact, been entitled 'Mr. Moore as a Dramatic Critic' and it was mainly a reply to Moore's criticisms of the repertoire of the New Century Theatre. Moore, as we have seen, had attempted to create an independent theatre in the 1880s, so it was accepted that he and Archer were on the same side. In the introduction, however, the novelist had written that, while Archer had made a good start when he opened his theatre with Ibsen's play *John Gabriel Borkman*, his essay into the realms of modern prose drama had not lasted. He had also accepted the work of Sir Arthur Wing Pinero, 'who is about as subjective as a clown', over that of Yeats or Martyn, and had thereby shown that his 'catholicity of taste means that he doesn't understand true art'.[5] In fact Pinero's *The Second Mrs Tanqueray* (1893) was considered a strong contribution to the 'new movement' at the time. With reference to *The Heather Field*, Moore remarked that 'Archer failed to perceive that Carden Tyrell is the first appearance of humanity in the English prose drama of to-day'. A mighty claim indeed!

Archer had always made a point of distinguishing between Martyn and Yeats, declaring Yeats to be 'as authentic a poet as ever lived' and *The Countess Cathleen* is a very beautiful poem ... a creature visible only to the eyes of the soul'. But he argued, with right on his side, that he had 'never been able to see that the best interests either of the stage or of literature are served by efforts to make the stage the vehicle for all literature that happens to be written in dialogue'. Moore protested, and Archer assured him that he had found 'not inconsiderable pleasure in the works of Edward Martyn' but that 'to take Edward Martyn's play for the New Century Theatre would be to do him an injustice'. In the *Academy*, Archer also wrote about Edward's work: 'Mr Martyn is at the present of all things derivative, an echo not an individual voice. He gives you the persistent symbolism of Maeterlinck, the eerie glamour and mystic whisperings.'[6] By 30 January Yeats, at the instigation of Moore, had taken up the cudgels and, in a long essay-style letter, concluded that they were looking not for large audiences

IRISH LITERARY THEATRE

"THE HEATHER FIELD."

It is impossible to speak in moderation of Mr. Edward Martyn's drama, "The Heather Field," which was produced by the Irish Literary Theatre last night. The power, the beauty, and the excellence of Mr. Martyn's work took everyone by storm. Readers of the play were

MR. EDWARD MARTYN.

universal in their admirations of it. But amongs them there were those who doubted whether the fine literary workmanship, and that rare breath of poetry which seems to blow in straight from the pure, fragrant heather-field would bear the fierce glow of the foot-lights and retain their charm and freshness. It was difficult, as it is always difficult, to say from the mere reading of the book how far the play would justify the hopes that had been formed of it. But within five minutes from the rising of the curtain folk began to realise that here was a fine piece of drama—drama purely literary, drama dealing with the every-day life of the people, drama written naturally in good, nervous prose, but brightened by the play of beautiful ideas, which imparted to that prose the charm of poetry. Nor was this all. It soon became apparent that the dramatist had chosen for his theme not only a domestic in-cident, but one involving a NICE QUESTION IN PSYCHOLOGY. Now, to the average reader, no less than the

16 Review of *The Heather Field*, published in January 1899. Later, George Moore admitted to helping Edward with the structure, but never the content.

for their plays but audiences drawn from 'different classes, which will add to a true understanding of drama an interest in life and in the legends on which our plays are founded so deep that it will give us that freedom to experiment, that freedom to search for the laws of what is perhaps a lost art'.[7] The flavour of this correspondence is that of the 'big guns', the 'in people' fighting for a cause. And while Moore is fighting for his own ideals, he is also fighting Edward Martyn's corner. Edward was not grateful.

Max Beerbohm, cartoonist, critic and writer, published a short critique of *The Heather Field* for the London published *Saturday Review* on 28 January, revealing a dislike of the published version which did not entirely manifest itself in his later review of the stage play. In fact, at this point, Beerbohm was more interested in the scrap between Moore and Archer than he was in the play. Also on 28 January George Russell's review appeared in the *Dublin Daily Express* and dealt with the spiritual significance of the plays. He put Edward in the same camp as those who were 'feeling their way half unconsciously to spiritual certitude through impalpable things and visionary longings, and the sights and sounds which penetrate our world from a world unseen'.[8] In this period Russell's imagination was much taken up with all aspects of fairylore. He did make the point, however, that he wasn't sure 'whether it is madness or spiritual ecstasy that comes over him [Carden Tyrell] in the end'.

Annie MacDonnell of *Bookman* also reviewed the book and praised the plays but noted that Edward was 'not a master of language'.[9] It had been hoped that Arthur Symons would do the critique for the *Saturday Review* but he wrote to Yeats: 'I failed to get Martyn's plays, for Max had already had a cheap sneer at them by the time your letter reached the office.' Beerbohm had failed to see any 'transcendent peculiarities' in Martyn's work. Symons was probably personally offended.

In February Martyn's article on 'The Modern Drama in Germany' appeared in the *Express*. It was, as Yeats put it, 'good enough as thought but curiously clumsy as writing'.[10] In it Martyn suggested the encouragement of state-subsidised theatres on the German model, which might afford 'high class plays' to be acted for very short runs, thus allowing for experimentation. He was slightly baffled that it was in Germany that this was presently happening where 'no person of discernment had ever given the German Emperor credit for much taste or judgement. His words and actions suggest an unpleasant suspicion of the modern vulgarian'. This remark reflects an underestimation of the birth and triumph of modern art in Germany, especially in Weimar during the Wilhelminian era, despite the limitations of the Kaiser. The bulk of the article, however, is devoted to the work of Gerhart Hauptmann, who was reputed to be a great admirer of Henrik Ibsen, but who later told Count Harry Kessler, the German aesthete and diplomat, that 'Ibsen had influenced him little if at all' and that it was Leo Tolstoy who had opened the door for him to his own work as a playwright. Ibsen's characters were all artificial, whereas Tolstoy's were genuine creations.[11] It was hardly surprising that it was Hauptmann's *Hannele* about which Martyn chose to write. It was 'the dream of life and the life of dream,' he wrote, with echoes of Calderón's *Life is a Dream*. The 'dream visions in this play go with simple pathos to the heart'. Hauptmann's most important play to date had been *Die Weber* (The Weavers) and on 4 March Edward was writing to the artist Sarah Purser explaining to her that it was a play about the factual events of the social struggle of the weavers of Silesia. 'All the weavers are the hero,' he told her.[12] This letter is in reply to a query by Purser, but there is no explanation of why she wanted the information. With the exception of a thank-you note for an invitation to dinner on 24 February, it is the first communication we have between these two aesthetes. Purser was about to become the fine art side of the cultural renaissance and they were still writing to each other in 1922. The friendship lasted until Martyn's death in 1923.

On 24 November 1898 George Moore wrote to W.B. Yeats with reference to *The Countess Cathleen*: 'Martyn thought there was something paradoxical in the idea of a woman selling her soul so that she might buy the salvation of the soul of others' … I said to Martyn: "I know Yeats is right but I cannot tell you why he is right but I will tell you tomorrow or the next day; and I did".'[13] He didn't convince him, though, and it was quite legitimate that a Catholic might question a situation where God excuses the deed by looking at the motive. *Cathleen* sells her soul to save lots of other souls. Her soul is, apparently, worth more than others! Martyn appeared to let it go.

They were trying to find actors to suit the various roles in the two plays but, even with the help of Florence Farr, Martyn and Yeats were failing. They didn't know what they were doing. Martyn was agreeing to pay bad actors good money for poor work and that alone was enough to spur Moore to action when they came to ask his help. He leaves us a wonderful description in *Ave* of them arriving at the flat in King's Bench Walk, but it is hardly the whole truth. By this time Moore had left the Temple and was living in his flat in Victoria Street. Nevertheless, describing the appearance of Yeats and Martyn as 'fantastic as anything seen in a Japanese print – Edward great in girth as an owl (he is nearly neckless), blinking behind his glasses, and Yeats lank as a rook, a dream in black silhouette on flowered wallpaper'[14] remains a lingering image. 'But rooks and owls do not roost together, nor have they a habit or an instinct in common,' the novelist reflected wonderingly. Was it then that Moore started planning his great trilogy? His first biographer, Susan Langstaffe Mitchell, poet and satirist, would have us believe it was.

Long-term planning notwithstanding, Moore was delighted to be accepted into this exciting cultural circle. Yeats introduced him to Florence Farr. He was very keen to work alone with her, insisting that Martyn 'knows no more about managing a theatre than a turbot from the North Pole'.[15] He didn't succeed and within a few weeks Moore and Martyn managed to have her removed as stage manager. She did, however, stay to do all the publicity for the theatre and was still very much involved with the production of the two plays. Relieved of much of the anxiety of casting for the plays, Martyn was able to relax and on 19 February we find him sitting for his portrait at the Yeats's home in Bedford Park. Susan Mitchell was living there at the time and John B. Yeats, the poet's father, insisted on her singing to him while he worked. The portrait is a pencil and wash drawing, signed by John B. Yeats, which Martyn gave to Augusta Gregory and is now in the National Gallery of Ireland. The elder Yeats was very keen to come to Galway to paint a full portrait of Edward. He wrote to W.B. urging him to arrange it.[16]

During this period Martyn was 'very chirpy,' as Augusta Gregory wrote in her diary. Indeed throughout that spring socialising was going at such a pace in London that no one was interested in Lady Geary's concern over Nevill, who was suffering from ulcerated feet in the humid heat of the African sun. Still, Gregory ruefully wrote: 'I hope I shaln't [*sic*] see Robert in exile for want of money.'[17] On 10 March Martyn heard tell of a report of Geary's death, but within a couple of days there was a telegram from the man himself assuring them to the contrary. Martyn was back in Dublin on 1 March for the inaugural concert of the Dublin Orchestral Society, which he had established with

Michele Esposito. Gluck, Mozart, Mendelssohn, Beethoven and Wagner were on the programme, but the audience was small.[18] It was an inauspicious start for a society that would only limp its way through its short life. Its foundation, however, and Edward's later involvement with the Pipers' Club, belies the notion that he was interested only in liturgical music, to the detriment of the cultural revival.[19]

Having no doubt forgotten Moore's letter of the previous year, it was on 21 March that Yeats heard again of Martyn's scruples about the theological orthodoxy of *The Countess Cathleen*. He had been entertaining Augusta Gregory in Woburn Buildings and, as he was seeing her out, he discovered a letter in his box. Martyn, still worried about the play, had submitted it for approval, perhaps to Cyril Ryan, the Provincial of the Carmelites in Dublin. It is not clear exactly whom it was that he consulted. He merely claimed 'a high authority' who had informed him 'that the play has many passages most objectionable to Catholics'[20] and he had thought so himself. He felt he could no longer support the Irish Literary Theatre financially or otherwise. His remorse – 'It was dreadfully mistaken and wrong of me not to have spoken of this at first' – was underlined in what was a very distressful letter. 'A thunderbolt', Augusta Gregory wrote. Martyn was their chief backer. T.P. Gill, a staunch Catholic, gave them the confidence to plough on, declaring that by no means must the scheme be abandoned. Moore spent much time jumping up and down with fury. Martyn 'keeps part of his conscience in his stomach, the rest around the corner,' he thundered.[21]

Yeats and Gregory set to work immediately. First they contacted George Coffey, who was, at the time, the Keeper of Irish Antiquities at the National Museum of Science and Art. He was also an amateur actor and had played one of the demon merchants in the tableaux vivants in the Chief Secretary's Lodge in January. He, too, had had some problems with the play and he had consulted Dr Gerald Molloy, eminent theologian and rector of the Catholic University, on what he considered might be heterodox passages but had had what he considered was a positive response. This gave them the confidence to do the same. On 22 March Yeats wrote to Martyn:

> My dear Martyn: you are wrong about the facts to begin with. Coffey told Gill that he supposed Dr. Molloy would omit what Coffey thought to be heterodox passages. Gill, whom I have just

seen, heard Dr. Molloys (reading) & listened very carefully because of what Coffey had said & assures me that (Dr. Molloy) he omitted nothing from the pages selected for him.

Now I am ready to omit any changes or passages which you may think objectionable. Taking into consideration the (enormous) extreme difficulties in which your backing out at this stage will envolve [*sic*] Lady Gregory, George Moore, Gill, the National Literary Society, yourself and my self & the miserable scandal it will make I think I have the right to ask you to do this. I am entirely convinced that the play contains no passage which can give offence to any Catholic. If you cannot (do this for) & do not wish to point out these passages, remembering your guarantees and the scandal your withdrawal of it (will) would make, (I must ask you) the suspicions this would throw upon the literary movement in Ireland and even upon peoplelike Horace Plunkett who have support(ed) that movement I am bound to ask you to take the only other course – to submit the matter to an arbiter, Dr. Barry, Dr. Delaney, Dr. Vaughan, Father Finlay or any other competent & cultivated theologian. I will take out or change any passage objected to by the arbiter. Of course I need not remind you we have little time to lose.[22]

The number of clergy that Yeats could call on in this matter reflects the strength of clerical interest in cultural matters of the period, and belies the notion that the clergy were entirely philistine. The most interesting of the suggested arbiters was Dr William Barry, priest, novelist, critic and essayist. He was a long-standing member of the Irish Literary Society and among his friends he counted Lionel Johnson, the late Count Eric Stenbock and Robert Ross. In 1905 he defended Wilde's *De Profundis* as an essentially spiritual work. After reading *The Countess Cathleen*, he wrote Yeats on 26 March:

I read your Countess Cathleen as soon as possible after seeing you. It is beautiful and touching; I hope you will not be kept back from giving it by foolish talk. Obviously, from the literal point of view Theologians, Catholic or other, would object that no one is free to sell his soul in order to buy bread even for the starving. But St Paul says 'I wished to be anathema for my brethren' – which is another way of expressing what you have put into a story. I would give the play first and explanations afterwards. ... Some one wise will say that you have learned from the Jesuits to make the end justify the means – and much that man will know of you or the Jesuits.[23]

Martyn had agreed to a compromise and wrote Yeats on 29 March: 'I am very sorry to have given all this trouble.'[24] He was more interested in Father Finlay's response than any other. Thomas Finlay S.J. was at this time working closely with Horace Plunkett in the Co-operative Movement. He was a literary activist and a founding member of the National Literary Society. Finlay recommended a few verbal alterations which Yeats carried out. Martyn was also pleased with Barry's reply, but couldn't help being a little petulant and ungracious. On 28 March he wrote to Yeats:

I must tell you that the chief objection was not the central idea of selling her soul to the devil in order to save other souls because the whole play is so mythical and undefined but the fact that there are several passages of an uncatholic and heretical nature that would over here create a scandal especially if the work was promoted and championed by a person like myself who everyone knows to be a Catholic. ... Dr. Barry does not seem to have realised it is *my* difficulty and not *yours*.

Unfortunately that was not the end of the matter. Moore was stirring the pot. In the draft of *Autobiographies*, Yeats wrote: 'I saw George Moore ... and exacted a promise that he would neither speak nor write to Edward Martyn on the subject 'till we had received our answers.'[25] As it happened, this was to no avail. On 31 March, Martyn wrote to Yeats:

I received from Moore a most offensive letter which I will not stand. He attacks my valued friend Dr. Healy [Bishop of Clonfert] in a manner that disgusts me. Now he is quite mistaken about that prelate. I never directly or indirectly consulted Dr. Healy about *The Countess Cathleen*. He knows nothing whatever about this row so you had all better be careful about mentioning his name. Now as to myself after Moore's words I shall pay either to you him or Lady Gregory £130 in aid of the LT or withdraw my play and leave the Literary Theatre altogether. I do not wish to be mixed up in the concern anymore. I have had too much trouble in various ways and cannot stand any more.[26]

Over breakfast in a Dublin hotel on 1 April Yeats and Florence Farr talked Martyn out of it. In the draft of *Autobiographies*, Yeats wrote that just as they had got off the boat from Holyhead, Martyn arrived. 'He was mopping his face with his pocket hankerchief for it was soaked with perspiration, and his first sentence was "I resign. I cannot possibly go on". Gradually, however, he talked away his misery and was soon busy with the preparations.'[27] Moore, it became clear, was furious with the compromise over *The Countess*. He had believed any attempted mollification of Martyn would be a failure and he had written an article that he had expected to publish in *Nineteenth Century*. 'It was', he wrote Yeats, 'to be called *The Soul of Edward Martyn*. It would have made a sensation all over Europe, no man has ever written so of his most intimate friend.'[28] Then, in his fury over the compromise, he sent Martyn the article in the form of a letter. For a while it seemed an unforgivable act, but all things pass. In his long letter to Moore of 28 September 1900 (already cited), Martyn reminded Moore: 'You wrote me a most insulting letter – but as you have expressed regret for having done so I will let that pass.' The article in question, in both forms, is lost to posterity, but it is interesting to note that John Healy blessed the Irish Literary Theatre and wrote Edward: 'I think your friend Mr. Yeats has been rather severely handled by the Theologians.'[29]

If we want to examine what it was that possessed Edward Martyn to behave the way he did, we have, paradoxically, to turn to Moore for some enlightenment. 'Edward', he tells us, 'yields completely to authority once he has accepted it.'[30] Back in 1886 when he had decided to live within the theological boundaries of the Catholic Church, it was because that was the place he felt safest. He had a sense of belonging. But this extreme reactionary Catholicism has to be juxtaposed with his attraction to, and will to be with, people drawn to the imagination and for whom the imagination is the route to the truth. Martyn desperately wanted to believe in his Catholicism with a simple peasant's belief, but

Art kept getting in the way. Dogma held no attraction for him. The 'drama of the mind' attracted him and that was something that Ibsen and Wagner understood. It was not something the Catholic Church had any truck with. He wanted to, and thought he could, compartmentalise art and religion. But what was he to do when they became intertwined? Others, as instanced by Dr William Barry and Fr. Thomas Finlay, coped.

It appeared that Edward Martyn didn't. When faced with a crisis he seemed to stop thinking. There is no evidence that he indulged in reflection on the basic tenets of Christianity and how they might come into conflict with the life that he wished to live, or with other beliefs that he held. Being an Irish Catholic was easy. Catholicism's notion of examining one's conscience, in preparation for the confessional, did not include a deep and profound look at one's life. For the Roman Catholic Church in Ireland, the acceptance of dogma was all that was required of its adherents. The questioning of it was not encouraged and this suited Edward Martyn. It did not interest him so he did not think of it. He took the easiest option and simply accepted. He did not want to examine his conscience and know himself; and the Catholic Church sanctioned this self-repression. This mode of living was not unusual in the era in which he lived in Ireland. But when his fourth play, *An Enchanted Sea*, appeared in 1902, it revealed much that was going on in Martyn's head that had little to do with Catholicism. The heather broke out in the manicured field and, as we shall see, it did so in its own peculiar way.

Though often timid, Edward Martyn was not frightened of people in general, especially of humbugs. 'I don't mind any number of Frank Hughs,' he told Yeats in early April. He was referring to Frank Hugh O'Donnell, a nationalist and journalist who had been elected MP for Galway in 1874, but had lost the seat because it was alleged he had libelled his opponent, and that he had used clerical intimidation to help him gain the seat. He went on to represent Dungarvan, County Waterford from 1877 to 1885. Always an egotistical and irrational man, O'Donnell spurned both Parnell and the Land League. After he resigned his seat in 1885, he concentrated on journalism and on 1 April 1899 launched an attack on *The Countess Cathleen* in the pages of the *Freeman's Journal*. He wrote from the Irish National Club in London, so it can be assumed that he was well aware of Martyn's misgivings regarding the play. He was out to do as much damage as he could to

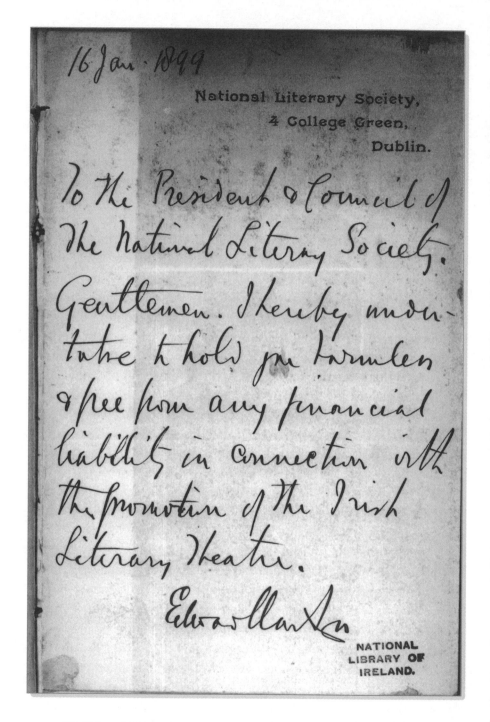

17 Edward Martyn's agreement to underwrite the debts of the ILT.

Yeats, and perhaps thought he might recruit Martyn to his cause. (In 1916 Edward Martyn and O'Donnell corresponded amicably about the theatre matters, when the latter submitted three plays for the Irish Theatre.) There was very little response to the first letter, so he wrote a second. When it was refused publication, he issued both letters in the form of a pamphlet with the title *Souls for Gold! A Pseudo-Celtic Drama in Dublin*. It was printed in London and dropped into letterboxes all over residential Dublin in late April. The first night of the Irish Literary Theatre was to be 8 May and *The Countess Cathleen* was the opening play. Florence Farr was in the throes of publicity for the event.[31]

Yeats did not panic. O'Donnell was an old adversary whose present gripe with him was his criticism of Thomas Davis, the leader of the Young Irelanders and co-founder of *The Nation*. Yeats was not happy with Davis's poetry because he felt that its propagandist nature led to a careless technique. This criticism was anathema to O'Donnell and many other patrons of the Irish National Club. But O'Donnell was also gunning for Yeats as a result of the poet's, and Maud Gonne's, repudiation of a pamphlet O'Donnell had published in June 1898 attacking Michael Davitt (Land Leaguer and ex-Fenian) as a 'renegade' who was working for the British government. As a result of this pamphlet, Yeats and Gonne worked hard to subvert his influence among nationalists and succeeded in getting the pamphlet denigrated by most of them and by all the relevant nationalist organisations.[32] Now this latest pamphlet, which reflected a cogent reading of *The Countess Cathleen*, sought to prove that Yeats was neither 'Celtic' nor 'Catholic'. 'Mr. W.B. Yeats's notion', O'Donnell wrote, 'of what is Celtic is everywhere illustrated by his harpings on his pet "Celtic Idea" that the Gaels of Erin have and had only the thinnest veneer of Christian religion and civilisation, and really reserve their deepest beliefs for demons, fairies, leprechauns, sowlths, tivishes, etc.'[33] He cites many instances in the play where characters behave as no Irishman could behave, such as when Shemus Rhua kicks the shrine of the Blessed Virgin to pieces or where the Demon, disguised as an Irish pig, hunts down and slays 'Father John the Priest' and then dumps his soul in a black bag. And there is the peasant woman who is false to her marriage vows. 'How Irish,' O'Donnell scoffs ironically, 'How exquisitely Celtic.' Indeed, Yeats did give him lots of ammunition and many of the Celtic Revivalists did believe that Ireland's Christianity was skin deep. Edward Martyn's fourth play, as we shall see, was highly 'pagan' in nature.

But the people of Dublin were well aware of O'Donnell's animosity towards the poet, and the *Freeman's Journal* and the *United Irishman* disparaged the pamphlet. On 6 May, however, the *Daily Nation* printed an editorial 'endorsing all the theological objections to the play'[34] and, in turn, it was attacked by the *Daily Express* for trying to outdo O'Donnell's 'hysterical pamphlet with the fervour of a Ghazi'. The *Daily Nation* article regretted that prominent Catholics were associated with the Irish Literary Theatre and warned that if the play was not amended, 'they will have only themselves to blame for the consequences which will ensue if "Countess Cathleen" is presented on Monday night'.[35] That evening (6 May) Yeats gave what Joseph Holloway described as 'a rambling discourse on 'Dramatic Ideals and the Irish Literary Theatre' to the National Literary Society at No. 6 St Stephen's Green. He effectively saw off the attacks on his play, to the satisfaction of the audience and then he 'rambled off without notes to speak of the drama' in general. When he was finished, 'Count Plunkett proposed in his usual pause-between-each-word-dreamy-way the vote of thanks and Mr. George Russell seconded it and went for Mr. Yeats's spiteful detractors and castigated the poor spite of those who published and circulated attacks on his work out of pure malice. Dr. Sigerson in putting the vote also had a go at the geese who will always screech, especially those of the Celtic breed.'[36]

The 'spiteful detractors' were far from finished. But Monday, 8 May, is upon us and the opening night of the Irish Literary Theatre deserves its own space – so bring down the lights.

9 · A Literary Theatre

T HE AUDIENCE WAS 'large and most fashionable' and there was 'a pretty little miniature stage, perfectly appointed', Joseph Holloway reported to his diary on 8 May 1899. The venue, as we know, was the Antient Concert Rooms in Great Brunswick Street (Pearse Street), described by Percy Fitzgerald in his *Recollections of Dublin Castle and Dublin Society* as 'a shabby tenement about the size and proportions of a moderate Dissenting Chapel'. *The Countess Cathleen* was the first night production. It was not just the furore caused by O'Donnell's pamphlet that excited the audience. They were more than ready to have their imagination struck and they were delighted by the notion that this theatre was going to be a distinctively nationalist institution. Trouble was expected, though, and it came in the form of 'an organized claque of about twenty brainless, beardless, idiotic-looking youths' who 'did all they knew to interfere with the progress of the play by their meaningless automatic hissing and senseless comments. Thomas Davis seemed to be the particular bee in their bonnet.'[1] They were, however, completely frustrated by the enthusiastic applause of the audience. James Joyce, who would later stage *The Heather Field* in Zurich, sat at the side of the balcony 'looking out with jaded eyes at the culture of Dublin in the stalls' and at the 'tawdry scene cloths and human dolls framed by the garish lamps on the stage. A burly policeman sweated behind him and seemed at every moment about to act. The catcalls and hisses and mocking cries ran in rude gusts round the hall from his scattered fellow students.'[2]

But Joyce was probably right about 'tawdry scene cloths and human dolls', for *The Countess* had been difficult to stage, especially with regard to the costumes. Afterwards Susan Mitchell, having listened to Yeats's dissatisfaction with the production process, summed up what his intentions for future drama might be:

> I for my plays will find a simple hall;
> My stage – shall I have a stage at all?
> My players' clothes I will have wan and plain –
> Ah, I forgot, from clothes they must refrain.[3]

Still, it had made for a great opening night. There had been much talk about whether it was an 'actable play' (John B. Yeats thought not) rather than a beautiful narrative poem. In the event it was, according to Holloway, 'incontestably proved' to be, substantially, a play. May Whitty was the Countess and 'spoke her lines with a delicious, natural cadence expressively and most distinctly, looking the rare and radiant maiden of the poet's dream to life'.[4] The protesters were a sorry sight in the end amidst the thunderous applause and the calls for the author. Yeats came on stage holding the hands of May Whitty and Florence Farr and, Holloway remarks, 'he must have felt very proud at the complete triumphing over his enemies'.

The next night it was Edward Martyn's turn. George Moore had not come to Dublin for the first night. He had seen Edward and the actors off at Euston station a few days before (all the rehearsals had taken place in London) and he vividly described the scene. Casting himself as 'baggage man', Moore wrote: 'Edward was splendid. Running up and down the station at Euston, shepherding his flock, shouting that all the luggage was now in the van and crying "the boy, who is to look after him?" … impassive, monumental, muttering fiercely to bystanders that he must count his money, that he had no intention of leaving till he was sure he had been given the right change', Moore waved them off.[5] Within a few days he had a telegram from Martyn, sent after the first night performance – 'The sceptre of intelligence has passed from London to Dublin,' it said. This version of the telegram is quite likely to be poetic licence on Moore's part. It does not sound like Martyn and, for Moore, its reception brought with it visions of what this new art could do for Ireland. He was 'inflamed'. Quickly packing a bag, he found himself in Dublin within a few days.[6]

To begin with, Moore's trip was an anti-climax. Nobody met him at the port of Kingstown (Dun Laoghaire) where he disembarked, nor was

18 The Antient Concert Rooms, Great Brumswick (now Pearse) Street, venue
for the inaugural performance of the ILT. 'Here', Moore pondered, 'Edward
thinks that heresy will flourish and put mischief into men's hearts'!

there anyone at the train station in Westland Row. Nor were they at the
Shelbourne Hotel to greet him. He had to eat dinner alone because
Edward had not even left a note inviting him to join him at his club,
which was just around the corner in Kildare Street. So after this, Moore
tells us, he made 'irritable steps towards the Antient Concert Rooms',
where, for him, the venue seemed 'a truly suitable place for a play by
Edward Martyn. The long passage leading to the rooms seem to bring
me into a tomb … and it is here that Edward thinks that heresy will
flourish and put mischief into men's hearts.'[7] It is highly unlikely that
Martyn was thinking any such thing, but it was impossible for him not
to be thinking of the success of his play.

It had been magnificent. The second night was even better than the
first. The audience had no bone to pick with Edward Martyn and they
were entranced by *The Heather Field*. Holloway, whose description is
noteworthy because of its immediacy, had read the play and thought

the dialogue very natural, full of beauty and keen observation. He was almost surprised to find it proved even better on stage. He liked the subject and was impressed with the love Carden Tyrell had for his brother, his son and his friend and felt that as a character study 'Carden Tyrell would be hard to better'. The influence of Ibsen was 'distinctly traceable'. The play was well staged and 'must be recorded as a triumphant success as an acting drama. ... Mr. Edward Martyn appeared on the scene several times to receive the homage deservedly due to him. ... *The Heather Field* has made the Irish Literary Theatre an unmistakably established fact, and an institution which all Irish people of culture and refinement ought to be justly proud of.'[8] But Joseph Holloway *wanted* to be entranced. What did the critics think?

By the end of the week most of the reviews were good, but not unanimously so. Yeats continued to be attacked by the *Daily Nation*. On 10 May it reproduced a letter from Cardinal Michael Logue, Primate of all Ireland, who condemned *The Countess Cathleen*, having neither read it nor seen it. But he had read O'Donnell's pamphlet and wrote that, 'judging from these extracts, I have no hesitation in saying that any Irish Catholic audience which could patiently sit out such a play must have sadly degenerated, both in religion and patriotism'.[9] Yeats replied on 13 May in a long letter to the *Morning Leader*. He defended his play and assured his audience that '*The Countess Cathleen* is a spiritual drama, and the blind bigots of journalism ... have called it a blasphemy and a slander. These attacks are welcome, for there is no discussion so fruitful as the discussion of intellectual things, and no discussion so needed in Ireland. The applause in the theatre has already shown what party has the victory.'[10] Of the positive reviews, Max Beerbohm's for the *Saturday Review* was the most treasured for he claimed Yeats had put beauty on the stage and 'I was, from first to last, conscious that a beautiful play was being enacted'.[11] Beerbohm wrote that he regretted disparaging the published version of *The Heather Field* for 'it turns out to be a very powerful play indeed. ... It has achieved a really popular success which must be most embarrassing to the founders of a Literary Theatre.'[12]

There was a mixed reaction in the Irish papers to *The Heather Field*, although most critiques were long and positive. The reviewer in *The Irish Times* found it 'wearisome because it has no action. Its characters are not deftly drawn and its reflection of Irish life is not very convincing.' The *Freeman's Journal* liked the idea that here was a play in which there is 'not the remotest suggestion in it of the disordered eroticism which is responsible for so many stage successes in London'. 'Disordered eroticism'! It is difficult to know what the critic means. Many would feel that the undoubted attraction between the two male characters which permeates the play was, in fact, 'disordered eroticism'. The play had 'pathos and power', the critic wrote. Later, when it was staged in London, the critic for the *Athenaeum* found this 'pathos' unhealthy and worried about the fact that it pervaded the play and in which we can read neither beauty nor significance.[13] A modern critic suggests that in *The Heather Field* the relationship between Carden Tyrell and his son Kit is informed by 'the wistful eroticism of a paedophile', implying, perhaps, that Edward Martyn was himself a paedophile.[14] Certainly, Edward liked boys. To what extent he sexually desired them, if at all, does not easily reveal itself to the biographer. The unlikelihood of his ever having physically fulfilled such a desire is, however, a given. As we shall see, the young men he later befriended all maintained a high degree of respect and affection for him.

On 11 May T.P. Gill hosted a dinner in the Shelbourne Hotel for all those involved in the production and many of its supporters, including Douglas Hyde, Standish O'Grady, Max Beerbohm and the elderly Fenian John O'Leary. Gill referred to Edward Martyn as 'a dramatist fitted to take rank among the first in Europe'. Moore watched 'dear Edward', who was, he tells us, 'as happy as a priest at a wedding ... chewing his cud of happiness, a twig from *The Heather Field*; slightly triumphant, I thought, over Yeats whose *Countess Cathleen* had not been received quite so favourably.'[15] Moore noted that Gill and Edward Martyn discussed the idea of founding a school of acting. This was something close to Martyn's heart and it put him at the front of the reformers of the period. In the long run, however, it was the Abbey Theatre that carried out these ideals and he had nothing to do with that.

Moore's set piece in *Ave* (the first book of *Hail and Farewell*) describing this gathering cannot be bettered. When Douglas Hyde stood up to speak he was, he tells us, 'interrupted by Edward calling on him to speak Irish' and as a result of this 'a torrent of dark muddied stuff flowed from him [Hyde] much like the porter which used to come up from Carnacun to be drunk by the peasants on midsummer nights when a bonfire was lighted. It seemed to me a language suitable for the celebration of an antique Celtic rite, but too remote for modern use.'[16] One is reminded of the shock the writer Flann O'Brien, a fluent Irish speaker, felt when he was introduced to Douglas Hyde, President of Ireland, many years later and discovered that he 'spoke atrocious Irish'.[17] It was a mark of the passion these people had for their cause that they sat quietly and listened.

Moore's greatest appreciation in those early days, however, was for George Russell (Æ) whom he regarded as 'someone who exists only in one's imagination, dreams, sentiment, feelings, than in one's ordinary sight and hearing'.[18] No doubt Russell affected people in this way, but at that time the poet's thoughts on George Moore were considerably more mundane. He had written Horace Plunkett on 8 May: 'If I see Moore over here, I will try and pump the true national spirit into him and instruct him in what is necessary for the good of Ireland.'[19] At the time Plunkett and Russell were engaged in writing a pamphlet regarding tenant problems in rural Ireland. It was Moore, the landlord, rather than Moore, the artist, whom Russell was concentrating on that day.

The celebrations petered out and life got back to normal. Yeats went to Coole where he worked on *The Shadowy Waters*. Augusta Gregory was making an attempt at her first play (*Colman and Guaire*) and over at Tillyra Martyn was working on *The Tale of a Town*, his third play. It wasn't going well. He was having trouble 'telling the plot'. Moore reflected on his friend in this period and what he might be feeling, a man who is 'shy, unobtrusive and lonely, whose interests are literary, and whose life is not troubled by women, feels intensely and hoards in his heart secret enthusiasms and sentiments. ... He is thinking that his dreams are coming to pass and believes himself to be the Messiah – he who will give Ireland literature and her political freedom.'[20] Grandiose thoughts for an 'unobtrusive man'. Hardly 'the Messiah' but Martyn did continue to believe, despite many setbacks to come, that he had something to offer in drama and literature. In June, however, when *The Heather Field* was played at Terry's Theatre in London, it evoked very lukewarm reviews, but it was considered by the critic of the *Athenaeum* as 'the most direct outcome of Ibsen our stage has seen but it had deep meaning only for the esoteric' and the audience was 'at least as mystified as it was pleased'.[21]

It was time for Bayreuth. On 28 July 1899 Moore wrote to Edward from Victoria Street: 'I have engaged rooms and I begged and prayed and exhorted Schults to get comfortable rooms for us. And now I do beg and pray and exhort you to be here on the first of August as I shall certainly require your [four?] days for the journey … I cannot travel all day. If the weather is like this it would be better to travel at night. But you don't like that.'[22]

They met at London's Victoria station. Edward arrived with only fifteen minutes to spare, 'huge and puffy his back to the engine … his straw hat perched on the top of his head broader at the base than at the crown'. There was an air of embarrassment for Moore, who tells us that he was conscious of the fact that he had written to Martyn to tell him that he did not like his third play, *The Tale of a Town*. But Edward, he writes, was not embarrassed. He angered Moore by non-

[By Max Beerbohm.]

CELTADES AMBO: MR. YEATS AND MR. MARTYN.

19 Max Beerbohm's cartoon skilfully reflects the relationship between Yeats and Martyn, in the context of the 'celtic movement'.

chalantly smoking a cigar while the novelist gave him the reasons for his dislike. He did admit, however, that the letter Moore had sent 'had spoilt the pleasure of his trip round the coast of Ireland in a steamer with a party of archaeologists'. Moore claims that he had written that 'there is not one act in five … which, in my opinion, could interest any possible audience – Irish, English or Esquimaux'.[23] The narration of this scene in *Ave* subtly puts Martyn in the wrong on what was to become a very distressing, almost cruel, situation. On the whole matter of this play, which we shall explore in the following pages, Moore's narration is suspect. On the trip to Bayreuth in general, however, it is not.

Before arriving at the Festspielhaus, the friends stopped at Aix-la-Chapelle, Mainz, Boppard, Nuremburg and Rothenburg. Martyn instructed Moore on both Gothic and Romanesque architecture; instruction that Moore did not take too seriously. He was struck by how much his friend preferred art and architecture to people. In Nuremburg they admired Lucas Cranach's nudes, both agreeing that he had an innocence that was not to be found in modern art (this was Cranach's early work; his later female nudes became highly erotic works of art). On this journey, as Moore tells it in *Ave*, the novelist worked out Martyn's antipathy towards women: 'his bias towards ecclesiasticism enables him to sympathise with the Middle Ages, and its inherent tendency to regard women as inferior, and keep them out of sight.'[24]

Their rooms in Bayreuth were clean and comfortable as well as being well situated near the Festspielhaus. Moore claims this didn't suit Edward because he needed to be near a Catholic Church so he could attend mass every day. They saw performances of the *Ring, Parsifal* and *Die Meistersinger*. On the return journey to London, they stopped at Antwerp where they saw Peter Paul Rubens's *Descent from the Cross* and met up with two English painters, Clara Christian and Ethel Walker.[25] All four travelled together to Bruges, where Martyn parted with them and made his way back to Tillyra to work on his play and to plan the second season of the Irish Literary Theatre.

In *The Tale of a Town* he wasn't keeping the women 'out of sight' and that was part of the problem. By late November things had come to a sorry pass. Augusta Gregory wrote to Yeats:

> What is going on about the play? My sympathies are with Edward now for I looked in at Tillyra coming back one evening from Castle Taylor and I found him very low, depressed and mortified. I stayd to dine and he cheered up a little and has been to see me since. Now he is off to Dublin again. I think it was just as much as his patience and temper would stand having the play rewritten at Tillyra but it was too much when Moore started again in Dublin writing and talking about it, and reading it to Gill and Russell. Then he had an interview in London at

which Moore seems to have been very offensive – claimed the play as his own and threatened to prevent the performance altogether this year, forgetting the £200 E.M. is responsible for. ... I told E.M. honestly that the play had to be altered and that it had certainly been improved up to a certain point, but that after that, both you and I thought Moore had run wild and written too much, and I quite agreed with him as to the commonness of Moore's writing . He says it is 'ugly' work now and that he won't sign it but I think ... he will sign it with Moore, which would be the best and most honest way. Do let me know what is going on before I see him again, for I am quite in the dark.[26]

In her diary entry for this period Augusta Gregory wrote: 'Some unpleasantness about E. Martyn's "Tale of a Town", Moore and Yeats having pronounced against it in the state he left it, he gave it over to them to alter – They did this at Tillyra, & made too much mystery over it, & vexed him till he "hated the sight" of both of them. ...'

A lot was happening. Martyn had been obliged to show Yeats and Gregory the play. It was needed for the second season of the Irish Literary Theatre which was fast coming upon them. In *Autobiographies* Yeats writes that when he and Augusta Gregory read the play, it seemed to them 'crude throughout, childish in parts, a play to make our movement and ourselves ridiculous'.[27] Yeats moved into Tillyra and, with Moore, set about converting Martyn's drama into an actable play. 'The finished work was Moore's in its construction and characterisation but most of the political epigrams ... were mine,' he wrote. On 7 November Moore had written to Augusta Gregory from the Shelbourne Hotel showing his exasperation: 'I have carried the play a step further and I send it to him so that he may carry it another step. Martyn writes so undramatically ... I beg you to save me from further emendations from our friend. I'm sure that they will be excellent but my sanity must be considered. ... He said in his letter this morning that the end of the second act of "Martyn's" play wanted a touch. Indeed it does and I shall have to rewrite the last pages of the act.'[28] Clearly, at this early stage, Moore no longer considered *The Tale of a Town* to be Martyn's play.

But what was this play? It was social satire in a middle-class drama. Soon Padraic Colum and Lennox Robinson would take up the cudgels for this sort of writing. In the meantime, Martyn had bitten off more than he could chew. He was entirely comfortable with his subject, but his play was dull and flat. He was trying, again, to apply Ibsenite technique to Irish subject matter and he was not succeeding. *The Tale of a Town* is set in a small Irish seaport that is in dispute with an English seaport, Anglebury. The English town had filched their contracts for the handling of American packet ships crossing the Atlantic. As the play opens, it is time for the Irish to fight back. This fight, however, is complicated by the fact that many of the Irish councillors agreed to Anglebury getting the contracts in the first place. They were, in fact, bought. But now they see the error of their ways and they have a new 'Young Turk', Jasper Dean, to fight their corner. Dean's aspirations are, however, complicated by the fact that he has just returned from Anglebury where he fell in love with, and became engaged to marry, Millicent Fell, daughter of the Mayor of Anglebury. Millicent does not like him in his new role as Irish patriot. He will have to choose between politics and romance. How will he choose?

George Moore had claimed that Martyn was having trouble 'telling the plot'. But there was nothing wrong with the plot other than its lack of drama. Jasper dithers, but in the end stays with Millicent. It is the central theme that makes this play such a highly topical and interesting work. Local government was only a few years old in Ireland.[29] The general public regarded it with cynicism. Most councils were made up of small manufacturers, grocers, publicans and property-owners. They had little interest in the welfare of the people. Jasper Dean's background was in the liquor trade, a trade 'highly honoured in Ireland'. Minor corruption was almost innate; vested interest and political apathy reigned. Edward wanted to satirise this situation and the divisions that were evident in the Irish Parliamentary Party at the time (this was a theme that Moore sharpened considerably in *The Bending of the Bough*). He was not attempting to create dramatic conflict and that was a problem, for it left the audience no reason to become emotionally involved with the characters (Millicent Fell is such an ineffectual character that nobody cares whether Jasper Dean loves her or not). But neither did he succeed in his attempt at satire. As with *Morgante the Lesser*, he quickly drifted into burlesque. Even if it had been less 'crude' and 'childish', it would never have been suitable for the Irish Literary Theatre. The scene in Act 5 where there is a scrap between the wives of the councillors it turns physical. It goes beyond burlesque to become indeed 'crude' and 'childish'. The reader is bewildered that a man, who exhibited a rare cultural refinement in so many artistic fields, including literature, should be unconscious of the paucity of this writing.

He handed over the text to Yeats. Then Yeats handed it on to Moore. It was developed into a good, though by no means a great, play. The plot remains the same, but the characterisation is immensely improved, especially that of Millicent Fell, who emerges as a strong and independent woman. The councillors are not all corrupt. Jasper Dean genuinely wants to do something for the town and he is supported in this by another councillor, Ralf Kirwan, an idealist. In fact, in Moore's version, the relationship between Kirwan and Dean becomes the central theme of the play. This is revealed in the third act, of which Yeats wrote to Russell: 'Moore told me he was going to tell you about "The Tale of a Town" – a great secret & our changes in it. Moore has written a tremendous scene in the third act & I have worked at it here and there throughout. If Martyn will only consent it will make an emmense [sic] sensation, & make our theatre a national power.'[30] This act shows how Moore's version was made into a suitable play for the Irish Literary Theatre. The playwright ponders the destiny of the race: 'I must believe in the sacredness of the land underfoot,' Jasper says. But in the end Millicent gives him an ultimatum. She sees the dangers of this 'idealism'. Abstracts have become more important to him than reality. She draws him back and, without explanation, he accepts her life of petty respectability and turns away from Ralf Kirwan. This greatly weakens the play.

Kirwan is based on Standish James O'Grady, whose version of Irish heroic tales had helped to inspire the Irish literary revival, but is also based, to some extent, on Edward Martyn himself.

In the long run, Lady Gregory and Yeats disagreed over the play. In reply to her letter, cited above, Yeats wrote:

Moore has really very much improved the play. He [Moore] has now rewritten again the third and fourth acts and has almost abolished Foley. I am sure he has done everything with a bad grace, but he has really made a new thing of the play even since you saw it. There is no use keeping fragments of Martyn's work merely because they were his. Of course one cannot help being sorry for Martyn and I wish very much you could get him to agree to put his name together with Moore's to the play. I have already urged this on Moore, who makes the lame excuse that it would make the play too important. The fact is that both he and Martyn are very cross with each other. I think Moore will not really however object to sign with Martyn. It is foolish of Martyn to call the play 'ugly', for ugly as it is from my point of view, and yours, it is beauty itself beside what it was; and as for 'commoness' [*sic*] in the writing neither of them know what style is but Moore can at least be coherent and sensible.

The next day he sent a postscript:

I saw Moore last night after all. He wrote while I was there to suggest to Martyn that they should both sign the play. I saw the letter and it was everything that could be desired. There is now almost nothing left of Martyn in the play except the foundation of plot – dialogue and characterisation are now all new. Moore sent Martyn Ben Webster's letter. Ben Webster says the play is now quite right. … Moore is very emphatic about Martyn being given no further advice as he is so afraid of what he may do but you will of course use your own discretion about this. He says that Martyn has left the matter now in his hands & and the thing to do is push on our arrangements. He denies ever having threatened to stop performances. He says he merely said that the committee would not he was sure agree to substitute a play of Ibsens [*sic*] for 'A Tale of a Town'. I found him very irritated with Martyn but I think I moderated him. He says his brother calls Martyn 'an old woman who ought to be given a parrot in a cage'.[31]

Moore was worried. He had written a good play but the plot and the characters remained Martyn's. The dialogue was changed but by no means in its entirety. Moore changed the title to *The Bending of the Bough*. The matter was not finished there. Martyn was hurting and was surely asking himself how his play had so quickly become 'Moore's play'. On 22 December Yeats wrote to Augusta Gregory:

20 Augusta Gregory, 1904. From Paris, in the last melancholy days of 1899,
Edward wrote her: 'You have always been such a kind friend to me'
and he looked back with 'a sense of sadness and loneliness'
for those they had both loved and lost.

Moore has worked a lot on 'The Tale of a Town', & I have a little, since you saw it & it is now extraordinary fine & he has done a fine preface too. It is now a splendid and intricate gospel of nationality & may also be epoch making in Ireland. A chief part of what I have done in it is that I have rewritten Dean's speech in the first act. My anxiety at the moment is how to get at the Dublin press as I shall not be there some weeks beforehand as I was last year; and I am afraid Martyn has been abusing Moore's play to people there. Mrs. Coffey told Mrs. Emery [Florence Farr] a week ago that Martyn said it was not good & she thought he might be right for 'you see Moore cant construct'. She would feel more easy if Martyn's version had been taken' etc, or 'if it were by Martyn' or something to that effect. I am afraid of this depressing her energy & others through her, and it shows me that we must not ask Martyn to work up the press.

Yeats did not consider Martyn's depression. He refused to sign the play. He didn't consider it was his any more, as, indeed, it was not. Moore felt no compunction. He claimed Martyn had given the play to him and Yeats to do with as they liked. And they had. They needed a play for the second season of the theatre and time was pressing. In the event, they were justified. *The Bending of the Bough*, as we shall see, was a resounding success. But that was not the last of it.

Luckily, for the time being, Martyn had other things to occupy him. He had started a correspondence with William J. Walsh, Archbishop of Dublin, with regard to the foundation of a choir for the Pro-Cathedral. Walsh was considering Vincent O'Brien as choirmaster and Martyn was certainly pushing his case, but this was only part of the argument in which the archbishop had to be persuaded that reform was necessary. 'In the first place the women singers would be got rid of,' Martyn wrote to Walsh on 29 November: 'Between 16 and 20 men tenors and basses would be employed to sing the Gregorian chant. Then on great festivals we could bring the fringe choir of the boys and do big masses by Palestrina, Vittoria, Lasso & co.'[32] He was respectful in his correspondence with Walsh but he was also confident. It was a timely moment, for William Walsh was almost as interested in polyphonic music (he had published a *Grammar of Gregorian Music* in 1885) as Martyn was and they both agreed that the government had neglected Irish culture. The Catholic Church, since the arrival of Paul Cullen back in the 1850s, had ambitions to be an agent of cultural reform and now it had a very generous patron to help it achieve this. Edward Martyn never baulked at spending his money on cultural interests. That, as he saw it, was what his money was for: the development of art and culture in the interests of the Irish nation. People close to him, however, were also interested in his own development. Susan Mitchell later summed it up thus.

> Martyn's from the Drama gone; up in the skies
> He sits aloft while choirs sing litanies;
> No female choristers impassioned noise
> But anthems masculine from nice small boys.

In fact he would never leave the drama. In the Martyn file in the New York Public Library there is an affectionate letter to Augusta Gregory, sent from Paris in December 1899:

> You have always been such a kind friend to me, and I can never forget the many good turns that Sir William did for me nor the interest he showed in what must have seemed to him crude efforts of mine. ... Although we are now entering a new era that is perpetually exploring new interests it is with a sense of sadness and loneliness that we look back on those days. Nevill Geary is taking his mother off to Japan. Our Nevill is always the same. I hope to be back in London on January 8th when I must begin work in earnest about casting the plays. I wish to goodness the thing was all over. It is charming here. I saw yesterday at the Française a superb performance of Molière's *Clare*. It would make you die laughing if you saw the caricatures of the English here.

Martyn was not the only lonely Irishman in that 'charming' city in those last melancholy days of the nineteenth century. Not far away Oscar Fingal O'Flahertie Wills Wilde was entering the closing scenes of his dramatic life and, within the year, would be defeated by his wallpaper.

10 • Political Drama

IN FACT EDWARD MARTYN was back in the Reform Club in Pall Mall on 3 January 1900 writing pedantically to T.P. Gill, who had just been appointed Secretary to the new Department of Agriculture and Technical Instruction. Horace Plunkett was the Vice-President. 'You have got the appointment all right,' Martyn wrote. 'I hasten to tell you how glad I am that you have got it. You will have a fine income now and I hope you will keep your eye sharp on it. With all your cleverness I do not think you have the worth of money. I hope you don't mind me saying this to you, you know what sincere friendship I have for you and your boys. I have got a really good cast for *Maeve*. The play is coming out very tense and dramatic in rehearsal and if all goes well it will be even better than *The Heather Field*.'[1] This letter is in marked contrast to Moore's version of Gill's appointment in *Salve*, where he assures us that Edward disapproved of Gill accepting the job.[2]

The Act creating the Department of Agriculture in 1899 reflected the nature of the change and progress that was occurring in Ireland. From being a net contributor to the British economy, Ireland was becoming a net beneficiary. As well as being responsible for Agriculture and Fisheries, the Act gave the Department a broad range of functions, including the supervision of the National Museum and the National Library of Ireland. It had several advisory bodies in which local government authorities were heavily represented. This was an honest attempt to bring the bureaucracy closer to the people, and the administrators were learning how to run a large government department. Such experience counted for much after the coming of independence. Possibly, though, it was too broad, for it wasn't always very successful and its failures were mostly laid at Gill's door. He was perceived to be

21 George Russell (Æ), *c*.1900.

'excessively cautious and sadly lacking in imagination'.[3] In fact, he was similar to some of Martyn's characters in *The Tale of a Town* or Moore's *The Bending of the Bough*. It is clear that Gill's brains were well picked for both these plays. Still, for all its faults, the Department made its presence felt. In time it controlled ten separate institutions, including the

Metropolitan School of Art where Gill, urged on by Edward Martyn, introduced classes in stained-glass. Students of this craft were vital to Sarah Purser in the foundation of her stained-glass studio, An Tur Gloinne.

Throughout the first six weeks of the year the rehearsals for the second season of the Irish Literary Theatre went apace. So did the socialising and the spite. In her diary entry for 22 January Augusta Gregory reports: 'on to a party at Yeats to meet Miss Milligan – whose play, or part of it, is going to be performed – but there was nearly a row as George Moore, who is resolving himself into a syndicate for the rewriting of plays, wanted to alter hers, & she refuses to let any hand touch it but her own'.[4] Two days later she tells us: 'Ed ... says the rehearsals of G. Moores [sic] version (of Ed's play!) is going very badly. ... Edward of course pleased, as he had foretold its failure.' He had, in fact, written to her on 15 January saying: 'It is awfully lucky for me that I remained firm about not signing the new play which is now called "The Bending of the Bough". It has come out just about how I told you – but more so even. I would not want to sign it for half of what I am worth.'[5] But he was hurting badly. He says, Gregory wrote, "he is being badly treated, never consulted, his opinion put aside, but he means to shake off "those chaps" – He says "the only one who was at all nice to me about my plays was you," and on 26 January she writes: 'At the rehearsal of "Bending of a Bough"... very amusing ... Ed. Martyn who has been requested by Moore not to make any more comments, made them only in depreciating whispers to me.'[6]

Things were fractious indeed. Edward was becoming the scapegoat for their bad temper. 'Yeats ... very angry with Martyn and with me for defending him – says Moore claims that no one can have more than one conscience, & his is an intellectual conscience – and no one with that can forgive Martyn's want of intelligence – I say if I have but one conscience it a conscience of friendship,'[7] Augusta Gregory told her diary. At this point they were arguing about whether or not Edward should be shown the first issue of *Bealtaine*, the organ of the Irish Literary Theatre. 'He might object to some sentence' is what they feared. Martyn had written a short essay comparing Irish and English theatre audience, which Yeats referred to as 'an excellent article'. Yeats then revealed to her what Moore had told him about the writing of *The Heather Field* and *Maeve*. Augusta Gregory regards it as 'a new story' but it must have given her pause for thought. In her entry for the following day she wrote: 'I begged him [Edward] not to publish "The Tale of a Town" as he intended, as it cd not hold its own with the others as literature whatever it may be as a play.'[8] He agreed not to publish, but soon changed his mind.

Rehearsals were being held in London, mainly in a small room at the Vaudeville and on the stage at Terry's, among other places. At the dinner table the conversation was as much about the progress of the Boer War as it was about the plays. The cultural nationalists were entirely pro-Boer, with the notable exception of Horace Plunkett. Plunkett, at a meeting of the Primrose League in Kingstown on 4 December 1899, had put forward a motion giving 'cordial support to Her Majesty's government in the policy they have adopted in regard to the war in South Africa'.[9] It is easy to sympathise with Plunkett at this time since he was trying to get his 'Department' off the ground and needed to be onside with the British government. He was also trying to hold on to his parliamentary seat in South Dublin, which he subsequently lost, sharing, as he did, the defeat of many who try to take the middle road. But Augusta Gregory was unforgiving. Perhaps this was because Plunkett also had said, in the same speech, that pro-Boer Irish Nationalists were 'un-Christian and unintelligent', which was clearly wide of the mark. The divisions of opinion on this war merely emphasised the growing nationalism of the cultural movement as a whole.

Martyn's relationship with Moore continued to deteriorate. Yeats had written to Augusta Gregory on 31 January 1900: 'Moore & Martyn have had another row but I cannot judge of its intensity from Moore's vehement account. Moore promises to raise a certain amount of money if Martyn goes out … . At any rate I shall do all I can to keep Martyn, but make plain that what is indispensable is the good work he may yet do & not the money which another may give as well as he & that if he goes nothing is changed except that his place is empty.'[10]

The first night, 19 February, was quickly upon them. The venue that year was Dublin's Gaiety Theatre in South King Street. It opened with Edward Martyn's *Maeve* and Alice Milligan's *The Last Feast of the Fianna*. The audience was, to say the least, underwhelmed. They were bewildered by 'Maeve'. Her cold, almost deadly, manner with its faraway look and visionary talk, provoked laughter in what Joseph Holloway tells us was a 'mostly kindly disposed audience'.[11] The symbolic idea of the gulf between Irish and English ideals did not fully translate on to the stage. It was, however, regarded as a 'nationalist play' because the heroine was prepared to die rather than marry the 'enemy' but, on the whole, the wag in the audience who declared that 'they ought to have clapped that one into an asylum' reflected the truer reaction. Alice Milligan's 'tawdry little piece' (Augusta Gregory's description) was well staged but very bad. It was saved by the fact that it lasted for only twenty minutes. Still, at the end of the evening Martyn took three curtain calls and Augusta Gregory could write in her diary: 'anyhow we are not discredited'.[12]

The next night Moore did not take his curtain calls. *The Bending of the Bough* was a runaway success. 'Acting splendid, meaning soon grasped & applause tremendous' Augusta Gregory wrote. 'Poor Edward came round rather sadly ... but he spoke very nicely, said it was a gr. piece of good luck this piece going so well it would save the venture – Maeve he says, truely, was very badly acted, & this very well – still he had been so confident that this would fail as an acting piece that he has had two defeats as it were, & bears it very well – with no sign of irritation or bitterness – There his real goodness comes out.'[13] As the week progressed, the production of *Maeve* improved, but the audiences dwindled and that was a major problem in a theatre the size of the Gaiety. But the papers, with the exception of *The Irish Times*, were kind. The *Freeman's Journal* on 20 February was quite sure in its review that the audience had fully understood the allegory in *Maeve*. There had been 'nothing so wonderful in the Irish theatre for many years' as the way in which the audience engaged with it. And, indeed, given the applause when Peg Inerny declares, 'I am only an old woman but I tell you that Erin will never be subdued', the audience were conscious of what Martyn was trying to say. This praise caused *Maeve* to be boycotted as a subversive play by the establishment at Dublin Castle.

But it was *The Bending of the Bough* that gathered the most enthusiastic plaudits and with it George Augustus Moore. According to the *Freeman's Journal* on 21 February: 'the audience felt that at last Mr. George Henry Moore's son that had been lost was returned again to the house of his father and they were prepared to kill the fatted calf on his homecoming'. The audience loved the satire and felt they could identify with many of the characters. But as the critic of the *Irish Daily Independent* put it, 'they laughed heartily at the countless epigrammatic sayings in blissful ignorance that some of these expressions were keenly satirising their very selves'.[14] The *Irish Figaro*'s review, taking into account that paper's loyalist sympathies, was most persuasive. The play, it perceived, had great merit and was a good acting play but it was not literature: 'It is of course a patchwork – bits of Mr. Martyn, Mr. Yeats, Mr. Russell and Mr. Moore and wants [i.e. lacks] unity.'[15] Indeed it was not literature, so it was a fair question to ask what it was doing in a 'Literary Theatre'.

Still, it was a topical idea and it had been Edward Martyn's. Many, especially I.P. Gill, felt that Moore should write to the papers informing them that the play was partly Martyn's. Unfortunately, Edward quickly forgot that he had claimed he was glad of its success. He started to abuse the play, saying that it was 'a poor and common thing, no better than a "Frou Frou" and not fit for a literary theatre'. He also said, Augusta Gregory reported to her diary, 'that in future the only help he wd give wd be, if a play of his were produced, he would guarantee the theatre against loss on it – but that he would not spend money on producing other people's plays – but he is out of sorts and has a cold and [I] feel sure his better nature will prevail in the end. ...'[16] Moore never wrote to the papers, declaring Martyn's interest in the play. He told Gill, 'I won't say anything & I won't write anything'. On 27 February he wrote to Martyn from the Shelbourne Hotel:

> My Dear Edward,
> I hear that a paragraph has appeared in the *Pall Mall Gazette* announcing the fact that you intend to publish *The Tale of a Town*. Without the slightest degree of laying myself open to suspicion of not desiring the publication of the play I may remind you that I never would have written *The Bending of the Bough* if you had not made a present of the play to the Irish Literary Theatre. Your words were 'I make you a present of the play, do as you like with it'. I remind you of the words not because I want you to refrain from publication but because it is possible that Fisher Unwin may object on the grounds of copyright. There are, I should say, fifty or sixty lines that are common to both plays, perhaps a hundred lines. The incidents are very different but some are the same ... .
> However, my [?] as author of *The Bending of the Bough* has been called into question and will be again called into question;

I have no objectionto raise, how could I have any – I have acted with perfect fairness in this matter and with perfect disinterestedness. I only ask to have my position in this matter safeguarded and this can be done by sending me a copy of *The Tale of a Town* of the text you submitted to the judgement of the Irish Literary Theatre – you submitted two versions, either will do. Do not think, my dear Edward, that a suspicion has crossed my mind that you could act in this or any other matter except straightforwardly but life is always shifting and the unexpected happens and misunderstandings happen if we do not take the necessary precautions.[17]

In the 1901 edition of *Samhain* (the journal that replaced *Bealtaine*) Moore did explain himself to the public:

I undertook to rewrite Mr Martyn's play *A Tale of a Town*, a play which the ILT did not think it advisable to produce. The public will soon have an opportunity of judging our judgement for Mr. Martyn has decided to publish the original text of his play. So much of the character of his play was lost in my rewriting that the two plays have little in common … . The comedy entitled *The Bending of the Bough* was written in two months and two months are really not sufficient time to write a five act comedy in; and at Mr. Martyn's request my name alone was put on the title page.[18]

The Tale of a Town, together with Martyn's fourth play, *The Enchanted Sea*, was published by Standish James O'Grady, Kilkenny and by T. Fisher Unwin, London in November 1901. The flyleaf contains the following: 'There is an adaptation of *The Tale of a Town* called *The Bending of the Bough* made by Mr. George Moore, with my consent, for the Irish Literary Theatre performances in 1900. Edward Martyn.'

The National Literary Society hosted a lunch for the Theatre in the Gresham Hotel on 22 February 1900. The tables were beautifully decorated with floral representations of a harp and a round tower, but the menu card was printed in Irish and was puzzling to many of the guests. It was a lavish affair. Douglas Hyde told the audience that the aim and object of the ILT was 'to embody and perpetuate Irish feeling, genius and modes of thought'. Mr Martyn's play 'represented the eternal illimitible passion of Irish memory, Irish regret, Irish Idealism'. George Moore informed them that he was not going to speak of the plays that had been performed that week but of the plays that were to come. In the coming year the ILT was going to put on a play in the Irish language. This was vital, he told them, because English was 'a declining language'.[19]

While all the consternation was going on about 'the play', Edward was in trouble on another front. At a Christmas concert at Tillyra the previous year he had refused to allow 'God save the Queen' to be played. It was a minor incident and he went away to Paris and thought no more of it. But others talked of it with interest. When Fanny Trench (wife of William Cosby Trench and niece of Augusta Gregory) asked Gregory if it was true, she replied, 'Yes and much worse than that, he would not have [Kipling's] "The Absent Minded Beggar"! which she [Trench] took quite seriously.' The diary entry continues: 'Lord Clonbrock [Lieutenant of County Galway] came up to E.M. in the smoking room at the club the other day and said he heard he had refused to have "God save the Queen" at his house – Ed said yes, he did not like songs that were party cries, & that someone else might have objected to "The Wearing of the Green" – Clonbrock jabbered a lecture at him and said he shld remember his oath as D.L. and J.P. – Ed said in that case he had better resign – Clonbrock got frightened, begged him not to think of doing so, & talked of other things.'[20]

This was too good an opportunity to let pass. Edward Martyn had never wanted to be a Justice of the Peace or a Deputy Lieutenant. Clonbrock had given him a chance to escape. After the exchange in the club, he immediately wrote to Lord Ashbourne, the Lord Chancellor for Ireland, tendering his resignation. It was not, however, immediately accepted. Catholic magistrates were not thick on the ground. Ashbourne wrote to Clonbrock from the Four Courts on 22 February 1900: 'I received the enclosed from Mr. Martyn. I do not like acting upon it until its been fully considered. Some years ago I met him at Lord Morris's, but have not come across him in recent times. I know that he is the head of an old Catholic family, and now a distinguished literary man. I wish you would let me know if the letter represents a final opinion, which I would regret.'[21]

The next day Martyn received a long letter from Clonbrock asking him to reconsider and enclosing Ashbourne's letter. Trying to persuade him to stay, Clonbrock wrote: 'First I should be sorry to see the head of your family withdraw from the position he ought to hold in this county; and secondly I believe it to be in the interests of the public service that you should act as a magistrate in your own district.'[22] Martyn, however, was adamant and went on to explain his position in detail to Clonbrock. Having assured him that it was not just the matter of 'God Save the Queen' and 'The Absent Minded Beggar' but that there were other deeper causes for his dissatisfaction:

> I now see that my opinion on many questions have been greatly changing since the time you were so good as to recommend me for the Commission of the Peace and as a Deputy Lieutenancy. I was brought up like most of my kind, in ignorance of my country, of her language, of her history, and in a sort of subservient acquiescence with England's account of her actions and position in Ireland. I was vaguely conscious that there was something unsatisfactory in my situation. It was not until a few years ago, when I read Lecky's 'History of Ireland in the Eighteenth Century ... that I really became aware of how false a position I, and those like me, were placed in with regard to our native country.

He explained how he saw England's 'habitual attitude' to Ireland in the sense of a 'fatal injury not only to the intellect and national spirit of the people but also to their material prosperity'. Then he wrote:

> I am no longer the sort of Unionist you believed me to be. I have realised that my own class, the landowners, are themselves as much the victims of that English state policy in Ireland, of which they have been the consistent upholders, as any other class in the country. Up to this hour they are impartially sacrificed when it suits the interests of British political parties. Now I am myself no politician. ... All I know is that I no longer share the views of the Unionist Party, in which I was brought up. In such matters what I want is absolute liberty for my thoughts and actions.

He assured Clonbrock that he had no disrespect whatsoever for the Queen but that

I wish to preserve my right of acting according to my own convictions in my own house as elsewhere and, if doing so, while retaining the Commission of the Peace and Deputy Lieutenancy, makes me liable to be taken to task in however friendly a way, by the Lord Lieutenant of my country, my only alternative is to resign those two posts. ... With many thanks for the invariable kindness you have shown me, I remain, my dear Lord Clonbrock, yours very sincerely. [23]

This letter was composed in the National Library of Ireland, with the help of Augusta Gregory, who had mixed feeling about the resignation. Nevertheless, it is a part of the flow of events that were all going in one direction and she was more in tune with this than most. 'We are not working for Home Rule, we are preparing for it,' she assured Martyn and Moore. On 24 March the *Irish Daily Independent* published the letter under the heading 'A Manly Irish Protest' and in its editorial on 26 March noted that the letter had created 'a profound impression throughout the whole country'. On 5 April Martyn wrote to Augusta Gregory from Pierce Mahony's house in Sutton, County Dublin, where they had passed a peaceful day while the 81-year-old Queen Victoria entered Dublin for the first time. Her royal yacht anchored at Kingstown and she brought with her little donkeys which she drove about the grounds of the Viceregal Lodge in the Phoenix Park. Despite much public opposition on the part of nationalists, including Yeats and Moore, the people were generally tolerant of the visit. They accepted, with equanimity, that Victoria had never liked the Irish. Referring to the visit, Martyn wrote: 'I assure you that Dublin is reeking with snobbery at present and is a most disagreeable place to be in.' But he was enjoying his own bit of notoriety: 'There is nothing but condemnation about my letter to Clonbrock, it has created a great sensation and may have tremendous effects. I get numerous letters from most unlikely persons such as a Protestant clergyman.'[24]

It was lucky he had some diversions for he could do nothing to please Moore or Yeats. They attacked him about Clonbrock and accused him of being timid. Moore wanted him to write 'a column & a half in the "Freeman's Journal" showing up the landlords and officials and declaring his political convictions'. He shut them up by informing them: 'My political convictions are those of the company I am in – and

I have no convictions but religious ones.'[25] As a consequence of his action, however, he was unofficially asked to leave the Kildare Street Club but this he refused to do. 'I have not the least intent of leaving this club,' he included in the letter of 15 April to Augusta Gregory. 'I heard that a few members held a consultation in the smoking-room and decided not to speak to me … it will not make much difference to me whether they speak to me or not. … This is not a political club and they cannot turn me out.'[26] At this time Daisy Fingall was asked to try to persuade her cousin to leave the club. She did try but he told her that it suited him to stay; he liked the food and 'anyhow I am not half as unpopular as Horace Plunkett'.[27] In the end it was Moore who wrote a long letter to the *Freeman's Journal*, dealing with Martyn's resignation, landowners, the Land Acts and the Boer War,[28] while Martyn wrote to that same paper in October championing Horace Plunkett, who was standing for election on a Unionist ticket, as 'a gradual convert to Irish Nationality'. Much later Plunkett wrote him: 'when you said I was becoming a Home Ruler they made a Solomon of you. Your letter did me some harm but I am grateful for it none the less. It was kindly meant.'[29]

But it was not just in the newspapers that the resignation made a splash. It was a major talking point at local government level. Local councils passed resolutions approving of it. Gort Rural District Council congratulated Martyn on his 'spirited action', while they bemoaned being 'deprived of his enlightened official advocacy of justice to our county and to our people'.[30] Loughrea Rural District Council expressed similar sentiments. On 23 April Martyn wrote a rather pompous and, in parts, silly letter to the Galway Urban District Council:

> Pray convey to the council my hearty thanks for its generous appreciation of my determination to uphold our National independence and individual liberty. This is the motto for landowners who wish to arrest the speedy extinction of their class to stand forward and resist a weak and alien Government that would view with indifference the ruin of its most consistent supporters. There are landlord conventions, I understand, in every county which are dying of inanition but which only require a spark of Nationalism infused into them to galvanise them into life. It is for the independent landlords … to form an All Ireland National Landlord Party which might be in touch with the people.[31]

22 Jack B. Yeats doodles on the cover of Augusta Gregory's copy of *Beltaine*, reflecting the state of play in the spring of 1900.

At the time he was writing this, Edward Martyn was in the throes of selling the bulk of his land, through the Land Commission, to his tenants. He had signed a disentailing deed on 6 August 1898. It was easier and more worthwhile for him to do this than for most of his fellow landlords since, thanks to the diligence of Annie Martyn, none of his estates were mortgaged. Getting rid of the land and resigning as Deputy Lieutenant was, for Martyn, all of a piece. The result of both actions meant that he would have less and less dealings with 'the people'. In January his tenants had been found at Gort Market 'attacking one another with sticks so that all the people in Crow Lane had to keep their houses shut'.[32] His tenants were always notably unhappy. It was hardly for him to preach to others that they might start a political party which would be 'in touch with the people'. The sentiments in this letter were very similar to those expressed by George Moore in his communication with the *Freeman's Journal* in April, when he referred to 'a class so stupid in its own interests as the Irish Landlords'. He urged them not to stand on the steps of the Kildare Street Club cheering the Queen but to 'join the National Party and adopt National Ideas'.[33]

Augusta Gregory was a 'landlord'. She made a point of telling Martyn she did not like his letter. A very telling cartoon by Jack B.Yeats, doodled on the cover of Gregory's April copy of *Beltaine*, shows a rather wretched figure of Martyn being physically dropped by Lady Fingall. It also depicts the Queen and George Moore ascending a staircase with W.B. Yeats furiously playing the organ. It is entitled 'In the graceful year of 1900 George Moore and Victoria returned to Ireland'. If ever Martyn was in the thick of it, he certainly was in the spring of that 'graceful year'. By August there were calls from the *Tuam Herald* for Mr. Martin [*sic*] to be found a seat in his native county. He would make an 'ideal member'. The Loughrea Rural District Council wanted to co-opt him on to the council, but he pointed out to them that this would be most unfair since he would be 'quite unable to do the proper work of it'. He had become popular, but popularity did not really suit him. He would get over it.

Still, for a while, it was liberating. The Piper Corley, a local musician, came to Coole and spoke much about the change in Mr Martyn and how it was now possible to go to Tillyra without fear. John Healy, Archbishop of Tuam, told of how one of his parishioners said to him: 'Mr Martyn is a great man' – 'What has he done?' asked the bishop' – 'He's after cutting the government adrift', was the reply.[34] So Edward was somewhat elated. Too elated, thought Augusta Gregory. But a letter from Charles Henry Meltzer in New York may have helped to bring him back to earth. In May Meltzer had produced *The Heather Field* for an American audience. 'It may not surprise you to hear', he wrote, that 'although a small minority was delighted with the play here [in New

York] the production was generally received with *resentful and stupefied amazement.*' Of the Boston production he wrote: 'even *The Master Builder* drew larger audiences than *The Heather Field*'.[35] Meltzer had promised to produce the play in New York, Boston, Washington, Philadelphia and possibly in Springfield, Massachusetts, which had been rather ambitious. The following year, however, when the *Tuam Herald* wrote about this, the newspaper loyally claimed that *The Heather Field* 'crossed the Atlantic and was presented with much success in New York, Boston and Washington'.

The summer wore on. It was full of interest. Artistic and political culture became interwoven. The Commissioners for National Education decided to reject bilingual teaching in areas which were largely Irish-speaking; the Gaeltacht. There was an outcry. A large meeting in the Rotunda on 19 July found George Moore, Edward Martyn and Cardinal Logue with Douglas Hyde attacking the culture of Trinity College, Dublin and its attitude to the Irish language. In August there was the Galway Feis and also the dedication of the memorial stone in Kileenan graveyard to the poet Antoine Ó Raiftéiri. Augusta Gregory and Edward Martyn had worked and paid for it. Hyde, Yeats, Gregory and Martyn were on the platform. Jack Yeats, the painter, and his patron, John Quinn, from New York were also there. Later Martyn wrote about the Feis in the *Leader*, praising its complete absence of 'vulgarity'. Indeed there was little 'vulgarity' in Martyn's world that year, but one would not be persuaded of this by reading this article, where he writes of women being 'the most vulgar creatures – from whom in fact all vulgarity comes'.[36] Except those at the Galway Feis, of course, and his growing band of women friends! A sensible editor would have known what to do with this copy but, as we shall see, David Patrick Moran, editor of the *Leader*, was many things but he was hardly ever sensible.

In September Moore returned to Coole to work with Yeats on their collaborative play *Diarmuid and Grainne*. It was to be performed at the third and last season of the theatre. He and the poet were, he tells us in *Hail and Farewell*, a pair of 'literary lunatics'. He had written to Augusta Gregory on 11 August with regard to Martyn: 'I am very anxious to be friends with him. The rewriting of the play was most unfortunate but you know I could not help it.' So when he arrived, Augusta Gregory noted: 'He went over to Tillyra to see Edward who received him cordially but refuses any guarantee, will pay for the production of his own play if accepted [there is no indication what this play is] but for nothing else.'[37] And despite the best advice from her, Edward Martyn, to his own detriment, did not budge from that position. On 1 October she records with reference to Moore: 'This morning he has a letter from Ed. Martyn [already cited] acknowledging his share in the "Heather Field", but hinting that he spoiled it! & also saying that he owed him no thanks as he had taken it up as a commercial transaction! He also says that he will not in future give any support to the I. Lit. Theatre, but if plays of his are accepted, he will have separate accounts kept, & will ensure the theatre being at no loss by them. It is sad he should cut himself away from what he had a share in starting, but for ourselves it is better to have a definite statement.'[38] Sad it was and the image of Edward Martyn, sitting in Tillyra that melancholy autumn, writing belligerent letters to Moore, is a lonely one. But he wasn't entirely alone. A letter to Sarah Purser on 19 November indicates that she was anxious for his company. And Augusta Gregory was always sympathetic. Not, however, on all levels. What she thought of Martyn as a writer is reflected in the fact that she did not ask him to contribute an essay to the book of essays, *Ideals in Ireland*, she was preparing at the time.[39] She did, however, ask D.P. Moran.

David Patrick Moran, who had been working as a journalist in London for ten years, returned to Ireland in 1898. While abroad, he had been involved in the Gaelic League and the Irish Literary Society. With a vigorous mind to complement his broad shoulders and leonine head, he had developed his own 'Irish Ireland' philosophy. The nation would be Irish-speaking, Gaelic and Catholic. Moran was a bigot, but his love of ideas often helped him surmount his prejudice. And so did his sense of humour. He didn't like women. His 'Irish Ireland' philosophy, where he pleaded for self-criticism and the development of the individual, was worked out in a series of six articles published in the *New Ireland Review* (later published as *The Philosophy of Irish Ireland*) between 1898 and 1900.

The *New Ireland Review* was a monthly publication of the Jesuits with Tom Finlay, SJ as its editor. The ideas involved in Moran's 'philosophy' also constituted the first editorial of the *Leader*, published in August 1900. His philosophy was refreshing in that he refused to blame 'the English Government' for the state of Ireland or the loss of the language.

Self-improvement and self-reliance were what was needed for Ireland to become 'a self-governing land, living, moving and having its being in its own language'. Making a copy of this editorial available to several Irish cultural leaders, including Martyn, in advance of its publication, Moran invited their comments. These, too, were published in the first edition. It was a bold, intelligent move and it launched a newspaper that became a leading critical review of politics, literature, industry and the arts for several decades to come. Moran's belief in criticism, however, soon led him into criticising almost everything, especially the nationalist movements. His lash could be vicious, but it was a few years before Edward Martyn fell under it.

11 • The *Leader*

B EFORE THE YEAR was out, George Moore and Edward
Martyn were friends again. When Moore heard that Lady
Gregory had not included any of Martyn's work in *Ideals in
Ireland*, he was, Yeats wrote to Gregory, 'filled with sorrow for Edward
and wrote an effusive letter of friendship'.[1] As a result of this, Martyn
came back from Rome early in the new year in 'exuberant spirits',
telling Gregory that George Moore had apologised for the letters he had
written him about the theatre. Moore had said that he was sorry to have
got into the controversy about the play but he had been 'lead into it'.
That it was, in effect, Yeats who was against him publishing *The Tale of
a Town*. Gregory kept silent since she knew that Yeats had indeed
dissuaded George Coffey from encouraging Martyn to publish the play
before he, Coffey, had read it, 'as it would be laughed at by literary
men'. Yeats was sacrificed on the altar of reconciliation.[2] Given Lady
Gregory's affection for Edward, it is unlikely that she would be
deliberately mean to him in any event, but a letter to Yeats dated 23
December 1900, à propos the staging of *Diarmuid and Grainne*, shows
some ulterior motivation for the keeping of her counsel: 'Edward's
present popularity ... will really do more for us just now than his money
would have done. He confers approval of [on] *Grainne*'.[3] It was true that
having Martyn on their side gave them an air of respectability in the
eyes of the Catholic Church and they were constantly aware of the fact.

No doubt Edward Martyn was disappointed that none of his work
was included in *Ideals in Ireland*, but he was being published in other
journals. Both he and Augusta Gregory were delighted with the arrival
of D.P. Moran and the *Leader*. Yeats was much less sure and, after a
while, Gregory realised that the paper, under Moran's editorship, was

not going to be an ally of the theatre. Replying to Moran's editorial, Martyn wrote, without a hint of irony: 'what we need are independent men who will speak out their minds and avoid personalities and guard against private wrangles. ... If some of us writers abuse England it is because we feel that unless she is steadily discredited as an ideal with the mediocre of this country all our efforts to establish a nationalistic artistic movement will be without adequate support.'[4]

On 10 October 1900 Martyn's Gaelic League pamphlet, *Ireland's Battle for her Language*, was published. It must have pleased Moran for its basic premise was that 'the fate of the Irish language is in the hands of the Irish people'. Be self-reliant and 'stop looking for scapegoats,' Martyn urged. He goes on to attack the National Education Board and, indeed, the entire establishment, but he is willing to stick with that 'establishment' for the time being for he tells his readers that Home Rule can wait, while 'the cause of the Irish language cannot wait'. But still, England was to blame for 'she first destroys what we have and then taunts us for our poverty and meanness'.[5] When he wrote about 'poverty' and 'meanness', Edward Martyn was usually speaking in the aesthetic sense. And the pages of the *Leader* afforded him an excellent opportunity to vent his anger about what, after the theatre, was closest to his heart: the state of liturgical music in Irish churches.

He started his campaign by writing that the musicians who should know better were 'too lazy to take the time to produce the proper liturgical music of the Catholic Church, or to collect a Boys' Choir which, in a large Catholic City like Dublin, ought to be easy'. But mostly it was the clergy he attacked: 'I have the greatest admiration for the clergy in Ireland ... but their greatest admirer could not, with any sincerity, say that they were gifted with aesthetic taste. ... I have only met one who gave me the impression of having a classical music taste and that is the present eminent and versatile Archbishop of Dublin. Aesthetic Taste is a born faculty which needs much cultivation if it is to be of any practical use.' Lest he leave anyone out of this offensive tirade, Martyn went on to give his readers his views on women in choirs: 'From a merely aesthetic point of view it is most offensive and reprehensible. The only proper place for a woman's voice, with its volume and passion and essential earthiness, is the stage. Women have always been unrivalled at depicting the violent emotion of life. ... But the liturgical idea is not dramatic. It is epic. It therefore requires a singing that shall be passionless ... with cerebral fervour. These are essentially masculine qualities.' If women were to sing in church at all they should 'sing in the body of the church, and the organist should accompany them from above'. He agreed that there would be an outcry at the removal of women. 'But what of that'? 'Is there not always an outcry from the philistines when some blemish on art is removed? So the sooner the outcry is manfully met and got over the better.'[6]

Not surprisingly, these views provoked a lot of reaction and, as was the custom of the time, it was not always obvious from where it was coming. Martyn's biggest critic in the pages of the *Leader* was 'O'. On 20 October 'O' took him to task for the fixity of his ideas and the 'weakness and contradictions of his own pleadings'. He didn't accept Martyn's criticism of the clergy and pointed out that 'it is the public above all who don't want to be sent back to the 16th century'. 'O' wondered whether His Grace, the Archbishop of Dublin, 'will be gratified at finding he is elevated to so solitary a pedestal in the Tillyra Valhalla'. When it comes to the women singers, 'O' is 'content to overwhelm our misogynist with himself' by exposing his contradictions: at one point Edward Martyn allows women to be only on the stage, but then he allows them in the body of the church. He begs that Martyn 'indicate the rubrics or decrees of canon law which concern the exclusion of women' from liturgical choirs.[7] 'O' then goes on to attack Martyn's notion that the liturgy is 'Epic' and not 'Dramatic', pointing out that in fact medieval drama grew out of the liturgical representation of the Passion on Good Friday. The notion that the musical service of God should be passionless is regarded as 'a purely Jansenist idea'.

This was strong stuff and in the weeks ahead Edward Martyn was lucky to have some supporters, most notably Henry Bewerung, the head of music at Maynooth College. Bewerung agreed with Martyn on the 'women question' and noted that it was hardly fair to blame the congregation in general for the lack of reform in church music, 'least of all the poor uneducated classes'. It was a few half-educated people who were preventing the reform necessary in the liturgy.[8] (E.M. was not grateful for Bewerung's support and in 1914 when the latter was made Professor of Music at University College Dublin, he was entirely against the appointment.)[9] It took the atheist and modernist James Joyce to sum up the ludicrousness of all these arguments. In his short story 'The Dead', Joyce deals with this controversy when Aunt Kate angrily tells her niece, Mary Jane: 'I know all about the honour of God, Mary Jane, but I think it's not at all honourable for the Pope to turn out the women out of choirs that have slaved there all their lives and put little whipper-snappers of boys over their heads. I suppose it is for the good of the Church if the Pope does it. But it's not just, Mary Jane, and it's not right.'[10]

And it seemed his Grace, Dr. Walsh, didn't mind a bit being put on a pedestal in the 'Tillyra Valhalla'. On 1 December the *Tuam Herald* reported a speech he had made at St Margaret's, Dublin. He acknowledged with gratitude 'the noble efforts of our distinguished countryman, Edward Martyn of Tullira Castle, to improve the standard of musical culture in Ireland'. The choir they had been listening to that day was the result of his encouragement and generosity. It was Mr Martyn who was behind their permanent organisation and continuous training. The standard was improving all the time. This was the Palestrina Choir, which was not yet an official choir of the Dublin diocese. They were still practising in St Mary's Place school, where the choir of forty boys had been increased by the addition of tenors and basses to bring the number up to sixty. They sang the liturgy of Holy Week in April 1901 in Saint Saviour's Church, Dublin, and got a wonderful reception, but the clergy, in general, did not like it. They accepted the choir, which sang without the musical accompaniment of the organ, only on penitential days. Martyn and his friends were regarded as 'faddists'. In reply to this he wrote: 'I do not mind what is said of me so long as I have my way.' In more gentle and reflective prose, he pleaded: 'There never was an age when it was so necessary for the church to put forth all her genius; and nowhere in her art does her genius shine so bright as in the vast collection of liturgical song.'[11]

A month later he was defending his other musical interest, the Feis Ceoil, from those who said it was not 'nationalistic' enough. The Feis, he wrote, 'is not the Oireachtas or any other provincial festival'; its wish 'is to foster a modern school of music. There is no danger of it becoming unnational'. He assured his readers that 'no amount of singing or playing Irish airs … will create a modern Irish school so long as our most talented Irish musicians abstain as a body from the task of composing genuine national music. Take the poems of *An Craoibhin Aoibhinn* [Douglas Hyde] and turn them into Irish madrigals,' he suggested.[12]

Just as it was fortuitous for Edward Martyn that William Walsh, with his particular love of polyphonic music, was Archbishop of Dublin at the time he wanted to found his Palestrina Choir, it was equally fortuitous for the Celtic Revivalists that John Healy was Bishop of Clonfert at the time of the building of Saint Brendan's Cathedral in Loughrea. Healy was an unusual cleric. He was a scholar and an intellectual who fully supported the Celtic Revival. A cultural historian, he lectured and wrote about Ireland's ancient monuments, doing all he could to encourage young priests to take an interest in their Irish heritage. For twelve years, while he was Bishop of Clonfert, he did not live in the Bishop's palace, but rented a house and 120 acres, at £50 a year, from Edward Martyn. This was Mount Bernard at Ballymacward, Andrew Martyn's land. Healy lived there in domestic harmony with his mother, his niece and his niece's children. He was known in the district as a first-rate farmer, who encouraged the neighbouring farmers to follow his example. The family continued to live with him when he moved into the Bishop's Palace in 1903, after he was appointed Archbishop of Tuam.[13] The Electoral College in Rome had not wanted this appointment, but he was the personal choice of Leo XIII, a Pope who believed that the Catholic Church should throw itself into the rising tide of democracy in order to regulate and direct it, in accordance with Christian principles. Healy didn't always reach these high ideals.

Martyn and Healy were close friends. The cleric often came to Tillyra and in 1897 they were together at the laying of the foundation stone for the cathedral. It was that year, too, that Jeremiah O'Donovan was appointed to the parish of Loughrea. O'Donovan was another unusual cleric who was dearly loved by the people. In 1985 in a radio documentary devoted to O'Donovan, Mrs Mary Conlon of Loughrea remembered him as: 'A very handsome, good-looking man. You'd love to look at him; a fine lively, lively looking man. Everyone loved him … lovely man.' And they had reason to love him for he was on their side. In April and May 1899 he published two articles in the *New Ireland Review* collectively entitled *Is Ireland doomed?* In them he called on the Catholic Church to show a social conscience and to provide leadership in secular affairs. Maynooth, the leading seminary in the country, was rich, while his new abode, Loughrea, was full of 'squalor, poverty and wretchedness'. Much of this misery was caused by the excessive consumption of alcohol. O'Donovan's first task was the foundation of the St Brendan's Total Abstinence Society, where he provided a library, reading room and gymnasium for the men of the parish. With the help and support of Horace Plunkett and George Russell, he redeveloped the crafts of lace-making and embroidery in the town. For O'Donovan, the provision of work for the people was the true patriotism.

After John Healy introduced him to Edward Martyn, he put them both to work on the decoration of Saint Brendan's. O'Donovan believed, as Martyn did, that the tool to use for the revival of Irish fine art was the Catholic Church. There was a spate of church-building in progress and they knew it would be no more costly to fill these churches with Irish fine art than with the usual English, French, German and Italian imitations. The backdrop to this thinking was as practical as it was idealistic. There was an impulse to revive the early Irish Christian and Romanesque art and relate it to Irish nationality, but at a practical level, Martyn was well aware of the scarcity of work for contemporary Irish artists and craft workers. Sarah Purser shared these ideals and she was just the kind of astute businesswoman he needed to help him achieve them. He greatly respected her as an artist and they both had a European taste and outlook. Moreover, she liked him. When she painted his portrait, she flattered him, but then she flattered most of her subjects. Saint Brendan's would be the spearhead of their campaign. O'Donovan showed his faith in Sarah Purser in a letter he sent on 25 April 1901, which included the reassurance: 'Hughes is doing the sculpture for the church. You will, I trust, will be decorator in chief.'[14]

John Hughes, who was the director of the sculpture department in the Metropolitan School of Art, had already been employed by Healy to do the carvings and sculpture on Saint Brendan's. He did not share with Martyn and Purser the notion that there was any 'National Distinctiveness in Art',[15] but he supported them in persuading T.P. Gill to institute classes in stained glass at the Art School. As already noted, it was these students who provided the foundation for a native enterprise in stained glass, that Martyn and Purser agreed was necessary for the production of work with a native aesthetic. Out of it would come Purser's stained-glass studio in Pembroke Street Dublin, An Tur Gloinne, for which Edward Martyn drummed up the orders, while Sarah Purser and her artists produced the work.

They used the pages of the *Leader* to promote their cause. Yet again Martyn offended as many readers as he could when he laid bare his extreme anti-democratic tendencies in his efforts to explain to people why they liked 'sham art'. The reason for the decay in the decorative arts, he wrote, 'can be traced back to the democratic educational movements of the early part of the last century, which sought to give everyone, irrespective of wealth, equal facilities of learning. Life was better when only the people who were rich, intelligent and stupid alike were educated. The intelligent were able to control the stupid unhampered by the uneducated masses ... the stupid rich were not numerous enough to vulgarize the world's literature ... education has made mediocre people "respectable", that mean English word that came into vogue with the decay of our own language – People became genteel and created a market for cheap sham.'[16] And yet when he goes on to tell people where they can go in Ireland to see beautiful stained glass, we can glimpse the social vision of a man who wants to make the world beautiful so that everyone can enjoy it.

In June 1901 he attended the consecration of two new churches and wrote about both in the *Leader*. The first visit was to Spiddal in County Galway, a town he knew well from visiting his cousins, the Morrises. There he found the early signs of change in church-building. The church had been designed by the architect W.A. Scott and 'the very style is at once distinguished, original and living. It is a development of the ancient Irish Romanesque for modern architectural purposes. In this way it may be said to begin a modern native architecture in Ireland ... a native school on strict principles may develop from this interesting experiment.'[17] Then he went to St Eunan's, the new cathedral in Letterkenny, County Donegal and felt obliged to write: 'It is not a perfect gem of art and nobody will dare say so. It is with great reluctance that I say so.' He castigated the decadence of 'Bad Italian'. But all was not lost. He enjoyed his trip to Donegal. The sermon in Irish was given by the Bishop of Galway and 'near the pulpit were stationed several altar boys, dressed in the white large cowled habits of the ancient Irish Culdees. They looked up at the preacher with faces lit by a poetry of sympathy and wonder and at the sight of them, and at the sound of the Irish language all the vulgarities around me seemed to melt away and, for a while, at least, I felt a strange contentment and peace.'[18]

After a quick trip to listen to Wagner in Bayreuth, in the company of Vincent O'Brien and George Moore, he was back writing for the first anniversary edition of the *Leader*. In an article entitled 'A Year's Work for the Leader', he wrote of what the paper and its philosophy meant to him. 'I liked it,' he wrote, 'its main idea was founded on criticism and satire of modern Ireland. That prospectus was very sympathetic to me. It expressed much that I had thought.' However, this praise was not unconditional. He was not pleased with the extreme criticism of his friends: 'I cannot but deplore certain opinions of the *Leader* in literature, as, for instance, its denunciation of symbolism [Arthur Symons's *The Symbolist Movement in Literature* had been published in 1899] or of the work of our writers, so much of which I sincerely admire.' D.P. Moran had been attacking Yeats throughout the year on the basis that the people could not understand his work. In an article entitled 'Literary Expression' he referred to 'a school of cant that threatens to do much damage to the revival of the Irish National Intellect'.[19] 'We are rough, homely and unaccustomed to the habit of sustained thinking,' he wrote. Edward Martyn wasn't any of these things. He was elitist and didn't at all like the respectable Catholic middle class of whom Moran wrote. Still, he concluded, 'I must recognise its [the paper's] enormous service in aggregate to the country.'[20]

In October Martyn wrote an excellent review of the 'The Two Irish Artists' exhibition, which was on at No. 6 St Stephen's Green, the work of John Butler Yeats and Nathaniel Hone. He gave the credit for the exhibition to Sarah Purser but she had had a good deal of help from him. In December, when he wrote 'Dublin at last the Capital of Ireland' and he called for the Catholic population to put their backs into the 'New Ireland', he was not being anti-Protestant. Even though he believed himself to be a true and ardent Catholic, he was incapable of sectarianism. He accepted, however, that the ascendency class, which was almost entirely Protestant, was not likely to relinquish its power easily. It would have to be taken from them by the majority, who were, obviously, Catholics. Not being sectarian made him something of a misfit on the pages of the *Leader*. He was very fond of D.P. Moran but he could never share his bigotry. Arthur Griffith, the founder of Sinn Féin, had the same problem. Initially he welcomed the new paper alongside his own *United Irishman*, but he soon got tired of Moran's bigotry, even though he was himself anti-Semitic. Did anyone, however, on the *Leader* share Edward's idealism? When Immal (J.J. O'Toole, a civil servant), the leading columnist on the paper, sat in the Catholic church in Killaloe, County Clare, to ponder the article he was writing on 'The Pubs of Killaloe' for the paper's anti-drink campaign, he shares his thoughts with us: 'Oh Edward Martyn – you have all your work cut out for you in your worthy aim of introducing something like an artistic soul into Catholic Ireland. Great actors cannot be made, even by Horace Plunkett or the Dublin Corporation.'[21]

The third season of the theatre was upon them, but Edward Martyn had had very little to do with it. He had written an article in the first issue of *Samhain*, reiterating his belief in what the Literary Theatre should be about: 'to put before the people of Ireland native works, also translations of the dramatic masterworks of all lands, for it is only by accustoming a public to the highest art that it can be led to appreciate art, and that dramatists may be inspired to work in the great art tradition'. But if he had any reservations about the plays he only expressed them to his friends. He took no part in the controversy that raged in the pages of the *Leader* and condemned *Diarmuid and Grainne*, calling it a 'travesty' of the ancient Irish fable. 'Mr. Moore and Mr. Yeats turned *Grainne* into one of those kinds of creatures that have been so prominent in the degenerate London drama against which the Irish Literary Theatre is supposed to be an antidote.'[22]

Joseph Holloway attended the first night on 21 October and found the play 'on the whole a beautiful piece full of weird suggestiveness, but lacking here and there in dramatic action'.[23] In the main people did not like it, but it gave Dubliners lots to talk about in the weeks following its first performance. The fact that they had used an English troupe, the Benson Company, was resented. They had been employed as a box-office draw, but it hadn't worked. When Martin Ross went to see it on the Friday night (it ran for one week), she reported 'a thin house'. She found the play a 'strange mix of saga and modern French situations – George Moore and Yeats were palpable throughout – the former in the situations, the latter in the beautiful writing here and there, and in the peculiar simplicities that arose'.[24] The London *Times* and the *Irish Times* both gave the play good reviews. For Augusta Gregory the success of the production was 'quite respectable'.

Douglas Hyde's *Casadh an tSugain* (The Twisting of the Rope), which played after *Grainne*, was not an unqualified success either, but people looked at it in a different way. It was the first time a play in the Irish language had been played in Irish in an Irish theatre and it was memorable for that reason. 'It was rather hard lines for those who went to see the Irish play and had perforce to sit out the other one,' the *Leader* declared. Hyde himself played 'Hanrahan', the wandering poet, and members of the Gaelic Amateur Dramatic Society supported him. It was produced by William Fay, whose brother Frank was the drama critic of the *United Irishman* and who found the use of a vulgar English company in the Irish Literary Theatre 'intolerable'. The Fay brothers were beginning to make their presence felt in the emerging Irish drama movement. They would become a force to be reckoned with.

In December 1900 Augusta Gregory had written to Yeats: 'George Moore is fated to be an embarrassment to his friends.'[25] On 13 November 1901 she was proved right. Moore wrote to the *Freeman's Journal* advocating 'ecclesiastical censorship of the theatre in Ireland'. His argument was that 'the intelligent censorship of the church will free the stage from the unintelligent and ignorant censorship of the public'.[26] Yeats immediately wrote to the paper declaring that, whereas he would be delighted to have it discussed, on the basis that discussion was

23 Max Beerbohm's cartoon of George Moore. He was 'fated to be an embarrassment to his friends', Augusta Gregory wrote. When he suggested, in the *Freeman's Journal*, ecclesiastical censorship of the theatre in Ireland, she was silent.

24 Vincent O'Brien, 1917; first director
of the Palestrina Choir.

a good thing, he wanted to lay down his marker. He would have nothing to do with 'ecclesiastical censorship' in the theatre. Writing to him from 21 Lower Baggot Street, Dublin on 16 November, Augusta kept him up-to-date with Moore's feelings: 'He says your letter is [injudicious] ... and that you have thrown everything into Edward's hands,' she wrote, 'but, in detail, this only means that if a National Theatre were to be started just now, Edward would be appointed manager and this does not seem a pressing danger. He considers *An Enchanted Sea* [E. M's fourth play] a "rotten play" and thinks of pressing Edward to perform it for the whole week, that he may have a real downfall. However, if Edward will consent to do it and *Heroes of Hegoland* in the spring he will be ready to keep friends with him. ... Fr. Dineen is rather sad about your letter; if literary men are to think they may write just what they like, what will the end be? I said I didn't know.'[27]

This is a very revealing letter. Although it is obvious that Edward Martyn's connection with the Literary Theatre went a long way to making it acceptable to the Catholic Church, the idea that this influence would be enough for to make him 'manager', should a National Theatre be founded, seems almost preposterous. It was certainly not what he wanted. When he did start his own theatre in 1914, his first task was to find a manager. And then there is the prospect of any of them staging *An Enchanted Sea*. Obviously, at this point, neither Yeats nor Gregory had read it. But even if they did produce it, it would not be part of the Irish Literary Theatre because that experiment had run its course. Yeats announced this in his article in *Samhain*, the journal that had replaced *Bealtaine*. In December 1901 it was not obvious that the 'collaborators' on the original idea had come to the parting of the ways, but that was, in effect, the situation. Yeats was attracted to the new ideas of the Fays and it was to them he would give his next collaborative play (this time the literary collaborator was Augusta Gregory), *Cathleen ni Houlihan*. There is no evidence that they minded parting with George Moore, but Yeats wrote to Gregory in January 1902: 'It will be a great pity if Martyn withdraws.'[28] It was hard on Moore, though, for he had left London to make his home in Dublin in the spring of 1901. George Russell found him a very pleasant Georgian house at 4 Ely Place, where he would entertain, and annoy, his neighbours and friends for the next ten years.

Martyn never fully withdrew, even though Yeats wrote to Maud Gonne on 28 January that Edward Martyn had given up the Irish Literary Theatre. These people were his friends and his loyalty to them remained constant, despite a later play that satirised their relationships in the period of the literary theatre.[29] Because he could not get his own way, however, he did not give them any more money. Even if he had, they would not have staged *An Enchanted Sea*.

An Enchanted Sea was Edward Martyn's fourth play and, in a way, it caused him more trouble than any of the others. For many it revealed his essential paganism, and there were other revelations which people noticed. In the letter cited above, Yeats wrote: 'Edward Martyn is being called a pagan at last.' This observation resulted from a review of *An Enchanted Sea* in the *Catholic Weekly Register*, a highly influential Catholic newspaper, published in London. The reviewer was Wilfrid Meynell, who wrote that Martyn's work: 'displayed a morbid and misty spiritualism, with a possible residuum of a kind of knowledge expressly and repeatedly condemned by the church'. The playwright, it seemed to Meynell, accepted legend as dogma. 'The chief work of the Irish Literary Theatre is, in essence, pagan.'[30] This was largely true but could this play, which was written by a presumed paragon of Catholicism, be offensive to his Church. It seems it could.

The play has been described as a homo-erotic tragedy, set in the west of Ireland in 1882. The critic Stephen Gwynn had doubts about it being a tragedy.[31] Lord Mask, who has just returned to Ireland from Greece, is in love with young Guy Font. Mask is a typical Martynesque, self-obsessed character. Commander Lyle, R.N. (a minor character) describes him as 'a selfish dreamer who would cramp the whole world into the mould of fixed theory – without affection – without love'. The young Font (he is only 15) lives with his aunt, Rachel Font, who hates him. She feels this way mainly because he is the legitimate heir to the property, 'Fonthill', where she lives, but also because she wants Mask for her daughter, Agnes. Rachel is a hard, domineering woman who will do anything to get her own way. She murders Guy by drowning him in the sea caves. When she is discovered, and subsequently realises that Mask will never marry her daughter, but intends to follow Guy into the sea, she hangs herself. That is the plot, but it is not the problem.

The central theme of the play is the sea. In this it owes something to Ibsen's *The Lady from the Sea*. After seeing Ibsen's play, Edward Martyn had written:

> *The Lady from the Sea* gives expression to that yearning and enchantment which the ocean has for certain natures. An enchanted sea! How can I tell the feelings that rise to the heart when we look afar to the sea from the barren coast in west Ireland for instance? The illimitable Atlantic with all its mastery and beauty calls … and we think of the old Irish saga
>
> Sea horses glisten in summer
> As far as Bran has stretched his glance.[32]

But, overall, the play is reflective of the more symbolic plays of Maurice Maeterlinck, the Belgian symbolist. Fairies are brought into the action at a very early stage. Mr Yelverton, who is Guy's tutor, collects 'fairy lore', but, more importantly, the 'sea fairie' was lately seen on

Mask Castle. This is ominous, for legend has it that a previous Lord
Mask had married a sea fairy who haunts the castle and the surrounding area. Being a fairy she never died but returned to her natural
home, the sea. In Act 1 Guy Font tells everyone of the appearance of a
white lady who had beckoned him down into the sea caves where he
saw the Celtic sea god Manannan. Commander Lyle tries to persuade
him that he is mixing this image up with a representation of Poseidon
that he had seen in Athens. But Mask says:

> Mask. If Manannan seems like Poseidon it is because the
> ancient Irish and Greek mythologies are akin. Some say
> our remote ancestry was Greek'.
>
> Lyle: But how could Pagan gods, who never existed, appear?
>
> Agnes: Perhaps they are fallen angels as the fairies.[33]

In a later act Guy questions Mask's true interest in him. It is clear
that Mask is more interested in things than in people (George Moore, as
we know, accused Edward of this).

> Guy: You needed me to give life to your beautiful things.
>
> Mask: Those distant passionless antique things – ought you not
> to glory in giving them life.
>
> Guy: What is the genius of the Antique?
>
> Mask: (*with abstracted exhalation*). Youth and form – pale marble
> form.
>
> Guy: Like the boys in the court of Manannan.
>
> Mask: I have dreamed it all in solitary days at Eton and
> Oxford, and now your genius has made me see in
> Ireland my dream of old Greece. How wonderful you
> are. You do not know how wonderful you are.[34]

Later in the act Mask continues his description and adulation of the
ancient Greek world:

> Mask: Youths and temples transfigured in plastic sunlight,
> galleys gliding like swans in the white Piraeus, while
> their oars break into the creamy waves, the blue marble
> of the sea.
>
> Guy: This is an enchanted sea.

And that is where they both end up. It is hardly surprising that the reviewer of a Catholic newspaper should question this play. Clearly the writer is attempting to marry the Irish cultural renaissance to the classical world of ancient Greece, the pagan world. As the play works out, however, while the lure of the Ideal is powerful, its pursuit and attainment prove fatal. Aside from the minor characters, the only real 'flesh and blood' creature in the action is Agnes, who was 'only a weak girl' but who was not made for the shadows and so is spared. In fact, despite some feeble dialogue, Agnes is a strong female lead and reflects the kind of independent-minded woman that Edward Martyn continued to meet, and with whom he was becoming used to dealing in his day-to-day life, women with whom he generally maintained excellent relations.

He was shocked by Meynell's review. On 7 January 1902 he wrote from the Reform Club: 'It is as a Catholic that I wish to deny some accusations on the score of unorthodoxy which he makes against me, and against the work that I have carried out. He says I accept legend as dogma. I absolutely deny such a charge. ... I believe folklore to be at the root of some of the greatest literature.' He goes on to defend the work of the Irish Literary Theatre against the charge of paganism and he points out that he doesn't understand what the reviewer means by referring to his work as 'morbid and misty'. He wants 'definite charges' brought.[35] This was published on 10 January.

In his reply of 17 January, Meynell appeared to pull back from his direct criticism of Edward, maintaining that he saw in his work, a mysticism very similar to that of Yeats, but 'I do not for a moment suggest that Mr. Martyn was conscious of the tendencies which seemed to me inherent in it, or would accept extreme developments of it.' Still, as he warmed to his subject, he was inclined to change his view. Reflecting on the theatre, he regarded it as:

> ... a movement singularly self-conscious and deliberate in its aims, and regarding itself as potentially at least expressive of the true genius of the Irish people, almost utterly ignored the existence of the Catholic religion; while it does show a very deep interest in those survivals of pagan beliefs which still linger on and are to some extent believed amongst the peasantry ... in none of the four plays by Mr. Martyn can I recall a line to show that the characters have any religion whatever. ... Two of Mr

Martyn's four plays seem to me to imply in their motif the literal truth of pagan legends or superstition. Of course the assumption of this for the purpose of the play does not mean that Mr. Martyn accepts the truth of the legends. But he is a leading member of a movement which is a very self conscious one believing itself to have a mission; he writes with a degree of earnestness and purpose which prevents our regarding him as interested merely in the literary aspects of his work. ... The legends contain some mystic lore or some peculiar reality which Mr. Martyn intends us to take seriously.[36]

There is no denying this, and Edward Martyn didn't. This play came out of what he continued to call his 'Hellenism', and which he believed to be a major part of his life. How he squared these beliefs with his professed Catholicism remains a mystery. Clearly Meynell thought that Catholicism was the lesser of the competing beliefs. It is unlikely that Martyn thought of it on that level, and it is difficult for the biographer to ascertain to what extent Edward Martyn's Catholicism was merely functional. He continued to believe in the play and in 1904, when it was very badly performed in Dublin, he wrote to Augusta Gregory from the Kildare Street Club: 'Thanks so much for your letter and kind good wishes which I regret to say were not fulfilled. ... *An Enchanted Sea* did not please the audience. Anyhow, I am glad it was produced as it really interests me more than *The Heather Field*. But I suppose writers are considered the worst judges of their own work.'[37]

Before leaving this subject, it is important to look at the homo-erotic content of the play. Lord Mask clearly loves Guy Font in an obsessive and possessive way, and it is equally clear that the playwright is happy with this. But Edward Martyn, regardless of what his most profound beliefs may have been, certainly wanted to live his life within the theological bounds of the Roman Catholic Church, and so it may seem surprising to find him dealing with the love 'that dare not speak its name' in such a positive way. Within the bounds of his Hellenism, however, this was a perfectly legitimate love. It was a form of Uranian love which for many, and almost certainly for him, was 'a mode of spiritual and emotional attachment that was, at some ultimate level, innocent or asexual'.[38] At this pure and intellectual level, it was the love that Oscar Wilde defended fearlessly from the Old Bailey witness box in

1895. There is no evidence that Martyn's aestheticism was a blind for a carnal appetite, but there is ample evidence that, from the great pleasure he took in high art, he had long since taken to heart Walter Pater's dictum to 'end the crucifixion of the senses and begin the renaissance of joy'.[39] This is the only way he could live. His Hellenism was no help to him in sexual matters for the Greeks of the period, like the Christians later, took a bitter view of sex. *An Enchanted Sea*, steeped as it is in 'literary aestheticism', was a play for the 1890s. The world, and art, had moved on and Edward Martyn never wrote like that again.

12 • Sacred Music and Art

IN JUNE 1901, at the same time as Edward Martyn was castigating the Catholic Church in Donegal for the paucity of its artistic values, he entered into a correspondence with Dr Walsh, Archbishop of Dublin, in an attempt to persuade him to put the Palestrina Choir on a 'permanent footing'. He felt confident in making his request since Walsh had already given him 'powerful moral support', but he had certain conditions: 'My offer is this: I agree to organise and defray the expenses of a choir of men and boys under the conductorship of Mr. Vincent O'Brien and ask you to be kind enough to appoint it to such a church in Dublin city as you may consider fit.' Appointing Vincent O'Brien as conductor should not be a problem, he said, since: 'If there is an organist already settled in the church we need not interfere or disturb him.' Edward's choir would sing only Gregorian Chant and the works of Palestrina and other masters of his time and school at High Mass and perhaps on Sundays and Holydays.[1]

At this time Edward Martyn and William Walsh were again on the same side on the battle for the language. A Commission had been set up to inquire into the system of Intermediate Education and there was a danger of the language being taken off the curriculum. Professor J.P. Mahaffy, of Trinity College, Dublin (later Provost), who was on the board, regarded the Irish language as a peasant *patois* in which it was 'impossible to find a text which was not religious, silly or indecent'.[2] Martyn and Walsh were writing to each other on a daily basis, with Walsh trying to find an opportunity to talk about the choir. It is quite obvious from the letters that he was, at the time, more taken up with the problem of the language. On 18 June Edward wrote: 'This treatment of the Irish language by the Intermediate Education Board ... may lead to very serious consequences. If people like Mahaffy ... persist in flying in the face of public opinion, they will certainly be met by methods other than argument. ... I look upon this language as one of life and death for the prospects of making the country a nation.'[3] He urged Walsh to go public on the debate, assuring him that he could easily be master of the situation. On 19 June he wrote that the Board needed reconstitution and Walsh was bound to have enormous influence with the Lord Lieutenant. Later that year, Walsh, in fact, resigned from the Board.

On 22 June they got back to corresponding about the choir. Edward Martyn had had an interview with Walsh who, it is obvious, was not entirely in agreement with all his ideas. After the meeting Martyn wrote: 'It occurs to me you might wish to have other works sung than those of the old masters, such for instance as the modern compositions of the St. Cecilia school. Now this could easily be managed if you wished. On ordinary occasions the choir could sing the St. Cecilia compositions and on great festivals the works of Palestrina and the masters. I will always be most happy to assist you in the production of the old masters.'[4] But Walsh had his own ideas and other advisers. He wrote to Martyn, who had set out on a musical pilgrimage to Ratisbon, in Lower Bavaria, in August: 'I have made my first move in the direction we had in view when you were last here. I am appointing one of the priests of the Pro-Cathedral to be "Choir Director". ... I have explained to him that we must move prudently but always in the right direction ... and that we must no longer allow the Protestant cathedrals in Dublin to be ahead of us in fidelity to the remnant they have of the old Church musical tradition.'[5] After the summer holiday we have Martyn replying to him in a rather subdued manner: 'I am much obliged to you for letting me know what you have done. I have no doubt it will lead after a little time to great changes for the better in the cathedral music of our Metropolitan Church – which if really fine could not but have a vast influence upon the reform of church music in Ireland.'[6]

On 17 October he wrote again to Walsh with regard to a visit of the Benedictines of Solesmes who wanted to visit Ireland. 'They might do great work in training Catholic organists and conducting a native school of church music.' He also committed himself, more definitely, to a very large financial support, for in December we have Walsh writing to him about costs: 'I have been endeavouring to ascertain how far it will be feasible to make a real reform to our church music in Marlborough Street [Pro-Cathedral].' He had got the information from a 'friendly source' in St Patrick's Church of Ireland Cathedral and he assured Martyn, giving a detailed list of expenses, that it would be heavy. He was, he told him, keeping Vincent O'Brien informed. And then he went on to make Edward Martyn very happy indeed with regard to the foundation of a trust. Dr Donnelly, the auxiliary Bishop of Dublin, had pointed out that 'the only way of securing the stability of the work would be to have a duly constituted *trust* set up, which would make it impossible for anyone, to the end of time, to divert the fund from the purpose intended by you as the founder of it. I happen to know enough of the law to be able to state with absolute confidence that the purpose is one for which a trust can be established in perpetuity.'[7]

Edward was delighted, but he wasn't yet ready to commit himself to a permanent endowment: 'Would it not be better for you and Mr. O'Brien to begin the work at once while I would supply money over and above what you could give? Or would you leave the work to Mr. O'Brien and myself, giving whatever money or help you could? At the end then of a couple of years or so, we could form some idea of what the amount of a foundation should be. ... I think it would be well if you could start Mr. O'Brien in the cathedral as soon after Christmas as possible, he should be preparing for Holy Week immediately.'[8] The archbishop didn't like this at all and impressed on Edward the necessity of looking ahead and planning on a permanent basis. Like Martyn he wanted to change things, but 'I don't see how I can break up the existing arrangement until we have something of a permanent character to put in its place,' he wrote. He pointed out that they had to consider public taste: 'I should of course wish to have *really great* music on as many occasions as possible, but even as a matter of cultivating a sound musical taste amongst our Dublin public in church music I think we ought not, especially at first, to be too lavish of what is really of the first rank.' (George Moore's assessment of E.M.'s achievement in the cultural renaissance was that 'he emptied two churches, he and Palestrina between them'.)[9] The archbishop was more in touch with 'the people' than Edward Martyn, but it was not the major stumbling-block.

That proved to be the appointment of Vincent O'Brien as conductor of the choir. Edward pointed out that unless he was given a permanent post he could hardly be expected to give up his present place: 'And it will be impossible for him to conduct the Holy Week music in the Pro-Cathedral while remaining organist of St. Saviour's.' The archbishop agreed with this and Martyn went off to spend Christmas in the Hotel Continental in Paris, for the third year running.

Back in Dublin in January Walsh wrote to him: 'I regret to say that we have encountered a hitch.' He could not ask Vincent O'Brien to give up his present job and start afresh unless the choir was constituted on a permanent basis. Walsh was putting it up to Edward Martyn: he wanted to see the colour of his money. Edward hesitated. On 20 January 1902 there is a very despondent letter to Vincent O'Brien. O'Brien had obviously heard bad news from Walsh and had sent it to Edward Martyn, who replied: 'I am well prepared for the bad news you tell me. … I fear it will be impossible now to do anything for some time unless he consents to appoint you to the cathedral at once, so that you can begin to get together a choir. … If he does not do this then the whole proposal is destroyed. Nothing more will be done as long as he is archbishop. If our business fails, as I expect it will, the only thing to do would be to look out for a parish priest with taste who would take you on as an organist and give you a free hand. Such a person may possibly be found among the younger men.'[10]

But it didn't fail. Martyn stopped dithering and decided to give the money. It would not be his choir unless he paid up. At the beginning of March he instructed his friend, Serjeant Charles O'Connor, to draw up a scheme for a legal endowment. The Archbishop, for his part, employed the best canon lawyers available for, as he pointed out to Edward, 'It would of course be useless to get a scheme that you and I would personally approve of, and that would also be approved of by the lawyers, if in the end it turned out to be unworkable on account of its being in some way at variance with ecclesiastical law.'[11] In the end Walsh looked after his patron's long-term interests with a stringency that did him much credit.

It was Edward Martyn's choir. It became the *Schola Cantorum* (in which there were no feminine voices, although, in later years, many female musical directors) but he couldn't help feeling sorry for Vincent O'Brien since he had to deal with 'the wretched acoustics of the Pro-Cathedral' when performing his work. 'How gorgeous it would all sound in a fine church like Saint Patrick's for instance,' Martyn wrote in old age.[12] He had parted with £10,000 (an astronomical sum in 1902) to facilitate its foundation. Arthur Griffith almost had apoplexy at the spending of this amount of money on a choir:

> Mr. Martyn's application of so vast a sum to the purpose of forming a choir, which not 2 per cent of the population will be able to hear and not one-half per cent be able to appreciate is simply monstrous. ... Mr. Martyn is a public man – a leader in the language, literary and industrial movements – all cramped for want of money. If Mr. Martyn arrived at the conclusion that the salvation of Ireland depended on the improvement of church music he would have done infinitely better by distributing the £10,000 among churches in the various districts of Ireland for surely Mr. Martyn cannot possibly believe that the establishment of a Palestrina choir in a Dublin church will affect church music in Donegal or Kerry. It is a deplorable fact that a gentleman who has shown a practicable appreciation of the situation in Ireland should now act in a manner as if he had believed the future of the country depended, not on the success of the national literary and industrial movements at work among us, but on the encouragement of foreign church music.[13]

But in the issue of 16 August Griffith decided to forgive him: 'Mr. Martyn means well,' he wrote, 'and the childlike innocence of his scheme for saving the country, vaguely reminiscent of Orpheus with his lute, deprives us of the power of hitting at it too hard.' Or perhaps it was that Griffith had an eye for the rest of what he called Mr. Martyn's 'superflous thousands'.[14]

In April 1903 Yeats's *Cathleen ni Houlihan* and Æ's *Deirdre* were performed in the hall of St Teresa's Total Abstinence Association in Clarendon Street. The plays were produced by W.G. Fay's Irish National Dramatic Society and were a success. Edward Martyn had been invited to be involved but he had 'prevaricated over the funding', so they went ahead without him. This was a great pity, for this performance led almost directly to the foundation of the Abbey Theatre. Having a performance in a Temperance Hall, however, had its drawbacks. Joseph Holloway complained that 'snatches of popular songs, erratic dance steps and the continuous sound of billiard balls coming into contact with each other wafted from the adjoining room, so that most of what the performers said was lost on me'.[15] Yeats asked Martyn to write to the *United Irishman* about the performance, an action he regretted.

In his letter to the *United Irishman* Edward commended the 'excellence of the plays themselves and the by no means incompetent manner in which they were performed'. While he thought Maud Gonne's acting of *Cathleen ni Houlihan* showed 'mastery over the difficulties of the art', he was not happy with the others. C. Caufield, who played Peter Gillane, 'did not play his part as a Mayo peasant perplexed and frightened by some vague terror impending ... but as an optimistic Dublin Jarvey'.[16] Yeats was furious. 'I got him to write to U.I. about the plays,' he wrote to Augusta Gregory, 'and he has written rather abusing the actors, whom one wants to encourage. He is going to bring English actors over for his play and is laying pipe.'[17] Martyn had told Yeats that Frank Fay had overacted his part, but when he went to see the performance himself, he disagreed. Then he wrote to the *United Irishman*: 'I do not agree with Mr. Martin [*sic*] as to the acting of Deirdre. I think the difference between us comes from the difference of our arts. Mr. Martin likes a form of drama that is essentially modern, that needs for its production actors of what is called the "natural school" the dominant school of the modern stage. The more experience an actor has had of that stage the better he is for Mr. Martin's purpose, and almost a certainty the worst for me.'[18]

Were Edward Martyn's plays *Maeve* and *An Enchanted Sea* 'essentially modern'? They were in so far as that they were about land, property and greed, but they also had large doses of mysticism as, indeed, did *The Heather Field*. Granted, Edward Martyn's 'mysticism' was closer to that of Henrik Ibsen than to that of W.B. Yeats; for the most part it was psychology not poetry. He always referred to it as the 'drama of the mind'. Fairies didn't interest him. He was very close to the land-grabbing materialism of human neighbours, and especially to that of Irish peasants. He was idealistic, but he was not romantic; somewhat mystical, he wasn't particularly spiritual. Despite *An Enchanted Sea* and *Maeve*, he would have been among those who believed that the 'Celtic Twilight' was nothing more than 'the mist that does be on the bog'. Still, he allowed himself to be enchanted by it. He wanted to be enchanted by it. An innate realism, however, continued to make him wary of a folk theatre centred on the life of the Irish peasant.

Yeats, nevertheless, had a powerful argument. 'Our movement', he wrote in the *United Irishman*, 'is a return to the people, like the Russian movement of the early seventies, and the drama of society would but magnify a condition of life which the countryman and the artisan could but copy to their hurt. The play that is to give them a quite natural pleasure should tell them either of their own life, or of that life of poetry, where every man can see his own image, because there alone does human nature escape from arbitrary conditions. Plays about drawing-rooms are written for the middle-classes of great cities, for the classes who live in drawing-rooms. ... We should, of course, play every kind of good play about Ireland that we can get, but romantic and historical plays, and plays about the life of artisans and country people are the best worth getting.'[19] Plays about country people came to be written in great abundance and, indeed, some of them were even set in drawing-rooms. But, by and large, they came to be known as the 'peasant play'. Romantic and historical plays were thin on the ground and since the folk plays were performed mainly to romantically minded city audiences, the 'countryman' gained little. Martyn clung tenaciously to the ideas he had started with in the Literary Theatre and on 26 July he published *The Place-Hunters, a Political Comedy in One Act* in the *Leader*.

This short, one-act sketch, which is about the middle-class establishment looking for preferment, and what they are likely to do to get it, was never staged. Perhaps if it had been well acted there might have been some comedy in it, but on the printed page this does not easily reveal itself. Still, it shows Edward Martyn examining the society he was living in and finding it wanting, and it reflects his realistic take on the position of the reformer in Irish society: 'Of course we don't expect any gratitude! It is only weaklings hanker after gratitude. Nation builders, working out their ideas, will think themselves lucky if they even escape assassination.'[20] Again, as in *The Tale of a Town*, the satire borders on the burlesque and, if the dialogue had been worked on and sharpened, it could have been of interest. Martyn, as a satirist, is at his best but his work rarely goes beyond the stage of 'amateur'. It is likely that this flaw in his creative work was pointed out to him by George Moore and it certainly was by Arthur Symons, but he was not listening.

That summer Dublin society was enthralled when Moore staged a performance of Douglas Hyde's play *The Tinker and the Fairy* in Irish in his garden in Ely Place. Douglas Hyde played the tinker and Sinead

Flanagan (later Mrs Eamon de Valera) played the fairy. John Butler Yeats sent his daughter Lily a vivid description of the event:

> There was a great crowd there. Tyrell, F.T.C.D. [Fellow of Trinity College Dublin] was the only F.T.C.D. there. I suppose Moore's attack on Mahaffy did not hurt *his* feelings [Moore had written an outrageous attack on Mahaffy's attitude to the Irish language]. The weather held up allright at the play. There had been a bitter black storm of rain in the morning but it cleared up. The play ought to have started at 3 o'clock when the sun was shining and it was quite warm, and that was the time appointed. But the delegates (I don't know what delegates) did not arrive. ... At last the wretches arrived and the play began, and though expecting every moment to be drenched through, we got safely to the end; though for a time all umbrellas were up. ... Fortunately this happened towards the end, when the musicians and singers (out of sight behind a screen of leaves) had the performance to themselves. Douglas Hyde was Tinker, the Fairy was a pretty young girl – Miss Flanagan.[21]

John B. Yeats had left Bedford Park in London and had lived in Harrington Street, Dublin for a few years before he moved permanently to New York. Edward Martyn was often at Moore's house when the painter made a visit. A keen observer of the human condition, John B. wrote to W.B. in early 1903: 'Last night I was at Moore's – Martyn, for half an hour, talked of nothing but your morality play [*The Hour Glass*] "Superb, magnificent, most dramatic, far the best thing he has ever done, and the things he has got into it". It was beautiful to see Moore's restlessness, the jealousy of the artist, which Blake says is like the sting of the honey bee. ... He questioned and questioned and was something relieved when he heard it could be acted in thirty minutes.'[22] But the elder Yeats loved Moore. 'He is the most stimulating mind I ever met,' the painter wrote to Charles Fitzgerald in January 1905. 'It is because he always keeps his own point of view – he is always like a man tumbled in among us out of some distant planet. ... It is all I suppose because he never learned anything at school, Nature having made everything safe for him by presenting him with natural industry and a good intellect.'[23]

Edward Martyn loved the company of the elderly painter. W.B. Yeats expressed surprise, in April 1903, when Martyn urged J.B.Y. to be 'rude and personal' in a letter he was writing to the *Leader* to defend himself against an attack on his work, and his aesthetics, by the critic Robert Elliot. Edward was obviously angry on the older man's behalf. Perhaps Yeats was surprised because he had just written a preface to Elliot's recently published book, *Art in Ireland*, which was mainly about ecclesiastical art and architecture. But, given the period we are dealing with, Edward Martyn was the obvious person to write such a preface. Of the author he later, rather earnestly for Martyn, wrote: 'His views are sound and excellent and ought to have a good effect on the much needed reform of church art'. Robert Elliot didn't like Jack Yeats's work either. He considered it to be 'a weak kind of happy-go-lucky' work. By this time Elliot was the art critic on the *Leader*. Perhaps Edward Martyn was jealous, but it was more likely that he was contemptuous of Elliot's criticism of art on the broader canvas.[24]

Martyn wanted to get *An Enchanted Sea* performed, and he wanted to revive his earlier work. He was also keen to stage a lot more Ibsen. In May he had been 'in treaty' about this, with Genevieve Ward, an American actress who was playing the Marquise de St. Maur, in T.R. Robertson's *Caste* at the Haymarket, but nothing came of it.[25] And then, in October, he tried to woo the Fays. 'Martyn has written a wonderful letter to the Fays,' Yeats wrote to Lady Gregory. 'He offered £10 at the end of a year if they played an Irish play at every performance and performed three times a week. He also told them that they must get the accent and manners of good society before they could do anything. They understood this to mean get English accents. Moore and Martyn are wonderful.'[26] Obviously the Fay brothers were not interested in this idea. They were about to bring *Cathleen ni Houlihan* to London and they would not be playing it with English accents.

Edward was, in fact, forced to fall back on the Players Club, a small amateur group founded by the Gaelic League. He was funding them in 1903, and they performed *The Heather Field* and Ibsen's *A Doll's House* for four nights at the Queen's Theatre. George Moore did the stage management and they were tolerably satisfied with their success. The critics, however, were not kind. 'Mr Carden Tyrell is neither a man nor a dreamer; he is not even decently insane; he is merely a monomaniac,' 'Spealadoir' wrote in the *United Irishman*, 'the power to see life steadily and to see it whole has been lost; blindness thereupon finds itself and promotes itself to a place among the positive virtues ... reason has capitulated to sophistry.'[27] This was a very fair review. W.B. Yeats wrote, from Coole Park, to John Quinn patron of writers and artists, in New York: 'Neither Martyn nor Moore would ever have been satisfied with our methods and they have their own distinct work in training a company for the performance of the drama of social life.'[28] Later the Players Club became the National Players' Society, with Maud Gonne and Arthur Griffith, along with Edward Martyn on the executive, but it was never a successful company.

On 1 January 1903 Sarah Purser's An Tur Gloinne was officially opened. The workshop was built behind the Georgian houses at 24 Upper Pembroke Street, Dublin. By mutual agreement, Edward Martyn was not officially a part of the business.[29] On 8 September 1902 he had written to Sarah Purser: 'I quite agree with you that I should keep outside the business, I would be in position to crack it up. There are two windows for the church here [Labane, his parish church] ... one of which I can give you and the other (on the part of my cousin) I can as well give you. My cousin's monument to her father (subject St. Andrew) should be done first.'[30]

The cousin referred to here is Mary Martyn, daughter of Edward's Uncle Andrew, who had married Fitzroy Hemphill in 1897. Mary was the only child of Andrew and lived, when she was in Ireland, at 28 Fitzwilliam Place, just around the corner from Pembroke Street. She had married into a very liberal family, with a strong sense of duty and public service. When her father-in-law, Charles Hare Hemphill, was created Baron Hemphill by Campbell Bannerman, the Liberal Prime Minister, in 1906, he became the only Irish Liberal in the House of Lords. But Mary's mother, Mary Dolphin of Turroe, County Roscommon, obviously had some reservations about the match. When their first child was born, she wrote, from Morpeth Mansions in London, to Archbishop Walsh in Dublin to assure him that the baby had been baptised in a Catholic church, and that he had Catholic sponsors and a Catholic nurse. The child was christened Martyn Charles Andrew Hemphill. Choosing a stained-glass window for the parish church at Labane was a fitting memorial for Andrew Martyn, who had grown up at Tillyra, not more than two fields distant from the church. The second window was almost certainly Edward's own memorial to his mother.

Sarah Purser was delighted with the extra commissions. She already had a lot of the work for St Brendan's Cathedral in Loughrea, but she

25 Saint Brendan's Cathedral, Loughrea, Co. Galway.

worried that being a Protestant might hinder Catholics from giving her commissions. Martyn assured her of the unlikelihood of this happening. 'You need not be afraid of a Catholic boycott,' he wrote. 'If Catholics, getting the opportunity either do not come forward or are inefficient there can be no help for them. It is impossible as yet to tell what my Christian Brothers' boys will turn out. The railways are a very different matter. Do you think anyone of average intelligence will be affected by a plea for bad art?'[31] All the artists who were working on Saint Brendan's Cathedral, Loughrea worked from Purser's studio. Alfred Child, when he was not occupied at the Metropolitan School of Art, where he worked part-time, started on his windows for Loughrea with Michael Healy, recently returned from Florence, and a willing pupil. Purser herself was also a pupil, not having any background or experience, in stained-glass. As the year rolled on, they went from strength to strength and in July Robert Elliot wrote a patronising review of their efforts in the *Leader*: 'One hardly knows whether to congratulate Mr. Edward Martyn, Miss Purser, Mr. Whall [a leading English stained-glass artist who taught Child] or the designer whom I take to be Mr. Child for there is such a delightful mystery about the responsibilities at this place; and, for my part, I do not care to know whether it is a firm, a fraternity, a workshop or a venture.'[32] In fact, for many years, Sarah Purser was the sole owner of An Tur Gloinne, but she ran it as though it was a co-operative and when she recouped her investment that is, in fact, what it became.

Five miles south of Pembroke Street two other women were setting up an enterprise which owed its initial growth to Edward Martyn, and to the decoration of Loughrea Cathedral. The Dun Emer Press, which was described in its prospectus as 'an arts and crafts manufactory ... to find work for Irish hands in the making of beautiful things', was established by Lily and Lolly Yeats and Evelyn Gleeson in 1902. Apart from the Press, the 'manufactory' was involved in weaving, tapestry and embroidery. Almost their first commission was the embroidering of the banners for St Brendan's, and they knew exactly what was required. On 28 April 1903 George Russell wrote to Yeats: 'I have been trying, with great pleasure, to turn a woman of the Sidhe into a Virgin for your sister to embroider on a banner. I think if I was allowed to I would do all the Sidhe as archangels and seraphim. I would dearly love to make a faery chapel, and put mystical figures so that the good Catholics who went there would become worshippers of the Sidhe without knowing it.'[33] In the end, the banners were designed by Jack Yeats and his wife Cottie, Pamela Coleman Smyth and Æ. They were large processional banners and sodality banners to be hung at the end of pews. It was the first showcase for Lily Yeats's work in Ireland.[34] When Saint Brendan's Cathedral was finally completed in 1905, the total cost was £30,000.

Padraic Colum, poet and playwright, of whom George Russell described to Sarah Purser as 'a new Irish genius', gives us a glimpse of what Edward Martyn and his friends were like in 1903. In *Ourselves Alone*, he describes the Óireachtas at the Rotunda in Dublin in 1902, when the proceeds of *Samhain* had been given to the Gaelic League for a special Oireachtas prize:

> An Craoibhin [Douglas Hyde] moves through the crowd ... like some king of the distant past going among his peers; the scarlet of his kerchief or his necktie brings out the darkness of his hair and moustache and strangely modelled features. And there is George Moore with his pallid face and blonde hair, an alert look in his china blue eyes as he takes mental notes of the characters around him, and makes some remark to that countrified gentleman beside him, Edward Martyn, who is humming a traditional air that some singer from Galway has made current that morning. And there is Yeats all in black with a black flowing tie, who is dwelling on a line that someone has translated for him from a poem in Irish that a blind man has translated for him. And there is Standish O'Grady (eagle like) and David P. Moran, a big man whose humorous and aggressive looks remind me of portraits of Daniel O'Connell and Padraic Pearse, a tall young man with a slight squint who had something exalted in his bearing.[35]

Later he describes Edward Martyn as 'an aristocrat, a man of station, open, sincere, cultivated. ... One of those squires who look the countryman, except for the liveliness of their movement and spruceness of their appearance. He was stout and ruddy faced, wore glasses, chuckled a good deal and spoke with a marked Galway accent.'[36]

13 • 1904

O N 2 APRIL 1903 Edward Martyn wrote to the *Freeman's Journal* to object to the pending visit to Ireland of King Edward VII. 'I understand', he wrote, 'that the British newspapers are already making capital out of the forthcoming visit of the King to Ireland, whom they declare the Irish people will receive as a welcome compensation for their deprivation of Home Rule. By this means England has once more thrown down the gauntlet to Nationalist Ireland. It is for Nationalist Ireland to take it up and tell the government with one voice that if they bring the King here under any other guise than as a restorer of our stolen constitution, they will regret their rashness.'[1] This letter was reprinted in the London *Times* two days later. On 9 April Yeats wrote to the newspaper in support: 'Royal visits with their pageantry, their false rumours of concessions, their appeal of all that is superficial and trivial in society are part of the hypnotic illusion by which England seeks to capture the imagination of this country.'[2]

Three weeks later Martyn wrote again to *Freeman's Journal*. This time it was in response to a resolution passed by the Baltinglass, County Wicklow Board of Guardians, which urged 'a cordial reception to the King, since the visit was another instance of the great interest he has taken in the affairs of this country'.[3] He described the resolution as 'one of the most deplorable exhibitions of incompetence by which Irishmen make themselves contemptible to foreign people'. This letter was supported by John Sweetman, a nationalist activist and later president of Sinn Féin, who 'supported Mr. Edward Martyn's manly protest against Ireland's grovelling before the King of England'.[4] Out of this agitation the National Council was born, and Edward Martyn was its chairman.

The National Council was, fundamentally, Yeats's idea. It started out as the People's Protection Committee and he persuaded Maud Gonne to recruit Edward Martyn. She was reluctant at first and wrote to Yeats on 7 May: 'I hesitated all day yesterday about writing to Martyn about the committee you suggested. I don't like doing anything politically from a personal motive & it seems to me for the reasons you gave me it might be one, but, on the whole, the usefulness of such a committee has outweighed all other considerations and I have just written to Martyn.'[5] The committee was quickly in place and it attracted a wide variety of supporters, especially among old Fenians, including the elderly John O'Leary. It was typical of the type of organisation that fell under the aegis of Griffith's Cumann na Gaedheal and would, in fact, be the foundation for Sinn Féin. Maud Gonne was an honorary secretary. By then she was married to Major John McBride, but the marriage was in a bad way and they would soon separate. The purpose of the Council was: 'to prevent the undue pressure which was brought to bear on the working classes particularly in Dublin, on the occasion of the visit of Queen Victoria to compel them to participate and to allow their children to participate in festivities and demonstrations of which they disapproved'.[6]

Their first task was to prevent Dublin Corporation from going ahead with its plan to present a 'loyal address' to the King, from the citizens of the city. In order to further this ambition, they sent a deputation to a meeting held in the Rotunda, on 18 May, by Dublin Corporation and the Irish Parliamentary Party. This turned out to be 'the most gorgeous row', where 'Martyn has heroism thrust upon him', Æ wrote to Yeats.[7] But, according to the *Freeman's Journal*, Edward lost his way in the mêlée: 'Martyn tried to hide behind Maud Gonne. ... Then someone in the audience threw a chair on the platform, and some injudicious person on the platform threw one back. The Deputation and Mr. Martyn made a rapid retreat from the platform, Mrs. McBride was an effective rear guard. The audience fought in small knots, and the Lord Mayor [Timothy Harrington] jumped clean off the platform and seized several of the protagonists.'[8] As a result of this, Russell wrote Yeats: 'Martyn's stay in the Kildare Street Club becomes one of the humours of Dublin. He says it is becoming serious for him for if they expel him he won't be able anywhere else to get a bed for 2/6 a night so comfortably.'[9] Maud Gonne was furious, on Edward's behalf, about the press reports and wrote Yeats: 'Mr Martyn was to have read a question but at the last moment got nervous about speaking, never having spoken at a big stormy meeting & handed the paper he himself had written to me. It was only nervousness about speaking for he was quite fearless and held his own splendidly. George Moore got afraid and backed out on the grounds that he was a man of letters and not a politician.'[10]

The day after the demonstration Edward Martyn wrote to the *United Irishman*: 'It is clear to every Nationalist that no Irishwoman or Irishman who values national dignity or honour, who realises the condition to which our country has been reduced – a shrunken and still shrinking population – a destroyed trade – a plundered and overtaxed people an impoverished country – nation with right stolen and still unrestored can participate in any address of welcome to the King of England.'[11] It is likely that much of this prose belonged to Maud Gonne, who was an extreme nationalist. She liked working with Martyn. She had met him for the first time in 'the pleasant green woods which surround Richard Wagner's Temple of Music at Bayreuth … when he was already dreaming of creating for Ireland the world's most perfect choir'.[12] Although she had been cross with him (on Yeats's account) for leaving the Literary Theatre, she never found him hard to work with. 'He loved God, Ireland, music and the theatre and never could dissociate his loves', she wrote. In the end they were successful. The Dublin Corporation voted, albeit by a small majority of three, not to present a loyal address. The National Council remained in being and Edward Martyn remained its chairman; a situation that led him into much conflict with his old friend and now adversary, David Moran.

D.P. Moran did not like the National Council, and he was especially scathing about what he termed 'the Rotunda rowdies', later to be called the 'Juvenile Party'. Martyn, as their chairman, would become 'King Edward VIII' or 'King Martyn I'. As far as the *Leader* was concerned, the King's visit offered great opportunity to the nationalists. 'England', Moran wrote on 13 June, 'was plainly making a bid to Ireland; and it was for Ireland, Nationalist Ireland, to play its hand so that it made the best use of the situation. If the King is favourable to Ireland his willing hand ought to be forced … our advice is – talk to the King fairly, openly and honestly and set out your appalling grievances, or keep a dignified silence.'[13] But Edward Martyn felt that, given his record, Moran's place was with the National Council. Griffith's policy, after all, was based on self-reliance, and the Union with Britain, in its present form, clearly prevented this. For Moran, as for Griffith, the only way a nation's salvation could be worked out was on the soil of that nation. On 3 October, in reply to a letter from the *Enniscorthy Echo*, Martyn wrote: 'I always admired and still admire, on the whole, the work of the *Leader* and think its editor a person of extraordinary natural talents and insight. However, he tumbled to pieces on the question of the King's visit because he could not bring himself, for reasons of his own, to work with the National Council.'[14] Directly to the editor of the *Leader* he wrote: 'The fact is, my friend, with all your cleverness, you have lost your way this time, because for once your fearlessness in following the course of your ideas deserted you. You have no right to use the insulting language you have used about the National Council, which consists of honourable and unselfish Nationalists, whose actions are as good as their words.'[15]

Moran was furious, mainly because there was some truth in what Martyn had written. The warmth of the *Leader*'s welcome for the King's visit ebbed and flowed. When Edward VII finally came in August, he got a tumultuous welcome in many parts of the country. He had made some very positive gestures, and had spoken harsh words to 'England's Faithful Garrison' (the Unionists), which pleased Moran. It was reasonable that he should think, and write, that maybe there was something here with which the Nationalists could run. His motives, however, were not entirely based on his belief in the merit of his argument. His feelings for the people who made up the National Council coloured his judgement. He despised Yeats, Griffith and Maud Gonne. He did not, however, despise Edward Martyn, and it was pity they quarrelled, for Martyn had far more in common with Moran than he had with Arthur Griffith. Although it is Griffith who comes down to us in history, while Moran is not quite so well remembered, the latter was the bigger personality, the more humane man. He understood Edward Martyn, but it took him a long time to forgive him for joining Griffith and his 'tin pikers'.

As it happened, Martyn hardly forgave himself. But he was genuinely attracted to Griffith's policies, especially to his 'attempt to fashion an Irish symbolism from the Hungarian Revolution of 1867'.[16] Griffith published his thoughts on this, *The Resurrection of Hungary: A Parallel for Ireland*, in a series of newspaper articles in the spring of 1904, and then in book form. He called it 'the Hungarian policy'. He argued that when Franz Déak, an Hungarian patriot, organised a massive abstention of Hungarian representatives from the Imperial Diet at Vienna in the 1860s, in an attempt to get a separate Hungarian parliament in Budapest, he had given to the Irish an idea of how they might achieve their independence from Britain. Deak had been successful and the *Ausgleich* (compromise) ultimately made Austria and Hungary two separate nations, linked by the Emperor. It was not as simple as Griffith made it seem and the two countries retained common ministries on war and foreign affairs, while the retention of interlinked economies meant that Hungary, the lesser partner, never thrived.

It was an attractive idea all the same, and it allowed Griffith to push his policy of Irish abstention from Westminster. There is a perfectly respectable Irish pedigree for the idea of abstentionism. Daniel O'Connell had considered it in 1843, as did Thomas Davis in 1844, on behalf of the Repeal Association, and it was urged on Charles Stewart Parnell by many of his party in 1881. Still, it was a hook on which Griffith could hang much and, as for Edward Martyn, he liked the 'European' feel of it. It allowed him to remain a 'constitutional rebel'. He maintained his romantic idealism for Sinn Féin for many years. In the summer of 1907 he wrote to John J. Horgan: 'Sinn Féin is above all an educative and intellectual movement and must proceed by educating the masses. By means of literature, the press and lectures, and by wide disseminating of branches all over the country. When we have thus got the country thoroughly imbued with our principles there will be no difficulty about its compelling the members to withdraw from Westminster.'[17]

But his old friend Standish James O'Grady, who at this time was editor of the *All-Ireland Review*, didn't quite understand the motives of this 'constitutional rebel' and feared certain members of the National Council, whom he regarded as 'revolutionists'. When Edward Martyn wrote: 'I am a strict constitutionalist, one of the few real constitutionalists in Ireland, Grattan and Charlemont[18] would have understood me', O'Grady replied that they would not have understood him at all, since they gave their allegiance to the King. O'Grady believed that Martyn's associates were deriving their principles, through Theobold Wolfe Tone, from the national convention of revolutionary Republican France. He wrote to Martyn:

They don't care about the things that you and I care for – the Constitution, the balance of power, the fundamental laws, the deep roots of our tree of liberty – for it is a 'tree' not a bare pole, like the French one. Do you remember Burke on that way of thinking and feeling, while it was still quite young and fresh, and so indistinguishable from a kind of divine revelation? If these people had their way they would strip life to the skin, nay to the bone with their 'Republican' simplicity. They have, no doubt, on their side an eternal truth, the equality of man, but like other eternal truths it becomes temporary nonsense and folly, when thrust violently into a world like this.[19]

This was a bit hard on Griffith's 'tin pikers', albeit that, within ten years, they did become 'revolutionists', long after Martyn had parted company with them. Still, Edward must have been struck by the eloquence of O'Grady's argument, and especially with the second part, which dealt so personally with his own (E.M's) background. For a short time he had not been using the 'Castle' part of his address, merely 'Tulira' ('Tulira' and 'Tillyra' have both been used through the years), and O'Grady took him to task for such silliness:

It was always known as 'Tulira Castle', he wrote, 'rightly so according to our rural manners and customs for your house is an expansion of an ancient keep, still cared for and inhabited. Was it the taste for republican simplicity which led you to discard that connecting link between the present and the past, between modern Ireland and that war-torn Ireland of the Middle Ages, when our fundamental laws were fashioning themselves in fire and blood. Is all our marvellous history to go by the board, and are we to begin everything with '98? You don't think so, I know, but like many clever, imaginative and sincere men you have temporarily allowed one thought, one emotion, to dominate your mind.[20]

Edward Martyn did not reply to this. He could not, for O'Grady knew him better than he knew himself. Tillyra, once again, became 'Tulira Castle', but Martyn, who has already told us his political convictions are those of the company he keeps, stayed with the National Council.

Politics were all very well, but the theatre still remained the most important thing. On 20 March 1903 Edward Martyn wrote to Augusta Gregory to complain of being deprived of his most pleasurable pursuit. He had not been to see her plays and he was in very bad fettle about it indeed.[21] 'I was very sorry not to have been able to see the plays', he wrote, 'but as I do not go to plays in Lent I thought that the extra pleasure that these would give me only a stronger reason why I should refrain from going. ... I do not think you should have chosen Lenten times for their production. It's only imitating Dublin Castle, which has its season at a time when in all other European Capitals there are no general gaieties. It is an insult to Catholic and Nationalist Ireland. And the Catholics who join in with it are about the worst types.' Then he mysteriously writes: 'I only hope your place has not been disfigured as much as mine.' Since Martyn went on to watch and produce many plays in Lenten times, we can only assume the bad humour was to do with the mysterious last sentence. This may well have been about the break-up of the land around Tillyra, which had been sold to the Land Commission and was, around that time, being distributed among the tenants.

In 1904 the Cultural Renaissance was at its height, and it seemed that the whole driving force of Ireland was in Dublin. When the Abbey Theatre opened its doors in December, for its inaugural performance, Padraic Colum wrote in *Ourselves Alone* that the audience was a congregation; everyone was singing from the same hymn sheet. Well, not everyone, but it was a community, a community with a shared history and conscience. At the beginning of the year Yeats had been in America. While he was away, and throughout 1903, the Irish National Theatre Society had gone from strength to strength. In May 1904, when it returned from a trip to London, Æ wrote Yeats: 'The Company have come back with the majesty which does befit kings after their visit to London. ... I am delighted they did so well from all accounts. I am sure it was an immense relief to you.'[22] Certainly, it had not been easy. In October 1903, when Synge's *The Shadow of the Glen* was first produced, Arthur Griffith and Maud Gonne let their displeasure be well known: 'The play has an Irish name, but is no more Irish than the Decameron. It is a staging of a corrupt version of that old world libel on woman-kind – *The Widow of Ephesus*,' Griffith wrote in the *United Irishman*.[23] (*The Shadow of the Glen* portrays Nora, the heroine, leaving her elderly, frigid husband, and potential second husband, to go into the wilds with a decent man, albeit a tramp.) A week after that, Maud Gonne resigned, in protest, from the National Theatre Society. She accused Yeats of forgetting that the majority of the Irish people were involved in a struggle for national independence. Yeats and Griffith also fell out. For the theatre movement it was a time of change; a time when discordant voices entered the scene. The Nationalists had always assumed that the theatre would be a propaganda tool for their movement, but Synge's realism would do nothing for that, and it was clear to everyone that Yeats favoured Synge. The loss of both Maud Gonne, and the support of the *United Irishman*, was a blow but, by then, Yeats knew that his friend Annie Horniman was going to give him a theatre, so he was quietly confident.[24]

He wasn't, though, overly confident. Edward Martyn, too, was looking for a theatre. In February 1904, when he was coming near the end of his American tour, Yeats confided in John Quinn: 'Miss Horniman writes saying that she is busy about buying Mechanics – I hope she gets it before Martyn.'[25] She did. The Mechanics Institute, which was fondly known as 'The Mechanics', operated out of a small theatre on the corner of Abbey Street, on the north side of the Liffey, just off the main thoroughfare, Sackville Street. She also leased the adjoining corner building on Marlborough Street, which had once been the city morgue, and she employed Joseph Holloway, who was an architect as well as a theatre fanatic, to turn it into what became the famous Abbey Theatre. There was no true rivalry between Martyn and Yeats for a theatre. This is evidenced in a letter from Yeats to Augusta Gregory, during the negotiations for a patent for the theatre: 'One barrister tried to prove that Ibsen and Maeterlinck were immoral writers. He asked was it not true that a play by Maeterlinck called "the Intruder" had raised an immense outcry in London because of its immorality. Quite involuntarily I cried out "My God", and Edward Martyn burst into a loud fit of laughter.'[26] They were still knocking good fun out of the adventure.

Back in the spring, however, it had not been funny for Edward Martyn. On 18 April the Player's Club staged *An Enchanted Sea*, under the auspices of the National Literary Society, in the Antient Concert Rooms. It was a total flop. Joseph Holloway wrote that it had proved 'a dreary monotonous play full of daft ideas of the most improbable kind.

Many a "back drawing-room theatre" would disown such crude acting as the Player's Club put into this piece of Martyn's. ... W.G. Fay put it on for rehearsal at the Irish National Theatre Society and, finding it impossible, withdrew it after the second rehearsal. It showed his good sense. Mr. Martyn, however, thought otherwise. ...'[27] Æ's report to Augusta Gregory was even more despairing: 'the fourth act was abominably acted, the actors didn't know their parts and one of them could not get out of the room and the audience laughed – I never felt sorrier for anyone than Martyn.'

Not even the *United Irishman*, which was very biased towards Edward Martyn at this time, could redeem it: 'It is a work remarkable in idea and construction, but it is absolutely frozen. There is hardly an emotional line in the whole four acts,' the critic wrote on 23 April. Since there is quite a lot of emotion in the play it must have been a very poor performance indeed. The critic of the *Irish Times* wondered why 'it did not strike a man of Mr. Edward Martyn's common sense to drown the foolish boy, and hang the murderous white haired aunt, in the first act', which would have been 'an act of real kindness to the audience'. Martyn was bowed but unbroken. Three days later he had the Player's Club produce Ibsen's *Hedda Gabler* at the same venue. Dublin theatre audiences were getting plenty of variety.

Other parts of the country were having their fair share of artistic treats too. During the summer the Palestrina Choir made a trip to Loughrea, all expenses paid by Martyn. On 16–19 August, Yeats, Augusta Gregory, Douglas Hyde and Edward Martyn were at the Galway Féis. That year it was called 'The Connacht Féis and Industrial Exhibition', and Hyde and Martyn were the adjudicators for competition in literature and music. In his capacity as a member of Coiside Gnótha, the executive of the Gaelic League, Martyn was embroiled in a fight for an 'International' Exhibition to run alongside a 'National' Exhibition', which was planned as a trade fair, but he lost. The Ard-Fheis (annual conference) of the League condemned 'the holding of an International Exhibition in this country as opposed to the development and true interests of our native industry'. It is hardly surprising that when he wrote to Augusta Gregory he was somewhat despondent: 'As usual I continue to narrow the circle of my acquaintances.'[28] This probably included any friendship he had had with Robert Elliot, who wrote in his review of the Arts and Crafts Fair, which was held on

19 November, that An Tur Gloinne was not well represented except for a small window with three lights, 'one of them in design is an affectedly medieval copy, and I trust the workers of An Tur Gloinne are not going to travel that road to unrealities'. In fact this was a 'colour study' after a window in Nuremburg, which sold for £5. Martyn and Yeats were also on the committee to develop a permanent Gallery of Modern Art in Dublin. The Hibernian Academy did not approve of the proposal presently on the table and wanted William Ponsonby, who was chairing the committee, to resign 'because there are such rebellious people on the committee as Edward Martyn and myself,' Yeats confided in Clement Shorter, the editor of the *Tatler*. If Yeats was, in this period, a 'missionary for art', so too was Edward Martyn.[29]

In September 1904 Gerald O'Donovan left the priesthood. He wrote to Horace Plunkett to tell him he had 'thrown up the ministry'. O'Donovan had become very much a part of the artistic lives of his friends which was all very well while John Healy was Bishop of Clonfert, but when Healy moved on, and Dr. O'Dea took his place, O'Donovan was ordered to curtail his artistic activities and to concentrate on his ministry. He refused, and confided to Plunkett that he could not stay and work with a man who had 'no knowledge of life whatever'.[30] He was not quiet in his leaving. The local people held a function to mark his departure and the *Western News* described it as 'one of the most spontaneous outbursts of genuine regret witnessed in the town for a long time'.

O'Donovan did not unfrock himself for four years. He worked as a journalist in Dublin and then in London, and got some financial help, and contacts, from Augusta Gregory and George Moore (Moore remained a friend for life). In 1910 he married Beryl Verschoyle and, two years later, he published his autobiographical novel *Father Ralph*.[31] In *The Times Literary Supplement* the review of 'Father Ralph' was headed: 'A Modernist in Ireland', and this was O'Donovan's own dilemma. He was a modernist in Ireland at a time when the Catholic Church was reaffirming the supremacy of its own doctrine of unquestioning faith. As a Catholic priest, at the time, Gerard O'Donovan was a hopeless case.

On Saturday night, 27 December, the Abbey finally opened. Neither Augusta Gregory nor Annie Horniman was present. They had not been friends and Miss Horniman cannot have been pleased that the patent, in the end, had to be issued in Gregory's name. It could only be issued to someone permanently resident in Ireland. This must have given Lady Gregory a tremendous sense of ownership, so it was surprising that she did not appear to see the production of her own *Spreading the News*. Perhaps she was sick, as she had said. Certainly, Edward Martyn believed her, as he made clear the following day when he wrote to give her a full account of the first night:

> Your comedy was a great success last night, and it deserved to be. I think it the best of its kind I have seen, admirably constructed and acted admirably. It is really humourous, what cannot be said of many productions of this kind. Everything went off very well last night. I like Yeats's new play very much. The Fays were excellent in it. Cathleen Houlihan would be quite good if it were rewritten from the part where the old woman goes out. The play goes to pieces from that point. I am very sorry to hear you have not been well. ...[32]

Edward Martyn's good nature reveals itself in this letter. Regardless of his own disappointments, he was nearly always pleased with the success of his friends. George Moore was surprised at his support for the Abbey, not understanding that Edward could support his friends, even if he didn't like peasant plays. When there was a problem with Synge's *The Well of the Saints*, which is not sympathetic to the Catholic Church, Moore claimed that 'dear Edward' had told him: 'All this sneering at Catholic practices is utterly distasteful to me. ... I can hear the whining voice of the proselytizer through it all.'[33] This is probably half true. As we have seen, Martyn did worry about offending the rites and mores of Catholicism in the theatre, but he did not associate it with proselytism. It is almost ludicrous to think of him associating proselytism, if he ever thought about proselytism at all, despite knowing, all his life, about the accusations around south Galway, regarding the Persse family and their reputation for proselytising, with Yeats, Gregory and, especially, the frail and sensitive Synge.

Almost everyone loved the first night. They had sat in the red leather seats, all 562 of them, knowing they were making history. All summer the workmen had worked on the site: 'The stained glass windows in the vestibule, with their celtic nut trees motif, had come from An Tur Gloinne. Behind them, distinguished visitors wandered around clutching elegant programmes decorated with Queen Maeve and her wolfhound. John Millington Synge, with his pale nervous face, sat on an upturned property basket rolling the inevitable cigarette. A deep-toned gong rang thrice to announce the commencement of the performance, and they filed into the horseshoe-shape auditorium where the small, neat stage was hidden by black and gold curtain. Maire ní Shiubhlaigh thrilled the audience with the "weird beauty and pathos" of her embodiment of *Kathleen* [*sic*] and Sara Allgood, as Mrs Fallon in *Spreading the News* was, the critics said, "an actress to her fingertips".'[34]

The critics on the daily papers were kind, but Arthur Griffith in the *United Irishman* and D.P. Moran in the *Leader* could not see anything 'Irish' in this venture. When he entered the Abbey, Moran felt, after he had viewed what he termed as the aristocratic, Anglo-Irish audience, he 'had strayed by mistake into a prayer meeting of the foreign elements in Ireland'. He had little to say about the plays, but concentrated on the patrons (he claimed that the theatre was only partially filled which was untrue). 'Mr Yeats', he told his readers, 'will never touch the Irish heart.' No Irishman had backed this 'illustrated chanting movement'. The National Theatre Society was not worth criticism in a widely read newspaper. Moran didn't necessarily mean all he wrote (in years to come he often held back criticism to allow Yeats to bring in an audience to a play. He was inconsistent in his view of the Abbey), but Griffith did. In the *United Irishman* he concentrated on the second night, which had opened with *The Shadow of the Glen*. He felt that Synge was as decadent as Petronius (the Roman author of *Satyricon*, a realistic novel of low life). Given what he had written about this play the previous year, Griffith must have smarted under Yeats's arrogance in showing it again so soon, and on such an important occasion.

Arrogance, of course, was a part of Yeats's strategy. In February 1905 when the Company introduced Synge's *The Well of the Saints*, it emptied the theatre. As we have seen, Edward Martyn had some reservations about Synge's work. It is likely he discussed them with Augusta Gregory. In this period she wrote to Yeats: 'Edward is a joy and will give you new notes for your diary. These RC's haven't the courage of a mouse, and then wonder how it is we go ahead.'[35] Later, when Martyn opened his Irish Theatre, he acknowledged this and set out to copy them. Gregory's comment, however, is unworthy of her. All over Ireland there were new movements, cultural and political, which were being led by real leaders with talent, strong character, unshakeable courage and who also happened to be Catholic.

These discussions with both Yeats and Gregory about Catholicism, and the response of the Catholic Church to what they were about, were not unusual. Joseph Hone, Yeats's first biographer, tells us that Yeats approached Martyn to talk about the possibility of a 'literary under-standing' with the Catholic Church. Would the priests help if a second Abbey Theatre specialised in religious drama? Martyn assured him that they would be far too suspicious. He agreed with the poet that if the Catholic Church did not encourage a distinguished, intellectual life the alternative would, ultimately, be to their own detriment. But he thought that the institution was not clever enough to realise the danger.[36] Sometimes he was brave enough to publish his thoughts on this problem, as instanced in the pages of the *Leader*, 4 June 1910, when he assured D.P. Moran that the behaviour of the Catholic Church, in this era, was not calculated either to produce 'staunch Catholics or valiant Irishmen'.

The Well of the Saints, which was first produced in Dublin on 4 February 1905, portrays a mean and miserable Irish Catholic com-munity. Many felt it was 'anti-Irish'. After its first performance Joseph Holloway wrote: 'Since I saw Synge's *The Shadow of the Glen*, I always thought that Synge would be the rock on which the Society would come to grief, and that time has arrived I am sorry to say.' Writing on *The Well of the Saints*, he concludes: 'No one, other than those involved with the theatre, has a good word to say for it, clever and all as it undoubtedly is, owing to its unsympathetic treatment and unnecessary loading with unpleasant speech all through.'

The 'grief' was somewhat alleviated by Augusta Gregory's intro-duction to her famous barm-brack. During the rehearsals for *The Well of the Saints*, Holloway tells us: 'She very kindly presented the Society with a huge barm-brack which she had brought from the country, and at the in-between acts the amount that vanished showed how thoroughly her gift was appreciated. I sampled it and found it quite to my taste.'[37] This became a custom that Gregory maintained for years. She and Yeats were right, of course, in their assessment of Synge's work; many would now argue that it was on his plays that the Irish National Theatre Society flourished.

In October 1905 Yeats wrote Florence Farr a long gossipy letter telling her his plans for the Abbey:

We are turning it into a private limited company. If all goes well
Lady Gregory, Synge and myself will be the Directors in a few
days ... the democratic arrangements have made it impossible
to look ahead and settle dates and all that kind of thing. ... I
have noticed by the by that the writers in this country that come
from the mass of the people who come from Catholic Ireland
have more reason than fantasy. It is the other way round with
those who come from the leisured classes. They stand above
their subject and play with it. The others, Colum and Edward
Martyn for instance, are dominated by their subject

Then he recalled that Edward Martyn came from the 'leisured class'
and continued:

Of course Edward Martyn, on his father's side, is one of the
oldest families in Ireland, but he always seems to have more of
his mother's temper, and besides he has taken the habit of his
mind from the mass of the people.[38]

Still, when he was in Coole, Yeats was always glad to 'break the routine
sufficiently to bicycle over to Edward Martyn's to dine there'.

14 • King Martyn and the Martynettes

IN FEBRUARY 1905 Maud Gonne filed for a French divorce from John MacBride, citing his drinking and adultery as causes of the marriage breakdown. It aroused considerable scandal, both in Ireland and in the United States. Yeats supported her consistently, which is hardly surprising, but what is interesting is the extent to which he was discussing the situation with Edward Martyn. On 25 February Gonne wrote to Yeats: 'I am glad Mr. Martyn is a friend of mine for I like and respect him very much. As for the others, when the verdict is given against John I suppose they will be convinced; anyhow it is not for me to bother about convincing them.'[1] During the summer Nevill Geary went to visit her in France and gave her advice, 'unofficially but kindly'. In September Edward Martyn was again on her mind: 'When I see Mr. Martyn', she wrote, 'I could console him on the religious side of the divorce question by telling him that Canon Dissard, who received me into the Catholic Church … when he heard all the facts and my reasons for asking for a divorce … could no longer advise me against.'[2] In the end, because of the legal difficulties about custody of her son, Seán MacBride, she did not get a divorce, but settled for a legal separation and this curtailed her visits to Ireland. When she attended the Abbey Theatre in 1906 with Yeats, peopled hissed, but there is no indication of any breakdown in her friendship with Edward Martyn. He was also present that night at the Abbey, and so was George Russell, who had been Maud Gonne's neighbour when she was living in Dublin. The friendship between Edward Martyn and Maud Gonne was enduring, for in the summer of 1918 Seán MacBride spent his summer holidays in Tillyra.

The year 1905 had been a busy one. In October Martyn's *The Tale of a Town* was performed, as a part of the annual Samhain celebrations of Cumann na nGaedheal. Then in November he wrote to John Horgan: 'I have been exceedingly busy over the Convention and meeting of the National Council ... the papers give you no idea of its success.'[3] When the National Council had remained in existence after the King's visit, the idea was that it would serve as a forum for all the disparate nationalist societies to meet and discuss policies. This encouraged tremendous activity, and it was soon obvious that a sense of cohesion was needed. At the Annual Convention, organised by the National Council in November, with Edward Martyn as chairman, Griffith decided to outline a detailed policy for the future of Irish politics. He elaborated on the economic policies of self-sufficiency which had always been his policy, and then called for the creation of a 'Council of Three Hundred', composed of MPs who would agree to abstain from Westminster, together with delegates from local bodies, to assume the power of a *de facto* parliament. Later this was reprinted as *The Sinn Féin Policy*, and in 1906 Griffith changed the title of the *United Irishman* to that of *Sinn Féin*. The party, simply known as Sinn Féin, did not come into being fully until 1908, when the Sinn Féin League (the Ulster Dungannon Clubs and Cumann na nGaedheal who held 'separatist' views and were committed to standing in general and local elections) joined the National Council, to form the one body.[4] By then Martyn was close to the end of his time as chairman. He had taken an unconscionable amount of abuse for the previous four years.

D.P. Moran, as we have seen, hated Sinn Féin. He was especially contemptuous of their cross-cultural agenda. He contended that it would do nothing to provide jobs for nationalists. He was particularly scathing of Griffith's romantic view of Henry Grattan's parliament of the late eighteenth century. But when he set out to wage a relentless war on what he considered to be the irrelevance of Sinn Féin, he personalised every attack. For two years Edward Martyn was the butt of almost every political joke in the pages of the *Leader*. An explanation for Moran's vindictiveness may be due to money. While there is no evidence that Edward Martyn funded the *Leader*, it is possible he had done so, and that he switched his money, and allegiance, to Griffith and Sinn Féin. Griffith felt he almost had a right to Martyn's money. But there was also Sinn Féin's anti-clericalism to annoy Moran. Edward

Martyn had been president of the Catholic Association and had resigned. Now he was president of Sinn Féin. It was puzzling since Martyn had told John Horgan that he had resigned as president of the Catholic Association to prevent a split, but did not elaborate on why there had been a split. Furthermore, Edward Martyn, a writer, had never written for the Catholic Truth Society.

It is clear that Moran wasn't sure what he was dealing with, but his anti-Martyn campaign got off to a good start when a by-election in south Galway enabled him to attack Martyn, for not standing. Moran said that he wanted Sinn Féin to prove itself by positive action rather than, as he saw it, hanging on to the coat tails of the Irish Parliamentary Party. When Edward Martyn did not stand, by virtue of his temperament and the policy of Sinn Féin, Moran represented it as cowardice on the part of 'the aspirant of the political leadership of the Irish race at home and abroad'.[5]

The editor continued his attacks relentlessly on both Sinn Féin and Edward Martyn. Sometimes his hyperbole was very funny. After Sinn Féin's interference in a by-election in North Tyrone in early 1907, the incumbent had his majority cut from nine to seven votes. Moran wrote: 'Jameson's raid is nothing compared to Martyn's foray into North Tyrone. We think that in the view of the great feat performed by Mr. Martyn's party, in pulling down the majority from nine to seven, Mr. Martyn may accept the result as a mandate from the country to step into the shoes of the late Mr. Parnell, and assume the leadership of the Irish race at home and abroad.'[6] Sometimes it must have been very hurtful. In May Moran wrote: 'Mr Edward Martyn is probably getting rather bored playing the unconvincing part of leader presumptive of the Irish race at home and abroad. Mr. Martyn had he been wise, which men born with too much money sometimes are not, would never have intruded into the field of politics; he would have kept playwriting; he might have been a first class dramatist; he can never be more than a ridiculous politician.'[7]

Of course Edward Martyn never thought of himself as a politician, and especially not as any kind of a leader. In January 1906 he wrote to John Horgan, who was documenting his life, perhaps with the intention of a future biography: 'I was never really a Unionist. I simply avoided politics.'[8] Indeed, the unlikelihood of him being a political animal is enhanced in the same letter when he writes: 'in Ireland what we have to

26 Kildare Street Club, Dublin, *c.*1900.

do is honestly keep to our principles, never relax them no matter what. Principles are no use unless they are held to in a crisis.' D.P. Moran knew that Martyn held these feelings, but he could not forgive him for becoming 'Edward VIII – president of that conglomeration of British civil servants, ex tin-pikers, fanatics and boys without a sense of humour who make up the Green Hungarian Band', and a follower of Arthur Griffith. The title of this particular article was 'The Cattle Drive of Tullira', where Martyn was accused of 'giving' his land to Lord Gough, 'one of the most tyrannical land sharks in Connaught', for grazing. The peasants in Gort were accused of 'driving the cattle off this land shark's land last Saturday night'.[9] Hardly surprisingly the people of Ardrahan, where the land was situated, were not amused and on 20 December, C.H. Foley, M.D. of Ardrahan, wrote in protest: 'Mr Martyn sold his estates at 18 years purchase before the passing of the late land act …

the only land Mr. Martyn now owns is within the demesne around his residence, … it is a bit too much that the people of this parish should be libelled via the *Leader*'. The piece of land in question had, in fact, been sold to Lord Gough after the 1903 Land Act and was then being grazed by cattle owned by Henry Persse.

Before this annoyance started, Edward Martyn had been expelled from the Kildare Street Club. In the letter of 26 January he wrote to John Horgan: 'For my speeches at the Convention last November I have been expelled from the Kildare Street Club. I am going to take an action against them.'[10] He engaged Tim Healy (later Governor-General of the Irish Free State) as his Senior Counsel, and wrote again to Horgan on 29 January: 'I hope to throw plenty of boiling water on that nest of wasps in the Kildare Street Club, but I fear I have not much chance of winning.'

Rumblings about Martyn's behaviour as a club member had begun at the time of his resignation as magistrate. He had wanted to resign his membership then, but Lord Gough had persuaded him not to do so. But the rumblings gained pace when he was reprimanded over his letters with regard to the King's visit. He was informed at that point that his letters 'in their opinion are derogatory to your station in society'. In reply, Edward Martyn wrote: 'I consider my political opinions as expressed in my various published letters or other works in no ways derogatory to my station in society, or to that of any other Irishman. I have no explanation to offer and retract nothing, and await with perfect equanimity the decision of a general meeting of the Club, should such be deemed advisable by the Committee to be called to decide a political matter in a club which is strictly non-political in its constitution.'[11]

The Club argued that it was not his political opinions, but his respect for the King that was in question. In reply Martyn pointed out that he did not agree with their estimation of the Sovereign: 'I do not think a Sovereign who is unconstitutional in this country comes, in the guise of, and with the assumption of the authority of a constitutional Sovereign to this country, I believe I have a perfect right to show him disrespect, and I believe my action in so doing to be a political action and, consequently, refuse to acknowledge the right of Kildare Street Club to dictate to me as to the propriety of such action.'[12] Under their current rules the Club could not deny this, so they set about changing them in order to argue their case on stronger grounds. The subsequent amendments were carried by a majority of 152 votes to one; Edward was in a minority of one.

When they came to get him, after the Convention, they must have felt they were on sure ground. In one of his speeches he had gone completely over the top, saying that: 'The Irishman who enters the Army or Navy of England deserves to be flogged.' D.P. Moran made the point that Edward Martyn would not understand that a man might join the army for money or adventure, but this is not so. His brother John had joined up for the latter reason, and many of his Smyth relatives were army personnel. The Club asked him to corroborate that he had indeed said this and, when he did, they set about a resolution that would expel him. War had been declared and Martyn decided to fight. He did not expect to win and many, including Moran, were baffled at his determination to carry on. The Club wrote to him politely asking for an explanation of his speeches. He replied that he had no explanation, so a circular was issued to all members of the Club informing them that a ballot to decide on his expulsion was to be held.

At his desk at the British Legation in Dresden, Lord Gough, Edward's near neighbour and old friend, took up his pen to gently rebuke him for his extraordinary behaviour. There were some things that he wanted to remind him of:

> I am not bothering you to concur, I am only explaining the position, or what I suppose is the position of our fellow members generally, which was yours till twenty years ago, that is, considering loyalty to the Sovereign as a part of religion. You should not think too bitterly, therefore, of people whom, however correct you may be, and however wrong we may be, you have grievously injured in a religious matter. To my mind a parallel would be a Club frequented by 500 Gaelic League friends of various religions and politics. Supposing that one of them, an extreme Protestant, went to public meetings and wrote to papers and devoted his talents to attacks upon His Holiness, that would be a matter with which the Club, as such, would be in no way concerned, just as little as the Kildare Street Club is with the Royal Supremacy. Who can, however, doubt that the members would resent it, as too excessively distressing to many of them. I cannot think of anything more to say but fully trust to your supplying the deficiency. It will be very interesting for

you to be confabulating with Mr. T. Healy. If he comes down to Tulira next summer, you must not fail to invite me to lunch. What fun if you bring him over to the next garden party at Lough Cutra: a bombshell for the archdeacon and the Miss O'Haras of Raheen.[13]

This must have given Edward pause for thought, but he went ahead anyway. He could not have known that Gough had also written to Lord Clonbrock pleading his case. 'Edward Martyn', he wrote, 'is saved in my eyes by holding the conscientious belief that the king could easily issue a [?] throwing off Scotland and England from his dominions, that is all he asks the king to do!'[14] Gough felt that many Home-Rulers felt this but were more reticent about saying it so baldly.

By now Edward Martyn was staying in rented rooms at No. 4 Leinster Street, not much more than one hundred yards from the club. His argument was that, as a member of the Club, he was entitled to hold whatever political opinions he wished and that Irish Nationalists were perfectly entitled to criticise, and denounce, the prevailing political situation, and not be treated as social outcasts. He had been informed by the Club that a meeting had been called and a ballot would be taken and he could make any submissions he wished. Then he was subsequently informed that there would be no discussion, only a ballot. It was on that point that the Club lost the case. It failed to comply with its own rules. It did not hold a meeting. After a trial, which lasted five days, Martyn won on that technicality. He had not attended the court and Moran, maintaining his vindictiveness, wrote: 'The leader presumptive of the Irish race at home and abroad did not appear in the box', and for months afterward referred to Edward only as 'Mr. Martyn of the Kildare Street Club'. The Master of the Rolls pointed out, in his summing up, that the Club had expelled him not because of his politics, but because he had deliberately insulted the majority of the members. This is true.

In his biography of Edward Martyn, written in the 1920s, Denis Gwynn describes Martyn's reaction to his victory as triumphalist. A suspect narrative (unusual for Gwynn) shows us Martyn deliberately embarrassing the Kildare Street Club by inviting in awkward visitors, such as belligerent Sinn Féin activists and long-haired Franciscan monks, who would have been very uncomfortable to be there. It doesn't ring true. Edward was, unfortunately, a stubborn man, but he was not a vulgar one, although it could be argued that saying people should be flogged, even when it was not meant, was the height of vulgarity. This was a case where, as Standish James O'Grady has already shown, Edward Martyn allowed one emotion to dominate his mind. Some of the members of the Kildare Street Club had, perhaps, offended him, but he also saw the fight as a service to the nationalist cause. Taking the case was not his finest hour. After 1907, while he continued to eat at the Kildare Street Club (they sent food out to him during Easter Week, 1910), he did not live there. Now, when in Dublin, he stayed quietly in his rooms at No. 4 Leinster Street, where we shall often find him with George Moore, and some new friends, in the coming pages.

The best insight we have to Edward Martyn's life in these years comes from his correspondence with John J. Horgan. Horgan was very close to politics and public affairs, especially to the Irish Parliamentary Party, where his father had been Charles Stewart Parnell's election agent. It was through Moran that he met Edward Martyn; they were all working to change the employment practices on the Great Southern Railway – Moran called it the Great Sourface Railway, possibly because of its almost one hundred per cent Protestant workforce. Jobs on the clerical staff were closed to Catholics, despite the great majority of the shareholders being of that faith. The staff was selected almost entirely from a Protestant orphanage, where one of the directors had connections. Moran exposed these affairs, and a committee of Catholic shareholders was formed, on which Martyn sat, and Horgan was the secretary. To an extent, John Horgan was a snob and a social climber, but he was also an intelligent and likeable man, who wrote an excellent memoir of his life and times, up until 1916. In 1906, however, like so many others, he was trying to write plays, and he was looking to Edward Martyn for help.

That summer he went to Tillyra. We catch a glimpse of how things were in that little corner of south Galway from Martyn's letter of invitation, and from Horgan's subsequent descriptions: 'Will you pay me a visit here', Martyn wrote. 'I wish you would. I have no establishment now and I could not do you as well as you did me, but you will be most welcome. I could meet you at Ardrahan station.'[15] There is a wistfulness, and a touch of loneliness, in this letter, for a man who was, apparently, so involved in politics at that time. Horgan's memories of

Tillyra, all the same, are good. He particularly remembered one occasion where

> ... the *dramatis personae* were, in addition to our host, Lady Gregory, Yeats, Musek, the chief comedian of the Bohemian National Theatre, and myself. Musek was a small man with beady eyes and funny features. His knowledge of English was slight and he had a large notebook in which he took laborious notes of Yeats's *obiter dicta* with a reverential air. Martyn objected to oil lamps, and Yeats, in the rather dim mellow candle light, after dinner, sat wrapped in clouds of tobacco smoke from Martyn's long churchwarden pipe, descanting like a prophet, in that delicate and fastidious language on the eternal verities in art and beauty. From time to time Martyn would burst in with some matter of fact, sometimes slightly malicious comment, which brought the proceedings down to earth.[16]

Horgan also remembered dinners at Coole where 'only Yeats and his work mattered', but the dinner-table talk ran freely, 'with such diverse subjects as the then comparatively recent tragedy of Wilde and the language of the Kiltartan peasantry'.[17]

It is not surprising that Horgan was impressed. Edward Martyn benefited greatly from his friendship. After the 1906 visit he sent him the present of a cap. In fact he sent two. 'I received your letter and two hats,' Martyn wrote, 'I have chosen the lightest of them size $7\frac{1}{8}$. I am very much obliged to you for so nice and useful a present.' And a few days later he wrote: 'I received the photographs. They have come out wonderfully well. The interior of the study is really fine although it is a bit dark.'[18] But Horgan was not above asking favours and trying to involve Edward in the sort of 'placehunting' he despised. On 18 June 1907, he wrote to Horgan, regarding the latter's request for 'Miss Patton's candiditure': 'placed as I am I could not ask for a government post, and least of all from a man like Killanin, when I am always chaffing about his politics. If I am asked I will say all I can in her favour, but I will not ask for the post.'[19]

Events in the theatre continued apace, but even there D.P. Moran found occasions to snipe at Martyn, often getting very personal. After the first performance of Yeats's *Deirdre* at the Abbey on 29 November 1906, he wrote: 'There was evidently a lot of the height of fine talking about the passion of love, though having cool heads ourselves we remained conscious that the gentleman who was the author of all this fine talk had passed into his forties and yet had gone through the world so far in a state of single blessedness. And another gentleman who loudly applauded and called for the author, Mr. Edward Martyn, is also a bachelor. Must not all that wild passionate loose talk about love, Pagan love too, have been rather of the nature of what the Yanks might call "fake" or we might call *raiméis* to these middle-aged bachelors.'[20]

By the beginning of 1908 it was clear that Edward Martyn was not a suitable person to be chairman of the new Sinn Féin movement. He believed in Sinn Féin as a cultural, educative and intellectual movement; he was totally against fighting for political seats. In June 1907 he told Horgan that fighting constituencies would only make them appear as another faction in Ireland: 'Winning two or three seats would be no advantage to us; a defeat would be a serious setback.'[21] During a by-election in North Leitrim he was removed as President (he later claimed that he resigned because it had become a political party and he still had an oath of allegiance to the King), and it was done very quietly. He wrote to Horgan in June: 'I have retired from the presidentship [*sic*] of the Sinn Féin movement and indeed from all politics as I think it better for me to stick to my own politics. I have much delayed in my new play, but I hope to finish it now.'[22]

Moran had fun. From the 'Chronicle of Hungaria' he wrote:

> King Martyn I, being terrified in his heart of the vanities of this world, laid down his kingship of the Martynettes and fled into the club or desert palace of Kildare Street. And the barons and the nobles of Martynettia were sore stricken and affrighted because of it, for it was even a custom in their land that the king should be chosen out of the richest amongst them, and the king had taken his treasure board and his monies to the desert with him; nor did the barons know how to fare without. Then did Sir Arthur Griffith, a right doughty Knight ... marshal his army and lead them forth to the desert that they might bring back the king, or at least get from him, what in their language they called a cheque.[23]

This would certainly indicate that Moran knew Martyn was funding Sinn Féin and, given that Edward believed it to be a cultural organisation it is likely that, at some early stage, he was. But there is no evidence for this conclusion, and the reader must always bear in mind Moore's dictum that Edward Martyn was a man who was not that easily parted from his money. Usually his purpose was art and then, mostly, high art. The explanation for the parting may simply be that, after the amalgamation with the Sinn Féin League, Martyn, and some of his friends who were regarded as the 'awkward squad' in the National Council, were simply forced to resign. Certainly he was relieved.

In December 1907 the *Irish People*, then edited by William O'Brien, MP, had published his one-act play *Romulus and Remus*. It was described as: 'The Makers of Delight: A Symbolist Extravanganza in One Act', and it allegorises the situation surrounding the rewriting of *The Tale of a Town* in 1899. It is a remarkably honest sketch, but it is not drama. It has a two-plot storyline (the destruction of his play, as he saw it, by Moore; and the relationship between Yeats and Gregory that appeared to leave everyone else out), and it is set in a hairdressing and perfumery establishment where Denis D'Oran (Martyn) has invented a wonderful perfume. He fears his colleagues, Romulus Malone (Moore) and Remus Delaney (Yeats), will pollute it by constantly adding ingredients:

> D'Oran: I have invented perfume before this which the best judges considered to be the best quality.
>
> Romulus: And if you have done how much help did I give you?
>
> D'Oran: Well you cannot say you invented any of the chief ingredients. You added your common ingredients, you adjusted others, in some cases spoiling the whole.

The other characters in the sketch are Daisy Hoolihan (Augusta Gregory) and Mrs. Cornucopia Moynihan (Annie Horniman). The relationship between Gregory, Yeats and Horniman is incorporated into the plot, with Daisy Hoolihan being jealous of Mrs. Moynihan, who is getting too close to Remus (Yeats). But it is D'Oran's reflection on his previous relationship with Daisy, before the arrival of Remus, which is revelatory:

> D'Oran: I considered myself most fortunate in Miss Hoolihan [A.G.] until he [Remus/WBY] came. She was an excellent steady shop woman. Now her infatuation with him has made her quite girlish until I can no longer stand her vagaries.

Edward Martyn was obviously feeling his exclusion from the relationship between Yeats and Gregory, and he was well aware what the intrusion of Annie Horniman might mean to Gregory, who treasured her intimacy with the poet. In one scene Remus tosses an odourless concoction of dead flies, which has been collected for him by Daisy, into the perfume mixture – an allusion to the folklore collected by Gregory for Yeats. It was a highly topical sketch, and the portraits were quite malicious – Remus is described as having 'long hair, divided like window curtains, down each side of his face. But when D'Oran tell us that 'people presume upon my easy habits ... they take me for a fool ... it is decidedly hurtful to one's vanity to be apparently rated so low', there is a whinging tone that is not characteristic of Edward Martyn.

On the whole the sketch reflects Martyn's growing ease in the company of women. When he writes a speech, however, in which Remus declares: 'My ideal of modern woman is physical force – the warrior ... such figures inspire the tonsorial artist to the loftiest investigations. That is how one gets dissociated from corporeal pleasures. One no longer thinks of the body', the reader wonders where this thought process is leading? W.B.Yeats never got 'dissociated from corporeal pleasures', and when he married George Hyde Lees, ten years later, she was made very welcome at Tillyra.

In April 1909, the 'Theatre of Ireland' (a small company of malcontents from the Abbey, along with Padraic Colum and Edward Martyn) put on *The Heather Field* at the Abbey Theatre. D.P. Moran did the review for the *Leader* and his sympathy, he wrote, was entirely with Agnes Tyrell, played by Sara Allgood, who was stuck in a marriage to an impossible man, Carden Tyrell, who was Edward Martyn. Trying to reclaim the Heather Field was 'as ridiculous as the Hungarian programme', he writes. 'Carden Tyrell is Edward Martyn carried to his logical conclusion. But the author has too much flesh and worldly sense to go anything so far as Tyrell. Mr Martyn is an idealist and thinks everyone wrong who doesn't agree with his hare-brained schemes, whether in art or politics ... he should stay at home in Tullira if he is a real idealist. The Heather Field of the author was "The National Council" ... Carden Tyrell would have stuck with it to the bitter end ... but our author made no such mistake. Carden Tyrell is really a satire on the moonstruck idealist. Edward Martyn knows where to draw the line.'[24]

Not always. The Kildare Street Club case was an obvious exception. But there was a positive side to that contretemps – Martyn got himself a home, of sorts, in Dublin. His 'cosy little flat', as Augusta Gregory termed it, remained the address at 4 Leinster Street, and it became something of a Mecca for a new crop of Irish artists. Thomas MacGreevy, poet and fine arts administrator, described it as a plain room with bare furniture and the solitary thing in the way of a picture, an unframed coloured print of the 'Madonna of the Eucharist', by Ingres, propped up on the chimneypiece: 'There the great men of the great generation of the first quarter of this century had all, at one time or another, gone to talk over some aspect of the nation's life with the generous, saintly, patriotic old crank.'[25] George Moore was one of those 'great men'. It is a very short walk from 4 Ely Place to Leinster Street, and the novelist often traversed it, watching out expectantly for a light in the window above the tobacconist's shop as he turned the corner of Clare Street. His visits were often late, after eleven o'clock, but he knew Edward Martyn kept late hours:

> Two short flights of stairs, and we are in his room. It never changes – the same litter from day to day … the same old and broken mahogany furniture, the same musty wallpaper, dusty manuscripts lying in heaps, and many dusty books. If one likes a man one likes his habits, and never do I go into Edward's room without admiring the old prints he tacks on the wall, or looking through the books on the great round table or admiring the little sofa between the round table and the Japanese screen, which Edward bought for a few shillings down on the quays – a torn dusty ragged screen, but serviceable enough; it keeps out the draughts … between the folds of the screen we find a small harmonium of about three octaves, and on it a score of Palestrina … and one can only think that it serves to give keynote to a choir-boy. On the table is a candlestick made out of white tin, designed probably by Edward himself, for it holds four candles. He prefers candles for reading, but he snuffs them when I enter and lights the gas, offers me a cigar, refills his church-warden and closes his book.[26]

Moore does not exaggerate the pleasure he found in Edward's company in these years. There are extant letters showing how often he sought it. He came regularly to the 'cosy little flat'. These were the years, however, when he was writing his trilogy, *Hail and Farewell*, which, for many, was a great betrayal of friendship. But Edward Martyn well understood the splinter of ice in the soul of George Moore. He put off, for as long as he could, the knowledge that would, inevitably, damage their long friendship.

15 • Melancholia

IN 1909 EDWARD MARTYN was fifty years old; he made his will and he bought a motor car. 'A splendid motor,' he wrote to Horgan. He was out of politics for good, and the sense of relief was tangible. 'If you and Mrs. Horgan would find your way to County Galway in this weather, and would put up with my somewhat primitive housekeeping, I should be delighted to see you, and could take you around some of our splendid sea-board.'[1] He was in good form, but that was in November. In February when he had made his 'last will and testament', things were looking much bleaker indeed.

'What drove him to those long prayers, those long meditations, that stern Church music? What secret torture?'[2] Yeats wrote of Edward, long after his death. Reading his will, across the years, the writer is in sympathy with the poet's searching questions. The document, for the most part, was straightforward, with some very generous bequests (Vincent O'Brien was left £5,000), but the legacy of £1,000 to the Cecilia Street School of Medicine was conditional. They would only get the money when: after my death and, before the cover of the coffin in which my corpse may have been placed may have been screwed down on, or otherwise affixed to said coffin, preparatory to interment, the proper authorities

> of the said Cecilia Street School of Medicine ... shall take my body (as they respectively are hereby authorised to do, and my executors are hereby directed to permit) and as soon as, but not before, decomposition thereof shall have set in, cause the same to be dissected in the Dissecting-room of the said school in the same manner in all respects as a subject acquired in the ordinary course for dissection therein would then be dissected, and, when

same shall have been fully so dissected, cause my remains to be gathered and interred with Christian burial, as simply as the remains of paupers are then usually interred.

It is the detail that gives one pause for thought. It may well be asked 'what secret torture'? for these were the instructions of a depressed and tortured mind. There is no altruism in his bequest to Cecilia Street school. He wanted to be absolutely certain of the destruction of his flesh, before it was planted in the ground. Whether this was a hatred of his own flesh, flesh in general, or bound up with his pathological fear of death, is an unresolved question.

In March 1909 Synge died; Yeats took it badly. Edward had been to all his first nights. When *The Playboy of the Western World* was first performed in 1907, he apparently liked it but, as a Nationalist, he was shocked that Yeats brought in the police to quell the riots. Some audiences felt the play was a slander on Ireland, and the Irish. In the face of what passed for criticism, Martyn's silence was eloquent. Joseph Holloway wrote: 'I maintain his play of *The Playboy* is not a truthful or just picture of the Irish peasants, but simply the outpouring of a morbid, unhealthy mind, ever seeking on the dunghill of life, for the nastiness that lies concealed there.'[3] This was reflective of most criticism but, as has already been noted, Edward Martyn could well conceive of a peasant 'murdering his da', and idealising it. As he moved away from Hellenism, he developed some sympathy with Synge's belief that 'no drama can grow out of anything other than the fundamental realities of life, which are never fantastic, are neither modern or unmodern and, as I see them, rarely spring-dayish, or breezy of Cuchulainoid'.[4] In Ibsen, Martyn had seen 'peculiar qualities of poetry coming direct through realism',[5] but he chose not to see anything of Ibsen in Synge.

Soon after the revival of *The Heather Field* at the Abbey, Yeats went to see Edward and, subsequently, wrote to his father in New York:

> Dined with Edward Martyn. He told me he has left the Sinn Féin organization, retired from politics altogether. He did not say, but I expect the collecting of shares for a Sinn Féin daily had something to do with it. Sometime ago ardent Sinn Féiners were called upon to refuse to pay income tax. He, poor man, and one other, were the only members of the party who paid any. He is busy writing as ever, is very amiable when one sees

him, but never goes to see anybody so far as I can make out. Moore is his only friend, and he thinks Moore is damned, and he has no responsibility about him.[6]

Yeats didn't seem to count himself as a friend. Moore, too, despite the closeness of their relationship, had to go seeking Edward out remarking: 'He has contributed few visits to the maintenance of our friendship.'

And it was *Hail and Farewell* that they were all thinking about. Moore had been writing the book since 1906, and he made no secret of his great work. In April 1909 George Russell wrote to John Quinn: 'I don't know what the fiend has written. Anyhow, we are good friends and I don't think he intends to say anything very hard. I think he is probably keeping most of his satire for the Church and W.B.Y.'[7] A few months later, however, Yeats wrote to Augusta Gregory: 'Last night Moore read out to me the chapter in his autobiography about the dinner at the Shelbourne, it was amusing and very bitter about T.P. Gill, quite amiable, though inaccurate, about myself and enthusiastic about Russell ... . I doubt his committing any indiscretion, except about Edward Martyn and his brother [Maurice Moore], whom he quarrels with perpetually about Catholicism.'[8]

Yeats was right about Moore's indiscretion regarding Edward Martyn. In a letter from the novelist to Martyn, written some time in the summer of 1909, there is this assurance: 'On the subject we spoke about last time we met there is not a word in my book.' If it refers to Edward Martyn's sexuality (Moore's biographer, Adrian Frazier, assumes it does, but is it likely they would be discussing Edward's sexuality?),[9] then Moore's betrayal is enormous. In the same letter Moore includes a P.S.: 'You are really [wrong?] about the book – It is not a lampoon. I'd be a fool to waste my time on work that might be ephemeral.'[10] The fact that Edward was forewarned cannot have lessened the shock of the frankness of Moore's revelations. In elegant and amusing prose, the novelist strips Edward Martyn's private life bare. 'Edward was a bachelor before he left his mother's womb,' he tells his readers. And lest they fail to understand, he explains: 'If the boy is a natural boy with a healthy love of sex, in his body, the wife or mistress will redeem him from his mother, but if there be no such love in him he stands in great danger.'[11] Throughout the book he constantly 'lampoons' what he considers to be Edward Martyn's misogyny, and his love of boys.

EDWARD MARTYN
'HAVING A WEEK OF IT'
IN PARIS.

GRACE GIFFORD

27 Grace Gifford's cartoon of Edward Martyn 'having a week of it in Paris', did not reflect his position in 1914 when most of his close friends were strong independent-minded women.

For the modern biographer of Edward Martyn this proves to be the book's weakness. By 1911, Martyn's relations with women had changed considerably; he had many women friends, whom he liked and respected and they, in turn, held him in great affection. They were usually strong, independent-minded women, such as Daisy Fingall, Sarah Purser, Helen Mitchell, Maud Gonne and, of course, Augusta Gregory. Later, he was very close to Grace Gifford and Maire ní Shiubhlaigh. If, in his attachment to these women, he was seeking to replace his mother, they gave no indication of knowing it. Certainly, they knew that he did not hate them nor, as Moore would have us believe, find them 'absurd'. The affectionate, and often wholly true, nature of Moore's portrait of Martyn in *Ave* is marred by the biographer never allowing his subject to grow emotionally, while, in reality, Edward Martyn did grow. All his life he liked men and boys, but he learned to love some women, and his affection for Augusta Gregory, revealed in the letters and diaries, often belies Moore's description of that relationship. The fact that everyone in Dublin who might be reading the book knew already much of what was likely to be in it, and of the attitudes and beliefs which the author held, would not have made its publication any easier for Edward.

It was a few years, however, before he had to deal with any of this, and we shall return to it. In the meantime, if he had any illusions about his next play, *Grangecolman*,[12] being a runaway success, Annie Horniman did her best to put paid to them. By 1910 Horniman had left the Abbey, and was running a theatre in Manchester. Edward Martyn submitted the play, for her consideration, and got the following reply:

> Dear Mr. Martyn,
> When I get plays sent in by office boys, all about titled people generally, I beg them to write about the kind of human beings they associate with. Now have *you* ever associated with lady doctors, even unsuccessful ones? If you want to imply that the worry of an incapable husband has upset a weak mind, you should have made it clear. If your play were put on the stage, it would justify another *Playboy* row, for you have made your fellow countryman in a light which may be true, but is not kind. To get oneself shot in order to annoy someone else is to carry out the saying 'to bite off one's nose to spite one's face', to the uttermost limit.
>
> If you ever come to Manchester, I'll show you the Gaiety and some most attractive lady doctors.

But in January 1912 when Dublin was, according to the Abbey actress Maire ní Shiubhlaigh 'drama mad', this play got quite reasonable reviews. It was produced at the Abbey by the Independent Theatre Company, and was directed by Casimir Markievicz. Constance Markievicz, who was then a member of Sinn Féin, played Catherine Devlin, a frustrated feminist doctor. She was criticised for the 'stodgyness' of her performance. The play is an attempt at Ibsen's 'psychological drama' in an Irish domestic context. There are strong women and weak men, and Catherine's character is akin to the Norwegian's most famous heroine, Hedda Gabler. It quickly runs into melodrama and, while the *Evening Telegraph* reported that 'the play runs along merrily for the first two acts, with some sparkling dialogue here and there, and the climax (Catherine is murdered) is brought about effectively', the critic in *Sinn Féin* was more astute when he wrote: 'Mr. Martyn can do large things in drama and does not do them, because he lets a little devil, compounded of perversity and sentimentality, run away with him in the end.'[13] Later, Edward Martyn paid tribute to this production of *Grangecolman*, which he felt had been produced by Markievicz with 'intelligence and success'. It gave him the impetus to carry on.

Throughout the first half of 1910 life had been full of the theatre. In March Martyn was in London, and wrote to Joseph Holloway: 'thank-you for the copy of the *Evening Telegraph* … containing the report of your very interesting lecture on the acting of the Irish players. I have, as you know, a very great admiration for their work. If some of the members of the company are flying away from Dublin that is, perhaps, a matter for congratulations as well as for regrets, and I only hope that they may be making comfortable nests for themselves elsewhere. …'[14] But if he was happier with the actors than he used to be, he wasn't so keen on the plays that were being performed. He consistently preferred the plays of Padraic Colum to those of William Boyle, whose work kept the theatre going. Boyle's plays, he felt, attracted the 'common herd of playgoers', and he told Holloway that he was not remotely interested in the filling the seats. Holloway decided, after a conversation with Martyn about this on 7 May, that 'Edward Martyn was a crank of the worst kind, and did not want a play to be a play at all, but a play to hang fancies and dreams upon.'[15]

Martyn went, nevertheless, to London with the Abbey Players and Boyle's play *Dempsey*, and wrote to Holloway from 5 Russell Mansions: 'I have to thank you for your kind and interesting letter. It gratifies me to find myself in accord with one who has evidently so much sympathy with the work of the theatre, and so clear an understanding of it as you have [it is unlikely that he really felt that about Holloway]. It is my firm belief that ninety-nine people in a hundred cannot tell good acting from bad, and being used to bad, acquire a taste for it, as they do for indifferent wives. You and I, my dear sir, are epicures in the theatre.'[16]

This slightly nasty missive was written at the same time as Edward Martyn had started an unusual, and equally nasty, correspondence with the editor of the *Leader*. In a long letter entitled 'The Wooing of Mrs. Moriarty', he sought to justify his foray into politics, and his leaving of it, to D.P. Moran. It is a very odd correspondence and, in it, he begs Moran not to be so hard upon him, just because he was 'interested in a policy [Griffith's Hungarian Policy] 'over the heads of all you noxious little chattering apes'. He and Moran had always differed in their perception of the character of the Irish people; Martyn's was always higher than that of Moran's. But, now he agrees that Moran was right; that the Irish are a 'tame people': 'Yes quite right, a tame, ineffective people, mostly all, except the peasants, they are by no means tame and ineffective. They surely are violent, beyond all codes of ethics, but effective as brigands in securing other people's property for themselves.' He continues by attacking 'our own Mother Church', for its intolerance, and quotes Frederick the Great – 'you do not know the human animal'. 'Man's unchecked instinct is to tyrannise,' he continues, 'whether he be landlord or ecclesiastic. You will therefore see, my dear, that you have no heroic people to deal with but "tame", as you were the first to find out.'[17]

He wanted to be friends again with Moran and wrote: 'you and I are never likely seriously to quarrel. ... Yeats, I think, is responsible for the aphorism – "the only friendship that are eternal are those founded upon mutual contempt". Indeed, I am always ready to forgive a great deal in a person if he does not bore me. You are indeed to me always that beautiful, if barren, type, the Widow Moriarty in her little place of business, surrounded by her battered marine stores and other general wreckage of her country, out of which she makes a genial living, while she gives to everyone indiscriminately, including the Liberator, the length of her tongue.'

In this first long letter Edward Martyn claims that he left Sinn Féin because he found out that his oath of allegiance to the King was for life. Sinn Féin had told him that he should not reveal this as his reason for resignation since 'no one would believe me'. And, of course, no one did, but Martyn, being utterly perverse, did go back to being a Grand Juror!

In his replies, Moran addressed 'My Dear Boy', and is glad that Martyn now realises that the idea of the Irish being 'valiant and noble', was but 'a figment of your own disordered imagination'. Moran agrees that he is, indeed, no more successful than Edward Martyn, except as a journalist. He writes: 'I am a success and I have left a deep mark – some might prefer to call it a blister – on the country.'[18] But Moran has the sense to point out that Martyn goes too far: 'I rejoice at your returning to good behaviour and civility, and at your having left the evil companions of the period of your political wild oats. In your present condemnation of your country you show a lack of restraint … in which I see more petulance than judgement.'

The correspondence went on for some weeks, with Moran appointing Martyn to be Mrs. Moriarty's Lothario. They were tedious 'tit for tat' (who was right about Sinn Féin, and whether the *Leader* came before the *United Irishman*) letters, and overly long. Martyn baited Moran that he should get into politics and become a 'Leader'. But Moran replies: 'Is not this leadership notion a pure figment of thy hot and wayward imagination, my poor perplexed Lothario?' But Martyn did not think so: 'Darling of the Philistines and of the ignoramus,' he wrote. 'Leader of the tames and the cantankerous, come out and show yourself to the people.'[19] Then the correspondence stopped abruptly, and it was almost certainly due to a letter of disgust penned by Edward Martyn's old friend and colleague, Alice Milligan, entitled 'A General Remonstrance'. She questions Martyn's 'want of faith' in the Irish people. 'Martyn's communication is very tragic and extraordinary,' she wrote. She wondered about his credentials as a nationalist, and taunted him with Tennyson's quotation: 'Faith unfaithful kept him falsely true.' She hoped that 'His Grace of Tuam [John Healy] had nothing to do with it'. As regards the oath, she pointed out: 'Mr. Martyn owes absolute loyalty and faithful service to his country, even if he has done no swearing with regard to that.'[20]

Milligan's remark about John Healy, given the time we are dealing with, was particularly pertinent. There was a debate raging regarding the Irish language and its place in the new National University. Healy was one of the strongest episcopal opponents to its compulsion. It was also well known that the priests at the local college of Saint Jarlath's, in Tuam, were prevented from speaking on the matter. Healy was unapologetic, and, in the summer of 1909, made himself even more unpopular when the Gaelic Training College, in Mount Partry, needed a new Principal. He owned the building and land on which the school stood and, in the light of that, insisted on appointing his own candidate; the school was largely financed by the Gaelic League, which had its own candidate. There was a battle and Healy won. The result revealed a nasty side of clericalism which, in turn, led to a rise in anti-clericalism.

On the question of the Irish language Healy was running against the tide of the popular ideal. It must have been hard for Edward Martyn, as a member of the Coiste Gnótha, to have his friend behave in this way. Perhaps this incident is what he had in mind when he wrote Moran about 'ecclesiastical tyranny'. Luckily his other friend, although they were never close, Dr O'Dea, was appointed Bishop of Galway in 1909, and joined him on the Governing Body of Galway University. O'Dea was 'sound' on the Irish question.

There is no explanation for the strange correspondence in which Martyn and Moran indulged; it did not lead to any real rapprochement. In August 1910 Martyn wrote to Horgan: 'The only way to tackle Moran is to humbug him. If you take him seriously you are done, that is why he sat upon so many people. We are far too huffy and serious about things that don't matter in this country.'[21] He did, however, continue to have work published in the *Leader*, and this included some rather bad poetry, which reflected, along with his very unsteady handwriting, that he was not well. In fact the content of his writing, at this point, reveals a highly depressive state. In November 1911, in a long poem entitled 'In the Woods', he sees himself as a 'luckless sage':

> And oceans of ugliness
> And hours of dark ennui
> Then a glimpse of ideal bliss
> Are the world as it seems to me

The poem had been written at Tillyra, as he wondered around the garden and the woods, known to him since 'childhood day', with a mind that is 'a satiric stage'. He is in a 'Greek mood,' and highly mystical. He did not turn to his Catholicism to relieve his dark moods, appealing, instead, to the dryads and the fauns to give him peace and rest:

> … To live where beauty reigns
> Like wisdom high austere
> A science meet for the pains
> Of poet or of seer.

> And now that young Greek's rays
> In the mists of the evening air
> Stream through the woodland way
> Like the golden threads of his hair

And I hear an army of wings:
The rooks come home to rest;
And the sound of their voices brings
Strange comfort to my breast.[22]

Rooks, for Edward Martyn, represented continuity. He had seen them come and go at Tillyra all his life. The postman came too, bringing with him news and affection from friends. On 26 December 1911 he wrote to Vincent O'Brien, thanking him for the telegram and Christmas card from the boys in the choir. He was 'very touched' by their concern and made the point that, 'perhaps I am sometimes exacting, it is only because of my deep interest in your splendid work that makes me anxious'.[23] In June he was still separated from them and the 'black dog' was not gone: 'I played sadly to-day the Duo Seraphin on the organ at about the time they would be singing it.' And he goes on to detailed instructions on how things were to be sung, closing on an admonitory note: 'keep an eye on William Dunne'.[24]

He had spent over a year doing everything he could to pick himself up off the floor. The poetry was a fairly typical attempt of a writer trying to ascertain what, if anything, he could write successfully. And the motor, too, was a great help. In July 1911 he wrote to Horgan: 'I must take some Gaelic Leaguers around the schools in Connemara in my motor. The Coffeys come on 4th July. Would about that time suit you, or would later be more convenient.'[25] An incident on that trip to Connemara is vividly described by James H. Cousins, poet and Orientalist, who was living in Clifden for the summer: 'One group came and made a stir. On an errand for herself to the town I thought I was "seeing things", or a play dressed up to take off the literary revival, or the Gaelic League or both – Edward Martyn, Patrick Pearse and the Honourable William Gibson in *Kilts*, standing in a triangle of frustration [they couldn't find a hall for their lecture]. They were on a tour on behalf of the Irish language.'[26] When Cousins suggested they get in touch with the bishop, who would have been Dr O'Dea, they declined, and left in a huff. Edward Martyn, in a kilt, in the summer of 1911 would have been a sight to behold. The 'bulky youth from Galway' had become considerably bulkier in the thirty-odd years since Moore had considered his sartorial non-elegance in a London drawing room. He had a major weight problem, which would grow into extreme obesity, and would indirectly lead to his early death.

Padráig Pearse, in the meantime, maintained a good feeling for Edward Martyn. In January 1912 he told Joseph Holloway that Ireland was lucky to have such men as Martyn, Moore, Russell and Yeats. He had considered Yeats to be 'a minor poet of the third rank', but now they were mere '"irresponsible beings"', that help to keep life fresh'.[27] A few weeks later Pearse stood on a platform outside the General Post Office in Dublin to support the introduction of the third Home Rule Bill, then being brokered by John Redmond, leader if the Irish Parliamentary Party. Four years later, he stood on the same spot and set out to undo the life-work of Redmond, while Edward Martyn, in his rooms in South Leinster Street, sat and listened to the guns.

In spite of a setback in mid-summer, Martyn was well on the road to recovery in 1912. His handwriting was still very wobbly, but this was more likely to be a harbinger of the arthritis that was to plague him for the rest of his life than a symptom of his mental condition. The production of *Grangecolman*, as we have seen, gave him the 'impetus to carry on'. The Abbey Players were in America, making a wonderful splash. They were known everywhere as: 'Lady Gregory's Irish Players'. The *Chicago Tribune* reviewer wrote that they were 'Magical'. The same paper, however, referred to Synge's work as 'belligerent materialism'. Edward Martyn watched it all with good-natured approval.

On 20 March Violet Martin, his cousin, wrote to Edith Somerville:

> Yesterday he and I [Jim Martin] drove over to Tillyra and left him [Archer Martin] with Edward Martyn, who was very civil and interesting, and amusing – and very like George Moore's description, and also like Bertie Windle – Tillrya beats all the houses I have seen here – rebuilt about twenty years ago, its splendid old keep embedded into a castellated grey limestone house and I saw the study up in the tower, and the chapel beside it. The staircase is quite away and beyond most.
>
> There are very good pictures, in fact it is a thing to see. His mania now is the Malboro' street choir in Dublin, on which he has spent £10,000 and it is wonderful I hear. He even offered to take me to hear his choir sing madrigals, and I was so taken aback that I said nothing – so I shall not be asked again – and perhaps that is as well. He and Jim were on the Grand Jury this week, and the resolution was passed, calling on the government

to demand a higher licence for firearms in view of the hideous state of affairs about Craughwell – Edward Martyn alone dissented – and I think Jim was a good deal disgusted. He and I did not get home till past eight.[28]

From the above comment one can deduce that most of the people who mattered had read, at least the first book of, *Hail and Farewell*, by 1912. In July 1913 Holloway wrote: 'Dr. Gogarty motored past with a lady in the motor (past Green's bookshop in Dublin, where Æ was scanning the books with his nose up against the glass), as I stood at the door of No. 6 St. Stephen's Green, and I thought of Moore's description of him in *Salve* [second book] as the wit of Dublin. To me he always looked like an overgrown schoolboy, who would like to be thinner, so that he could readily take part in games.'[29] Moore himself wrote to Edmund Gosse on 11 April 1913, from his home in Westport: 'I leave to-morrow and hope that all the characters in *Ave* and *Salve* do not come to meet me at Broadstone.'[30] But had Edward Martyn read it?

He put it off. He did not want, he told friends, to fall out with *Mon Ami Moore*. In the very early days of his friendship with Yeats, the poet had pointed out to him that Moore had good points. Edward Martyn had replied: 'I know Moore a great deal longer than you. He has no good points.' Ironically, one of Moore's more obvious 'good points' was his love for Edward. But, of course, his ambition for artistic achievement superseded everything; Edward Martyn was the best copy he was ever likely to come upon. He managed not to read the book for some time, but knowing that it was there, and that everyone else had read it, must have contributed to his nervous problems in these years. It would be hard for him to give up the company of Moore, so he put it off as long as he could.

Lady Hemphill (E.M's first cousin) told Philip Rooney, the actor and writer, that she remembered dinners in her mother's house, after the publication of *Ave*, when they were both present: 'Well they always used to talk to each other, you know, because they'd meet at my mother's house at dinner. They'd be quite friendly on occasions like that. But Edward always used to say that he never could have the same feeling that he had for George before the book was published.'[31] For the same article Rooney interviewed Owen Linnane, Edward Martyn's manservant and chauffeur, who told him: 'I can safely say I was at the last meeting of Mr. Martyn and Mr. Moore. It happened in 15 South Leinster Street, Dublin. Mr Martyn was then living in that house. What actually happened was this: I let Moore into the room. And he stood there in the centre of the floor, and he said "Good morning Edward." He used to call Mr. Martyn Edward. Always. But at this time Mr. Martyn did not answer him in his usual friendly way. He was silent for a minute, and then he said: "What kind of tomfoolery are you going on with now, Moore? Tomfoolery." With that, he turned his back and picked up his book and went on reading. For a few seconds Moore stood there, in the centre of the floor. But he could see, I suppose, that he wasn't wanted. And he knew Mr. Martyn too well to have any hope of making him change his mind. So he turned around and went his way. And I think that was about the last meeting they ever had.'[32]

No doubt Owen Linnane's recollection is reasonably accurate, but there is ample evidence that Moore and Martyn continued to see each other on a fairly regular basis. Still, the old closeness was gone. Moore had done his best and done his worst and, in the end, Edward Martyn would forgive his friends almost anything. He still had a life to live which, as so often happens in troubled lives, improved immensely in later middle age. Moore didn't begrudge it him. In 1920, when Martyn was writing the introduction to his *Paragraphs for the Perverse*, he came back to Moore and referred to him as 'that Donnybrook Fair type of Irishman, who, by constituting himself my Boswell, has reaped a notoriety … which, it is certain, none of his other works could bring him'. He compared him to the infant Morgante who, 'when he misbehaves himself, clapping his little hands laughingly shouts "I did this because I knew it would annoy you". But it does not annoy somehow. I suppose it is because it is *Mon Ami Moore*. Nay, it was eagerly relished for its *monamimooring* of me by our mutual relatives, and other dreadful people, who were never known to read a book in their lives before.'

16 • Hardwicke Street

O N 27 JULY 1914 Edward Martyn wrote to John Horgan:
'What awful news from Dublin this morning.' He was not
referring to the mobilisation of Serbia, which occurred on 25
July, when the Austrian ultimatum led to the outbreak of the Great War.
While Europe was about to be plunged into darkness, they had been
having a very nice time at the Oireachtas (Gaelic League Festival) in
Killarney, where a photograph was taken for the *Cork Examiner*. It shows
a healthy, happy Edward, dressed like a parish priest. No, he was not
then thinking about the breakdown in relations between the cousins
who represented the Great Powers of Europe, but more with the
repercussions, and fall-out, from the work of one of his own cousins.

In September 1913 Edward Carson, who was then the Unionist MP
for Dublin University, had set up a Provisional Government in Ulster.
His sole motivation was the defeat of the third Home Rule Bill. Carson
knew he would not get the support he needed from the Protestant
minority in the south, many of whom were, by now, supporters of
Home Rule, so he moved north and, from then on, resistance to Home
Rule developed into an almost purely Ulster movement. An Ulster
Volunteer Force had been founded in January, after the third Home
Rule Bill passed its third reading in the House of Commons. Carson
subscribed £10,000 to it. Ulster intended to fight. John Redmond, and
other members of the Irish Parliamentary Party, assumed Carson was
bluffing, but others in the south, were inspired. On 25 November
Professor Eoin MacNeill, a prominent member of the Gaelic League,
and Laurence Kettle, brother of the poet and writer, Tom, founded the
Irish Volunteers. Their manifesto stated that the object of the Irish
Volunteers was: 'to secure and maintain the rights and liberties common

to all the people of Ireland. Their duties will be defensive and protective, and they will not contemplate either aggression or domination.' They were not really expecting to fight, at least Eoin MacNeill was not.

The Irish Volunteers were prepared to imitate their Ulster counterparts, whom they admired for their determination, and to import munitions. It was the 'Howth gun-running' that Martyn referred to in his letter. Guns were landed from Erskine Childers's yacht, *The Asgard*, in Howth (a coastal village close to Dublin), and brought into the city by some Volunteers, who were ambushed by British Army troops. The Volunteers managed to get away with most of the weapons, but the troops, returning to their barracks, were set upon by an angry crowd. In the mêlée that followed, three people were killed and thirty-eight injured. Violence had come to the streets of Dublin and it would be many years before it went away. Edward Martyn hated it; he was very frightened of physical force; he didn't like anything about the Volunteers. When they had been given short shrift in Cork, for their attitude to the Irish Parliamentary Party, he had written to Horgan: 'I am very glad Cork knocked the bottom out of the Volunteer Movement – a most dangerous movement at this time, but a very good one after we get Home Rule.'[1] He must have felt that he had some part in it all the same for his letter of 27 July continues: 'I knew they would take *us* seriously and disarm us. They don't fear anything Carson does because he is on England's side. The Volunteers are playing the Carson game. It is all going as I thought.'[2]

On 18 September 1914 the Home Rule Bill became law. It was accompanied by a Suspensory Act, which prevented its operation until the end of hostilities in Europe. Britain and Germany had been at war since 4 August and, on 20 September, John Redmond made a speech at Woodenbridge, County Wicklow, committing the Irish Volunteers to serve anywhere in the theatre of war. It caused a catastrophic split in the movement. Not many people knew that it had been split to some extent anyway, because the supreme council of the Irish Republican Brotherhood had developed an inner circle, which pledged: 'to free Ireland by force of arms, to use the Volunteers to that end, and to secure arms from Germany'. England's trouble would be Ireland's opportunity. The people who were on the inner circle of the IRB were also very close to Edward Martyn for the next two years; their involvement in dramatic art was intense and, for some of them, the Easter Rising of 1916 proved to be the final curtain.

28 At the Oireachtas in Killarney, July 1914. From left: John Horgan,
Edward Martyn, Mary Horgan and Douglas Hyde.

There was no premonition of tragedy on that scale in April 1914 when Martyn wrote an article in the *Irish Review* entitled: 'A Plea for the Revival of the Irish Literary Theatre.' In it he paid homage to W.B. Yeats and Lady Gregory for their success at the Abbey. Then in his slightly inimical fashion (which only ever appears when he takes up his pen), and with a certain amount of tongue in cheek, he poured praise on Yeats, whom he genuinely believed to be

> ... a fine poet and a subtle literary critic, ... and Lady Gregory, although not intellectually profound, is intellectually acute in the most extreme degree. She has a knowledge of mankind, and a social mastery and tact, that can only be described as genius. A combination of two such efficient and unique personalities for the special work they had to do, I suppose, the world has never seen before. The result is that they defied opposition, and have built up, from nothing at all, a remarkable and lasting structure.

The manner in which they commenced the work always seems to me, who have had some experience in such concerns, as particularly wonderful. We all know how useless it is to push a person without talent ... but these are the sort of persons, however, whom Mr. Yeats and Lady Gregory triumphantly succeeded in pushing. ... Mr. Yeats discovered some people trying to act in a little hall among the by-streets of Dublin ... and pounced upon these most unpromising players and proclaimed a wonderful discovery. He proclaimed their merits in his most dictatorial vein, until they actually got to believe in themselves and even show signs of some improvement, and eventually much good work was gradually done until the Abbey players are now recognized as the best actors of peasant plays probably in the world.

Making it clear that he is going to found another theatre, he informed his readers that he intended to closely study and copy the work of Yeats and Gregory, but his theatre would be different. 'If I could have written peasant plays, which I could not ... I have no doubt I should have found my place naturally at the Abbey. ... So what is my project then? ... It is not original. It is simply to apply the methods of the Abbey Theatre to an organization of the most talented amateurs, for the encouragement of native Irish drama, other than the peasant species. ... Our plays ... shall be those not usually acted by professionals. We will also act plays, co-operating with the Gaelic League Players, in the Irish language. ... We will not expect to make money.'[3]

Martyn had written to Ernest Boyd in the same vein in July. Explaining the difference, he told Boyd: 'I do not want to interfere with the society in any way, I only want to carry out the idea of the Irish Literary Theatre.' It was not named the Irish Literary Theatre, however, but the Irish Theatre, and it lasted for six years. In 1912 Thomas MacDonagh and Joseph Mary Plunkett, who were both on the editorial board of the *Irish Review*, were trying very hard to create an Art Theatre. In her memoir, the actress Maire ní Shiubhlaigh describes Dublin as a city full of small halls and concert rooms, together with the Abbey and the Rotunda, when they were available for hire, and the Queen's provided a stage for little amateur groups of the most varied kind. These were not important, but they were interesting to watch, if only because of the people whom they managed to enlist as members, players, writers or producers. 'In Dublin poets, writers, artists, revolutionists were all interested in the theatre.'[4]

When Thomas MacDonagh was in correspondence with Frank Fay in 1912 with regard to the foundation of a theatre, they discussed, in very negative terms, Maire ní Shiubhlaigh. They didn't rate her as a great actress (later MacDonagh would have good reason to rate her as a great patriot), and made the point that they didn't want her in their new company. At the time she was being paid over £5 a week by Edward Martyn to, apparently, research and read plays. But he wasn't happy. In an undated letter he wrote to her: 'Do you think I am honour bound to continue this salary when the gentlemen who asked me to pay it have done nothing on their side to promote that dramatic society for the production of plays? ... I know I am bound to you until February 16. I don't grudge it in the least, if I could see some results.'[5]

In 1912, in fact, it was Evelyn Gleeson, who had been an original founding member of the Dun Emer Industries with Lily and Lolly Yeats, who was the feminine force in a push for a new Art Theatre. But the attempt to interest Frank Fay came to nothing and, by the time Martyn wrote his article for the *Irish Review*, it was agreed that he would fund the new theatre. Thomas MacDonagh wrote to his brother John offering him a job as actor-manager. 'We would have to put on Martyn's own plays (which would require good acting),' he told him. John accepted and, in the long run, did valiant work for Edward Martyn.

Thomas MacDonagh and Joseph Plunkett were both poets and patriots, but they very different characters. MacDonagh, at the time, was in his mid-thirties and employed as an assistant lecturer in English, at University College Dublin. He was an extrovert; well built, with light-brown hair and a fresh complexion, his eyes lit up easily with wit. Every point was animatedly expressed. A gay spirit, he was always well dressed, either in dark suits or kilts. When Maire ní Shiubhlaigh wrote of him, long after his death, she presented him as a popular figure, well liked in Dublin. But others felt differently. The critics didn't think much of him as a producer, and the popular actress Una O'Connor made the point, with a hint of acrimony, that 'Martyn was a good and kindly man, but MacDonagh ruled the roost.' Beneath the bonhomie, he was a man who liked to be in control, and some felt that he was arrogant. Joseph Holloway believed him to be 'devoid of theatrical instinct'. He had had two of his plays performed, one by the Abbey Players and one by the Theatre of Ireland. His friendship was one of the late blessings of Edward Martyn's life.

Plunkett was twenty-six. A tall, slightly built man with a pale, earnest face and sporting heavy spectacles, he was a gifted musician, poet and actor. Maire ní Shiubhlaigh described him as 'rather mysterious with dark hair, long, tapering hands and penetrating eyes'.[6] He had spent most of his short life travelling in Europe, both for health reasons and on behalf of the Irish Volunteers. His father, George, was a Papal Count, who was descended from the Catholic martyr Oliver Plunkett. Joseph was shy and sensitive, with a quiet wit. It is believed, however, that he was deadly serious when, as Director of Operations for the Volunteers, he often instructed his subordinates with the following: 'You will meet a man in X outside the Railway Hotel, he will polish the radiator of a car with grass as you approach, you will ask "Are you Thomas?" He will answer "Do you come from William?" You will reply "I am William." He will salute and say "I will now lead you to Thomas in his house behind the Market Square."' His men usually simplified such instructions to: 'I'm So and So. Take me to Tommy Mac.'[7]

In the meantime, however, the Plunkett family did a great service to the theatre movement in Dublin by supplying a suitable home for the new Irish Theatre. The property at 38 Hardwicke Street was, in fact, owned by the Countess Plunkett. In its time it had been a convent, a Catholic chapel, a Methodist chapel and a school. The Plunkett family had converted the auditorium into a theatre and rented it out to amateur dramatic societies. In 1912 Evelyn Gleeson parted company with the Yeats sisters in Dundrum and took her Dun Emer Guild (the department of the industry that made tapestries and carpets) to Hardwicke Street, where she occupied the back of the building. It soon became a gathering place for writers, including George Russell, Joseph Campbell and Padraic Colum. When Martyn took over the lease of the auditorium it needed further renovation, especially to increase the size of the stage, which was never adequate. Micheál Mac Líammóir, who started his Irish theatrical life there, wrote of it: 'The stage was inadequate. I painted a mountainside set for one of Martyn's own symbolic plays – a quaint Ibsenic affair [*Regina Eyre*, E.M.'s female *Hamlet*] in which Maire ní Shiublaigh gave a memorable performance. The seating was haphazard in arrangement … and even the lighting was of that sad

29 Poster for the Irish Theatre, Harwicke Street, 4–9 January 1915;
Anna Kelly remembered sitting on hard seats
learning how to be intellectual.

and glacial quality one associates with political meetings of the intimate and conspiratorial nature.'[8]

But ní Shiubhlaigh herself thought of it as 'a dainty little theatre, rather on the French style'. She also saw its first importance 'since the beginning of the dramatic movement itself, for it indicated the path that Hilton Edwards and Mac Líammóir later took when they founded the Dublin Gate'.[9] Mac Líammóir, writing for the Dublin Cultural Relations Committee in 1950, noted: 'Although the movement never grew into a popular one it did the invaluable work of preparing the palate of a growing minority of the public for new and adventurous tastes. ... Their work indeed came near to being as valuable to the development of Ireland's maturing theatrical intelligence as the early work of the Abbey had been.'[10] What Anna Kelly, one of George Moore's secretaries, remembered in 1937 was that 'they used to sit on hard seats in the Irish Theatre, learning how to be intellectual'.[11] In August 1915, however, Edward Martyn wrote to Ernest Boyd: 'I am sorry to say we are not discovering playwrights at all.'[12]

But Hardwicke Street wasn't ready for the new theatre's first production. Everything else was in order. The Articles of Agreement had been drawn up naming Martyn, Plunkett and MacDonagh as the partners, and Article 20 stated: 'It is agreed that of the number of plays in the English language, original or translated, produced by the partnership ... at least one half shall be plays written by Mr. Edward Martyn, if so many be available.'[13] A tall order, but he made a relatively good start. *The Dream Physician* opened in the Little Theatre in O'Connell Street on 5 November 1914. There were several press releases alerting people to what was to come. The *Evening Telegraph* on 31 October informed its readers that: 'Criticism and satire rarely produce fine literature ... but the directors [of the Irish Theatre] are confident that Mr. Martyn's satiric comedy is of the lasting kind. It is Mr. Martyn's longest and finest play, having in it that strange quality of symbolism which gave its peculiar worth to *The Heather Field* and, at the same time, an unsuspected satirical power of ridicule, and common sense combined, that makes one see in a new light of sanity, many things in recent Irish movements, which under the hypnotism of a few clever writers we were beginning to take for granted as having a real relation to life.' A few days later there was another release assuring the public that: 'The Irish Theatre will present no peasant plays, but will endeavour to stage psychological, satiric, heroic and poetical works of literary worth. *The Dream Physician* … is full of allusions to men and matters connected with the recent developments of politics, literature and art in Ireland.'[14] It was, in fact, Edward Martyn's revenge.

The Dream Physician is a play in five acts which could satisfactorily be stripped of four. If it had been pared down to just the fourth act, it could have been sold to a Dublin audience as a very funny and very successful sketch. But it would not, of course, have been suitable for an art theatre. As it was, the audience did get the joke, although they did not all like it. *The Dream Physician* satirises George Moore as someone who believes himself to be a 'great writer' and who will, through his writing, remake Ireland in the image of his own ideal. To a lesser extent it satirises Yeats for his, in Martyn's opinion, naïve take on Irish society. There is also a character who is quite clearly based on James Joyce, although there is no other hint in Edward Martyn's life that he knew the great modernist, while there is much evidence that Joyce knew of Martyn's work, and of his passion for Ibsen.

The play hangs on the tale of the chief female protagonist, Audrey Lestor, who is married to Shane Lestor (this character is almost certainly based on the politician Shane Leslie). Shane joins the Separation and Plunder Party (Sinn Féin) and Audrey, who is a Unionist, loses her mind. Audrey has a brother, Otho (James Joyce), who is in love with Miss Martha Moon, the grand-niece of 'that funny old Mayo journalist, George Augustus Moon' (George Moore). Martha Moon writes under the pseudonym 'La Mayonnaise' and is, in fact, one of George Moon's alter egos. Otho thinks 'La Mayonnaise' is a beautiful name. It suggests: 'grey mullet, Paris, beautiful possibilities'. To which his father replies: 'Very well then; if you like being the mullet in the mayonnaise sauce.' These are good lines in the early part of a play which has a serious and a comic theme; the serious one being the situation of an ascendancy family when a member turns nationalist; the comic one being the satirising of those who aim to change Ireland through literature and art (Martyn, obviously, had no problem with this but he wasn't so sure about the way Moore and Yeats were attempting to do it).

The two themes are brought together in the fourth act by way of some very funny dialogue. The serious theme, however, is not developed, and the fact that Audrey Lestor regains her sanity because she realises that Moon and Beau Brummell (Yeats) are not real is rather peculiar, even though she has dreamt of Moore and he is her 'dream physician'.

Martyn's stage instructions for Moon's appearance were that he be 'a little old man with a plump body, short thick legs, very broad hips, very sloping shoulders, a long neck and a pasty, almost featureless face surmounted by what was once very red but is now sandy hair, streaked with grey'.[15] His room was to give 'the effect of a cheap boudoir', and he was to sport 'a look of absent-minded vacuity'. There is a strong implication that Moon sees himself in the same league as Jonathan Swift, so Shane Lestor tells him: 'Swift was a terror to his enemies, you have only succeeded in being a terror to your friends.' When everyone is collected in Moon's rooms for the fourth act, Brummell arrives, and the stage directions are even more outrageous. Brummell is 'tall with red hair, brushed back from his forehead, wearing a black frockcoat and trousers, a green waistcoat, a large black stock showing no collar, and a tall hat with a flat brim'. He carries a banjo in his left hand and a whip in his right. Brummell, Martyn explains, 'is a musical dandy, all exquisite exteriority, no more real than one of those long misty figures one might imagine straying, accidentally, from out of a picture by Burne Jones'.[16]

The fourth act opens when Moon has just taken delivery of a washhand-stand. He had recently written an article declaring that all Ireland's problems could be solved, when people learned to appreciate a good washhand-stand. He was very disappointed, however, that the one he had now got was not a Sheraton. But Brummell liked it (because of his inferior middle-class tastes), and decided that it might even have oracular virtues:

> Moon: It would take no less a person than you Brummell to
> discover the oracle of the washhand-stand

But Audrey's nurse, Sister Farnham (played by Maire ní Shiubhlaigh, she had written directly to Martyn for a job), is very anxious to sit on the stand, and to be the interpreter of the oracle. This, she feels, may well produce the cure that her patient, Audrey Lestor, needs.

> Brummell: Meander cor chios adelphos kai delon seisma

Sister Farnham screams, while Miss Whelan (Moon's secretary) calls for prayers.

Brummell: I wish I knew some prayers but this may well do (*loudly solemn*) 'Of man's first disobedience and the fruit of that forbidden tree whose mortal taste. ...'

The oracle interrupts Brummell:

Oracle: I see a funny little old man and he with a gutta-percha face. He has the heart of a flunkey the way he does be toadying imitation English Blackbeer and satirizing what his countryman often fed him of a Sunday night. He does be making terror for his friends but his enemies, leastwise if he has any–aren't in dread of him at all, at all.

Brummell: This is the language of genius. Yes, yes. Go on, go on.

Oracle: Ochon, ochon, ochon – Oh traveling tallow face with parsnip hair. ... You dance the world like a willow the wisp and you playing vanities foreninth soupers and other blackguards.

Moon attempts to remove Sister Farnham from his wash-hand-stand:

Brummell: If you attempt to interfere with her I will call the police. You have not made the sacrifice for art that I have (*clasping his banjo to his breast*). Art for Art's sake.

The audience knew exactly what was going on in this scene and, by and large, enjoyed it. But they were baffled by the play in general. They had been told, however, that the Irish Theatre was going to be about experiment, so they were very forgiving, albeit in the hope of better things to come. In fact, they had been spared much. *The Dream Physician* had not been an easy play to bring to the stage. J.M.S. Carr, who played Beau Brummell, told Seamus O'Sullivan, critic, that 'they had to cut some nasty dialogue out of it. Martyn has a Rabelaisian strain that comes out in his writing'.[17]

The critics were less forgiving. The critic in *Freeman's Journal* wrote, on 3 November: 'a telling drama has been spoiled in the telling. It is a fine drama, but the "satire" turns this strong material to other purposes, and does its best to waste it.' In the *Evening Telegraph* on 31 October, the critic had written: 'Mr. Martyn's new play should be described rather as a play in four acts and an interlude than a play in five acts. The fourth act is something of the nature of a play within a play. It differs from the other acts too in being the lightest of comedy, while they are for the most part serious and grave.'[18]

The opening night did attract a big audience of literary people. There was a call for the author. The *Irish Independent* reported: 'Martyn in an unbending way thanked the audience and, in disjointed sentences jerked out with pauses between, tried to explain the object of the new Irish Theatre. He has a bad method of delivery.'[19] Yeats went to see it on 6 November, but there is no evidence that Moore saw it at all, although he was in Dublin. Much later, in 1943, John MacDonagh recalled visiting Edward Martyn in his rooms in South Leinster Street, and finding Moore there. Martyn introduced MacDonagh by saying: 'Now George, here is the man who has all Dublin laughing at you', and Moore replied: 'Indeed'.

If there is a doubt on whether Moore went to see the play, it is certain he did not attend the celebration dinner on the Saturday night, when Edward Martyn was seated between Una O'Connor and Maire ní Shiubhlaigh. Grace Gifford presented him with a wonderful cartoon of 'Cupid and Psyche', in which Venus's winged bold boy is Moore pointing his arrow at Susan Mitchell, who, it was well known, was writing a portrait of the novelist. Mitchell was sitting at a desk which would be more fitting in a boudoir. Edward was embarrassed by so much attention and, looking at the cartoon, told Grace that she was another Max Beerbohm (there is a famous drawing by Beerbohm of Yeats introducing Moore to the Queen of the Fairies), before folding it up rapidly, and putting it away.[20]

There is evidence that Moore was still looking out for his cousin. In October Martyn received a letter from Barrett H. Clarke, an American drama critic and playwright, who was very interested in what he was doing. This connection almost certainly came through Moore, who knew Clarke and his wife quite well. Edward Martyn replied to his letter on 12 October, enclosing a copy of his article in the *Irish Review*, and telling him how they were progressing in the Irish Theatre. He was in a boastful mood: 'I fancy I have written more plays than anyone else in the Dramatic Movement, with the possible exception of Lady Gregory who, as far as productivity at least is concerned, is undoubtedly the Irish Lope de Vega [the Spanish dramatist who claimed to have written 1,500 plays].'[21]

30 'Cupid and Psyche' by Grace Gifford – Venus's winged bold boy is George Moore pointing his arrow at Susan Mitchell, who was writing his biography. Presented to Edward Martyn after the inaugural performance of the Irish Theatre.

As the season progressed, the company did, by and large, accomplish what it had set out to do. In January 1915 it moved into Hardwicke Street. Martyn had spent £100 on the renovation and, while it was not perfect, it meant that the little company developed a sense of belonging. Those who found their way there liked it. But the location, away from the city centre, would always prove a problem. From 4 to 9 January they had a programme of four one-act plays, which included new Irish writing and European greats (Chekhov's 'The Swan Song'). They were not especially professional, but neither were they pretentious. With the exception of Edward Martyn, they were all young bohemians (he was an old bohemian), as is evident from Joseph Holloway's description of Eimar O'Duffy, author of *The Phoenix on the Roof*, after its first perform-ance: 'Encountered the young writer mounting his bike to pedal his way home through the dark streets – how boyish he looks with his round schoolboy face and hair.' There was tragedy in O'Duffy's life. He was already cut adrift from his family because of his membership of the Irish Volunteers, and his refusal to join the British Army. His brother, who did, was killed at Suvla Bay just a few months later. In April O'Duffy's *Walls of Athens* was performed and, in May, there were, as promised, plays in Irish, including *Iosagan* by Padraig Pearse and Douglas Hyde's *Casadh an tSugàin*. They got consistently good reviews. Not so for their final production of the season. Bringing what Martyn called Chekhov's 'coherent incoherence', in the shape of *Uncle Vanya*, to the fledgling theatre was almost a step too far.

Uncle Vanya was an enormous undertaking for such a small company in so small a Theatre, but most agreed that it was admirable that they had done it. Louie Bennett, the trade-union leader, wrote in *New Ireland* on 7 July: 'The company must be congratulated for giving those in Dublin, who are interested, an opportunity of witnessing an extraor-dinary play.' Moore agreed and he wrote to the *Irish Times* to support it. John MacDonagh played Vanya, and William Pearse (brother of Padraig) played Professor Serebrakoff. Martyn rehearsed most of it. There are reports of him rushing around the place, behaving in a very similar manner to Yeats at the Abbey. During the intervals he was seen to scurry between the hall and the backstage 'enveloped in a big fur-lined coat of the Yeats pattern'.[22] He had become very theatrical. Holloway, seeing him in the street one day, remarked that he was got up like Herbert Beerbohm Tree, playing Demetrious in *The Red Lamp*. In that play, by W. Outram Tristram, Demetrious was the head of the secret police and he was a 'clumsily proportioned, white-haired, drowsy-eyed, sinister figure, who walked with the aid of a stick but moved with feline softness and celerity.'

Before the first performance of *Uncle Vanya*, Thomas MacDonagh told the audience that it would be almost impossible for them to understand the play unless they had read it beforehand. 'The truth of this was made manifest afterwards,' the critic for the *Independent* wrote. And the *Freeman's Journal*, not to be outdone, reported: 'The whole thing is like one of those post impressionist pictures, which looks just as well if turned upside down.' But everyone agreed that some of the scenes were extremely well done. For Holloway, however, who rarely had anything good to say about this theatre, 'the characters are mostly eccentrics who are always grunting and telling how old they are … they all moved about awkwardly, spoke listlessly and were mightly depressed – one could imagine people wanting to shoot each other in Russia.' When he left the theatre 'the night was as dreary as the Russian House Chekhov had created in his play'.[23] Even after the final curtain came down, *Uncle Vanya* continued to be a source of amusement for Dubliners. At the Theatre Royal, Percy French, in his variety show, did a parody of the production to show 'how Dublin does it'. He called it *Gloom* and it ran twice – the second time being in the Little Theatre in January 1916.

The image of the theatre was formed with the production of *Uncle Vanya*. This was an odd place, where odd things happened. All the literati congregated to see this Chekhov play. Sarah Purser was in the audience on 3 July. Clearly it was not a theatre that would ever attract a large audience but, in a small way, it did become 'the temple of Thespis in Hardwicke Street'.

17 • Easter 1916

BY AUGUST 1915 Edward Martyn was in a bad way with arthritis. In April, Holloway had seen him 'looking fit and well pleased with himself and the world, his clerical soft hat was turned up in the front in quite a devil-may-care way, making its wearer look droller than ever'. By June, however, he was struggling out of his car. He begged Holloway not to touch him, and he sat in a wheelchair beside 'the satin clad Grace Gifford',[1] the cartoonist and friend of Joseph Plunkett. In September he wrote Vincent O'Brien that he was 'very ill, crippled with arthritis'. Still, in October, he could write, 'Dr. Foley says I am much better. He is doing all sorts of things to cure me, chiefly burning out the acid from the joints with electricity.'[2] Evidence that he was a little better came when he told O'Brien that he planned to motor up to Dublin on the 26th. But to Thomas MacDonagh he wrote: 'I … may be a day or two late owing to medical treatment. I am sorry to say there is little improvement, if any, in my crippled condition … stick at rehearsals, without rehearsals it is impossible to do anything well.'[3]

His crippled condition showed in his wobbly writing, but he was in good form. In a rather mysterious letter to Sarah Purser in October he wrote: 'I fear you cannot get *monamimoore* out of your imagination. What a talent he has to fascinate. Think of little pigs!' And Yeats was attentive: 'I saw a lot of Yeats lately. He is greatly improved, talks more interestingly than he ever did before.'[4] At the same time, he wrote to Ernest Boyd: 'I have never fought with George Moore [which was hardly the whole truth]. He came to see me in my crippled condition in Dublin and was full of projects for my [?]. One does not take him seriously otherwise he would be almost wholly objectionable.'[5]

The rehearsals he writes of are for his play *Privilige of Place*. During the summer the MacDonagh brothers, Thomas and John, had been to Tillyra, helping Martyn to tidy it up. It is impossible to say to what extent they achieved success. There is no extant copy of this play in the public arena, but there are some pages in Thomas MacDonagh's archive in the National Library of Ireland.[6] The press release on 6 November in the *Evening Telegraph* tells us that it was 'a comedy of Dublin life, dealing with officials in high places, students, an idealist, an artist, a good girl and a policeman. The central theme is serious and far reaching.' The critics did not agree. 'Martyn became tired before he finished the play,' R.J. Kelly wrote in *New Ireland*. He described it as a Rabelaisian comedy, resembling *Morgante the Lesser*. There were bad reviews all round.

In March 1916 they staged August Strindberg's *Easter*. The critics loved it. Ireland had experienced Strindberg before, but not *Easter*. It was described as 'an exquisite little passion play', which is what it is – a play about betrayal and redemption. It is hardly profane and yet, Joseph Plunkett wrote to John MacDonagh: 'Edward and Tomás had no right to produce this piece of contemptible profanity', and resigned from the Irish Theatre.[7] In response, Edward Martyn merely remarked: 'Well really, Plunkett is a strange fellow.' He had never had a close relationship with him, always preferring the company of the MacDonaghs. But Plunkett was not alone in his dislike of *Easter*. On 7 March Grace Gifford sent a card to Holloway: 'Isn't the play at Hardwicke Street horrible?' This reaction in Gifford is more understandable, since the play does stress life as a 'vale of tears', and includes such lines as: 'everyone must suffer on Good Friday'; the sins of the father are visited on the children. There was sadness in Grace's own life and she might have identified, to an extent, with the melancholy strain in Strindberg's stricken family. The play's characters, nevertheless, are moving inexorably towards the light, while Joseph Plunkett was approaching the dark (it was less than six weeks to the Easter Rising, and Plunkett was executed on 4 May, a day after marrying Grace), and who knows what Grace Gifford knew.

Holloway showed his usual philistinism by noting: 'He [E.M.] loves crank foreign masterpieces, such as *Easter* and Ibsen, and can see no merit in aught else on the stage, save his own weak imitations.'[8] In retrospect, one ponders the motives of Thomas MacDonagh putting on this play a few weeks before an uprising that has gone down in history as a 'blood sacrifice'. Perhaps there were none, but Joseph Plunkett's reaction was, indeed, 'strange'. What we can be sure of is that Thomas MacDonagh was a man who was in love with life; it is unlikely that there was ever a morning he woke up thinking he might die that day. As for Edward Martyn, he knew nothing of what was to come.

Or did he know something? On 22 April 1916 Holloway reported to his diary: 'saw Martyn at his writing desk in his room over the tobacconist's – he now wears a white beard and looks strangely unlike himself'.[9] Within two weeks he would be the only remaining director of the Irish Theatre.

The Rising of 1916, which, for the most part, took place on the streets of Dublin, did not have the support of a majority of the Irish people, but it did have the support of most of the later protagonists of this narrative. Even Edward Martyn's great antipathy to violence was washed away in his loyalty to his friends. That Easter Monday morning, 24 April, when he first heard the guns from north of the River Liffey, was a beautiful spring day. The city was thronged with bank holiday crowds and race-goers. Maire ní Shiubhlaigh, who was a member of Cumann na mBan (the feminine arm of the Volunteers), got wind of what was about to happen and took the tram from her coastal home of Glasthule, in south Dublin, to the city centre. On the corner of Grafton Street and South King Street she saw: 'Joe Plunkett. He was in uniform. His hat bound tightly to the crown displayed a white bandage.' He had had an operation and had come straight from a nursing home. Later he would assist Padraig Pearse in the GPO, with Michael Collins as his *aide-de-camp*. Farther on, at the corner of York Street, Tom MacDonagh stood talking with a man in civilian clothes. This was 'Major John MacBride, Maud Gonne's estranged husband'.[10] Later ní Shiubhlaigh made her way to Jacob's Biscuit Factory in Bishop Street, where Thomas MacDonagh was commanding the second Dublin Battalion of the Volunteers. 'We have no provision for girls here,' he told her. But she stayed, and was still there a week later when MacDonagh told her they must surrender.

At two o'clock in the afternoon Joseph Holloway ventured out onto the streets. He was 'in blissful ignorance of anything unusual happening in the city'. On his way to the matinee of *Shall Us*, at the Empire, he stopped at the canal end of Mount Street Bridge, where he noticed 'knots of people had collected and were chattering earnestly and

31 (a) Thomas MacDonagh in Irish Volunteers uniform, *c.*1916.
His friendship was a late blessing in Edward Martyn's life.

excitedly and a man enquired of a woman as he passed, "Is there anything up" and she said, "It is them Sinn Féiners, or whatever you call them, are about".' The Empire was not performing a matinee, so Holloway carried on walking northwards: 'I passed a hoarding and read a Proclamation pasted up. It had a Gaelic heading and went on to state

31(b) Sackville (O'Connell) Street, April 1916.

that Ireland was now under Republican Government and they hoped with God's help etc. etc. It was signed by seven names ... it was a long, floridly worded document, full of high hopes.'[11] Holloway was prevented from entering Sackville Street by the gunfire, so he went round by Marlborough Street, thus passing the Abbey, which was closed for matinees. In O'Connell Street Padraig Pearse, one of the leaders who spearheaded the insurrection, had taken control of the General Post Office and declared it to be the seat of the Provisional Government of Ireland. Thus it remained until 29 April, when he signed a surrender document, 'in order to prevent the further slaughter of Dublin citizens and in the hope of saving the lives of our followers ... the members of the Provisional Government have agreed to an unconditional surrender, and the Commandants of the various districts in the City and Country will order their commands to lay down their arms.'[12]

They were hopelessly outnumbered, as they had always known they would be; they did not necessarily expect to die, but they were prepared for it. The speed with which it came about was astonishing. The courts-martial of the leaders were held on 2 May, and MacDonagh and Pearse were executed the following day. Then there continued a week of executions, including William Pearse, Padraig's younger brother, who was a member of the Irish Theatre. The writer Piaras Bèaslaì, who was with MacDonagh the day before his death, tells us that he 'chatted gaily and told them all that the Germans had landed in England'. Bèaslaì concluded that MacDonagh 'could not then have had the slightest idea that he was going to be shot the very next morning'.[13] Joseph Plunkett was executed the day after MacDonagh.

Augusta Gregory was worried about Edward, so she wrote to him. On 19 May he replied:

> I am as well as a man can be who has had a lot of his friends executed and deported. We had an awful time up here. I thought I would be starved, but Kildare Street Club came to the rescue and sent me some excellent food. ... Arthritis is still crippling my limbs. I have had the most heroic treatment ... injections, electric baths, massage every day almost. I now go to St Ann's Hydra in Blarney, a preliminary to returning to that horrid Tillyra. [Martyn's home had played a small part in the Rising. After the surrender Liam Mellows, Commander of the Volunteers in the west, called a final halt when he reached a safe haven in Tillyra]. I am glad Robert is going on so well. ... I did all that I could to dissuade those unfortunate volunteers from their folly. But they simply looked at me. From the very first I told them what would be the end of the volunteers.[14]

This does not mean that Edward Martyn knew anything specific but, as the company had been rehearsing in his rooms in South Leinster Street in the week leading to the Rising, and since the Volunteers had 'special training' every Wednesday evening in the Hardwicke Street hall, he had been very close to events.

To John MacDonagh, who was interned in Frongoch Prison in north Wales (he had been in Jacob's biscuit factory with his brother, but had left early in the week, with the result that his life had been spared), Martyn wrote:

Alas for your poor dear brother and the others. It was an awful shock to me, such great talents and high ideals, only the jobbers and place hunters left. I am trying to carry on the Theatre, but what can I do without your brother? Father Condon showed me his last letter to the family, it made me awfully sad. Those executions were abominable. I passed a horrible time during the rebellion thinking of you all, and listening to the never ending shooting. I think it is even sadder now, when one reflects on all our losses. I am much the same since I saw you last. I fear mine is a bad case.[15]

But John MacDonagh wanted to keep the theatre going, so while Martyn went to Cork, for his treatment, matters were left in the capable hands of their new, young, aspirant playwright, Henry B. O'Hanlon, who also happened to be a solicitor.

Martyn got through the summer feeling very sorry for himself. The friendship of the MacDonagh brothers had been a boon to an increasingly lonely man. In June he wrote to Vincent O'Brien, from Cork: 'Indeed I miss you very much and am very lonely here.' When he got back to Tillyra the Horgans came to visit, and he rewarded John Horgan for his loyalty by giving him some extraordinarily interesting letters 'from Miss Edgeworth, the celebrated Irish novelist ... another is my cousin John Woulfe Flanagan who had a hand in the "Parnellism and Crime articles in the Times". There are two of Æ [George Russell] and several of George Moore and Lecky.'[16] Things were definitely looking up. John MacDonagh was soon back, and Holloway noted: 'the Hardwicke Street Theatre would be resumed, though poor Martyn had to be rolled about in a wheelchair'.[17] The Company, which had never been a properly structured 'Theatre Company', was intact (with the exception of Willie Pearse, only the directors died), and they opened the 1916/17 season with a revival of *The Heather Field*, which got rotten reviews.

By December they were back on track, putting on three plays, all original Irish work by Irish writers. Edward Martyn's 'Symbolist Extravaganza', *Romulus and Remus*, came first and, despite a full house, this comedy review 'caused no laughter during its performance and the applause at the end was very faint indeed,' wrote the critic of the *New Ireland Review*. Holloway had seen Martyn coming to the theatre and

32 The characters in Edward's sketch *Romulus and Remus* at
the Irish Theatre, 1916.

noted: 'Martyn got out of his car and walked feebly in and got seated in the front row … looking for all the world in his black skull cap and bearded face like a money changer in the temple scene in biblical pictures'. He certainly didn't like Martyn's play: 'E.M. missed fire in his symbolist extravanganza. It was a relief to get to the morgue in Henry B. O'Hanlon's nightmare.'[18] This short play, *Tomorrow*, was O'Hanlon's first, and was about the last night of a drunken morgue attendant's life. After that it was a pleasure to get to John MacDonagh's comedy of manners, *Just like Shaw*. In *Paragraphs for the Perverse* Martyn wrote that this play was 'touched with an original humour that was as felicitous as his own volatile personality'.[19] Joseph MacDonagh, brother of John, played Shaw, and proved himself to be a fine actor. Everyone agreed that it had been a truly Irish evening.

In south Galway, in 1917, the pace of life quickened when Yeats finally bought the tower at Ballylee. It was but a stone's throw from both Tillyra and Coole. Fifteen years had passed since the friends parted company over theatre business, but Augusta Gregory remained Edward Martyn's nearest neighbour and friend. Yeats was still a regular visitor to Coole, and he was especially glad to bring his young bride (he married Georgie Hyde Lees in 1917) to Tillyra, while they watched over the work in progress on Ballylee. Neither Gregory nor Martyn fully approved of Yeats buying this ruin, even though it was Gregory who had first told him about it. Martyn offered him his own Dunguaire Castle in Kinvara, which was in far better condition, but the poet was adamant and, indeed, George Yeats also fell in love with the tower.

Martyn had recommended the architect W.A. Scott to Yeats. Scott had helped to remodel Tillyra, built the parish church at Labane and designed Edward's beautiful little parochial hall in Gort, which was later burned down by the Black and Tans (the part-time auxiliary soldiers, who were sent to Ireland to aid the RIC during the War of Independence). Scott had also been the architect of the Catholic church at Spiddal, and he designed the Morris's house. He didn't prove a great help to Yeats but, as Martyn remarked to Gregory, there was no one else.

When the work started on the tower, Edward Martyn motored over on a regular basis to inspect it and to lend his not inconsiderable advice on the merits, or otherwise, of living in a Norman tower. The newly married couple went to Tillyra most days, where luncheon was often

33 Yeats's Tower at Ballylee, Co. Galway. Once the restoration work started, the poet took his new bride to Tillyra almost every day for lunch; it was often drawn out until seven o'clock in the evening.

drawn out until seven in the evening. Martyn worried that he bored them, but he didn't, and they were all very relaxed together. George Yeats refused to believe the tales she had heard from her husband, and Augusta Gregory, about Martyn's legendary misogyny. She claimed that he complained to her of them putting it about that he hated women. She assured him she didn't believe it.[20] A year later they were still very close when Yeats, who was looking after Seán MacBride (Maud Gonne's son), sent him to Tillyra for his summer holidays. [21] While there he helped Martyn compile his *Paragraphs for the Perverse*.

In 1917 John MacDonagh considered a revival of *An Enchanted Sea*, but Martyn refused to allow it. He told MacDonagh that George Moore had suggested a disgusting connection between two characters, which made Martyn want to burn every copy of the play. So they revived *Uncle Vanya* instead and revealed, with considerable insight, something of the mood of the time, when their advance notice explained: 'In Russia and

Ireland we meet like characters – people of lively imagination and soaring ideals, struggling for expression, but live in a bog of uncongenial surroundings and vanished hopes.'[22] After that, MacDonagh had to bully Martyn into doing a production of Ibsen's *An Enemy of the People*. Edward pointed out that the Hardwicke Street stage was too small to accommodate the cast of twenty-two, but his reticence was more likely to do with his not liking this quasi-political play. His Ibsen was the mystic and psychologist, not the politico-social reformer. In the event, the production got very good reviews all round, especially for MacDonagh's stage management, and Paul Farrell's depiction of Doctor Stockman. Dublin, by this time, had seen a good deal of Ibsen, so this was the only work, by the Norwegian to be put on in Hardwicke Street. By now the ensemble was being admired for its courage, and its talent. Even Martyn's *Grangecolman* fell in for moderate reviews, as John MacDonagh 'playing the tired Devlin [the heroine's husband], yawned through his part convincingly'.[23]

'Sinn Féin is going through the country like an epidemic,' Edward Martyn wrote to John Horgan in July, with nicely strengthened handwriting; the arthritis was obviously under control. It was remarkable how soon after the Easter Rising was over it began to be known as the Sinn Féin rebellion. It had not been so, although many Sinn Féiners took part, but now the demand for complete separation from Britain was what a significant number of people supported. They were standing for election. People, in general, had metamorphosed from being mildly apolitical to being highly motivated. There was a feeling, throughout the country, of extreme revulsion at the executions of the Volunteers, so it was not surprising that the first seat won, by the advanced Nationalists, was by George Noble, Count Plunkett, father of the executed Joseph, in Roscommon. Soon after this, more by-elections were won, most notably the seat in East Clare, by Eamon de Valera, who was the only leader of the Easter Rising to survive, by virtue of his American birth. The old Parliamentary Party could no longer speak for the Irish people, and the Home Rule movement was all but dead.

The world was changing rapidly. In 1917 the United States entered the world war under the leadership of Woodrow Wilson, who had been re-elected president the year before. This was highly significant for the Irish nationalists, because Wilson, even before America's entry into the war, had declared his belief that 'every people has the right to choose the sovereignty under which they shall live'. This was the new creed, and the Sinn Féiners would cling to it. But first they had to do battle with the British government, to keep Irishmen out of that war.

The conscription crisis of 1918 came very close to the end of the First World War. After the German offensive of March 1918, the British government desperately wanted to raise 150,000 men from Ireland to go to the front. It proved impossible, and they were warned, from every quarter, not to try to get them on a compulsory basis. 'All Ireland will rise against you,' warned John Dillon, who became leader of the Irish Parliamentary Party after the death of John Redmond. They passed the legislation to enforce conscription anyway, and it galvanised people into action. Violence spread throughout the country, but so did politics and, the war being soon over, the conscription crisis became irrelevant, other than as a vehicle with which to arouse people's anti-British feelings. After the Armistice there was a general election and, even though there was a low turn-out, Sinn Féin won an overwhelming number of seats. Many of the new MPs were in jail but the party, nevertheless, set about convening an independent Irish parliament. When it met for the first time on 21 January 1919, it coincided with the opening shots fired in what was to become the Anglo-Irish War. The scene was in Soloheadbeg, County Tipperary, quite close to south Galway. Life soon became very dangerous in rural Ireland and Edward Martyn would be trapped in 'that horrid Tillyra'.

His biggest worry in spring 1918 was that his driver might be conscripted, and that he would be abandoned. 'You might well ask what is going to become of us,' he wrote to Horgan on 3 February. What had become of one of their most beloved came hard on the heels of this plea; the news of the death of Robert Gregory was heartbreaking. Robert had joined up, with public-school enthusiasm, at the outbreak of hostilities. He was a very happy RFC pilot but, while inspecting aero-dromes, he was tragically shot down, in error, by an Italian colleague, in February 1918. The telegram came to Augusta Gregory when she was alone at Coole and she had to make the journey to Galway, by train, to tell her daughter-in-law and grandchildren the dreadful news. She later wrote of how she longed for the train to 'go slower', so terrible was the news she was bringing.

Martyn and his motor, always so generously available to Lady Gregory, were in Dublin, overseeing a revival of *An Enemy of the People*. In April

34 (a) Edward Martyn by Sydney Davis, 1917.

they put on Henry B. O'Hanlon's play *The All Alone*, for which Edward had written the preface. He considered O'Hanlon to be 'a writer of extraordinary imagination and dramatic power'. The critics didn't agree. O'Hanlon's work was generally considered to be too 'talky' and much too 'gloomy', but when it was revived in the following season it got very good reviews. It continued to do so long after Edward Martyn's death, and the dissolution of the Irish Theatre. It was, yet again, an imperfect imitation of Ibsen. Reflecting on this, Seamus O'Kelly, who

34 (b) Grace Gifford by Sydney Davis, 1918.

was then the editor of *Nationality*, confided his thoughts to Holloway: 'The Norwegian carried out his psychology in his plays unflinchingly and, as he is a master of stagecraft as well, usually gets his message across. Martyn, though he possessed psychological insight, and often said good things, lacked dramatic craftsmanship. In most of the plays at the Irish Theatre all the characters are mad.'[24] To see this madness Mr and Mrs Jack Yeats were in the audience for the first night of O'Hanlon's play and, despite the warmth of the June evening, Edward

Martyn sat beside them, wearing 'a peaked cap and a wool caped coat'.[25]

What could the aspiring playwrights do? When a prize of £10 was offered for the best new play, the entrants were told: 'The author must eschew the peasant, the gombeen man, the crossroads publican, and all like characters whose bones, handled and examined for years by students of the drama in Ireland, lie on the dissecting table awaiting the decent burial their long services deserve.' The prize was won by Martin J. McHugh for *The Half Sir*, but it was never performed. Before the season was over Maud Eden, the critic for the *Irishman*, wrote: 'The Abbey Theatre has taught us to know ourselves. It reveals average everyday Ireland. It stands for complete independence in the management of our own affairs. Mr Edward Martyn's theatre stands for something more. It stands boldly, and uncompromisingly, for an independent Ireland, taking her place in Europe, interested in European culture. In the Irish Theatre nationalism and inter-nationalism meet.'[26] What more could they want?

Well, some recognition from Lennox Robinson would have been nice. Robinson, who started the Dublin Drama League in the autumn of 1918, completely ignored them. A simple acknowledgement of their existence, as an art theatre, was all they sought and perhaps the alacrity with which Robinson pinched Martyn's actors was this acknowledgement. Since Robinson had been appointed stage manager of the Abbey, in 1910, he had wanted to produce more realistic plays, and the foundation of this new company was a logical realisation of this aspiration. In September 1918 he wrote to James Stephens: 'For a considerable time now I have been thinking and talking about the desirability of establishing in Dublin some organization for the purpose of securing productions of plays, which we otherwise have no chance of seeing.'[27]

They had had some chance; Edward Martyn had given it to them. He was hurt, and he complained to Holloway that 'the Drama League ignored the work his company had been doing for years'.[28] Many agreed with this, including the playwright T.C. Murray, and didn't join Robinson's new society because they disliked 'their way of ignoring Martyn and his efforts altogether'.[29] But perhaps that wasn't the whole story. On 23 October 1918 Edward wrote to Ernest Boyd regarding the Drama League, and included: 'My difficulty always as to [?] patronizing newspapers, and part membership of theatrical organizations, is that I might be made responsible, against my will, in the production of views, or works of which I might extremely disapprove. I have complete control at the Irish Theatre.'[30] And, in the end, that's how he liked it. It did mean, however, that Hardwicke Street was no longer the only art theatre in town. Holloway predicted that the Drama League would not last, since it was being run on a highly democratic basis, but he was wrong.

Mícheál Mac Líammóir joined the League at its inception. It would become the embryo of his Gate Theatre, founded ten years later. Robinson wrote, in his history of the Abbey, that he had gladly stepped aside to make room for the Gate. But before Mac Líammóir parted company with the Irish Theatre, he did some good work for Edward Martyn. In September 1918, at the opening of the season, they put on John Galsworthy's comedy *Joy*, in which he played the adolescent lover. It was the only play by an English writer that they produced, and it was a success. Mac Líammóir was 19 years old, and very ambitious to learn everything he could. A few months later he designed a mountaintop set for Martyn's last play. It was 'unusually elaborate'.

18 · The Final Curtain

IN THE SUMMER OF 1919 it was reported that Edward Martyn had moved from his flat in South Leinster Street, to rooms in Clare Street. This address has also been described as above an art and furniture shop in Nassau Street (the three streets adjoin each other). But his letters to Barrett H. Clarke, in the summer of 1920, are still from the South Leinster Street address. Both addresses would have been convenient to the Kildare Street Club but, suffering from an extreme form of arthritis, why he chose to live in rooms that required him to climb stairs is odd. The poet Oliver St John Gogarty used to watch him get in his motor to go not much more than fifty yards, from his rooms to the club. He still lived in Dublin in the same monkish austerity that he had once enjoyed in the tower in Tillyra, with plain oaken chairs, a table and churchwarden pipes galore. 'His austerity appertained to everything except his appetite', and Gogarty, being a surgeon as well as writer, knew this would soon kill him. His 'protein-crippled' limbs would not, for much longer, sustain the 'carnivorous festival of rheumatism and gout' he enjoyed in the Club. Watching him of an evening, Gogarty often saw 'the trousers striped grey and black and the short black coat disappear gradually into the motor'.[1]

It is possible that Martyn moved into a slightly bigger and warmer flat in Dublin because he intended spending a lot more time there. He was terrified in Tillyra and he was very anxious to sell it. In April 1920 Augusta Gregory notes in her journal that she met him at the Abbey and he was 'very gloomy'. He was trying to sell Tillyra, but 'the Hemphills will not give his price'.[2] It would have been precipitate for the Hemphills to 'buy' Tillyra from Edward Martyn, since they were going to inherit it anyway. In his 1909 will he bequeathed all his estate, and his mansion, to his cousin or, should she predecease him, to her son, Andrew Hemphill. This also included Dun Guaire Castle, which the Hempills sold on to the Reddingtons for £90, and they, in turn, sold it to Oliver St John Gogarty for £90. There was no right of succession on Tillyra, so this was simple family loyalty, and it did not change. Lady Hemphill inherited Tillyra, and she didn't give Edward Martyn any money for it. Still, he had a right to be fearful. In early 1919 there was a breakdown of law and order; local peasants simply assumed ownership of his land and pushed out the legitimate grazing tenants. He took his case to the new 'Sinn Féin Courts'.[3]

These 'Dáil Courts' which, from 1919, supplemented the British machinery of justice in a large part of rural Ireland, started out as simple 'arbitration courts', set up to meet the flood of litigation regarding land. As the First Dáil, the independent parliament set up in 1919, developed, however, so did the courts and they became relatively powerful in some parts of the country. Edward Martyn's case was one of the first to be arbitrated in the Sinn Féin Court in Gort. They found in his favour, but it made little difference. Augusta Gregory noted that when the grazing tenants came back after the judgment, they were pushed out and 'those that bid for hay at the Tillyra auction without leave are in their beds since'.[4] Later, sometime in 1921 during the 'Black and Tan' terror, Martyn asked John MacDonagh to help him deal with his tenants. MacDonagh spoke to Michael Collins, then head of the IRA, but little could be done, given the chaotic times in which they were living. Edward was lucky that he could get away from his fear by thinking of other things.

Regina Eyre was his last play to be performed in his lifetime but, in 1922, he wrote Barrett H. Clarke that he had just completed 'a new play in five acts called *The Family Tradition*'.[5] It was a play that never saw the light of day, let alone the footlights, and that was a mercy, for *Regina Eyre* was not a success, and people close to Edward Martyn were getting weary of his poor dramatic attempts. 'A Drama in Elective Moods' is how he described *Regina Eyre*, and the critics had fun with the fatuity of the description. Even John MacDonagh, with the best will in the world, was puzzled. When he read the script, he suggested to Martyn that it seemed like *Hamlet*, and Martyn replied: 'I'll make a confession to you – that's what I tried to do – write a female Hamlet.'[6] It was never published.

From a rehearsal script, however, Stephen F. Ryan wrote a summary,[7] and many of the critics documented what the play was about, in so far as they could understand it: Regina is the daughter of Magnus Eyre, who lives near Carrantuohill, County Kerry, the highest point in Ireland. At the opening of the play she is studying in Germany, and her mother dies in her absence. When she returns to Ireland, she finds that her father has already married his sister-in-law, Dympna. Dympna's husband has died under suspicious circumstances and Regina's friend, a young female doctor, tells her that there was a question of poisoning in both deaths. Then Regina has a dream in which her mother tells her that her life's task must be to avenge her death. She tells her, also, that her father and her aunt must repent. In the shelter of Carrantuohill (this is the mountain-set, designed by Mícheál Mac Líammóir, which most people came to see) Regina contemplates what she must do. She is joined by Magnus, who now suspects Dympna of murdering his wife, and by the lover, Colm Joyce, whom she rejected before going to Germany.

Dympna becomes aware of Regina's suspicions and follows her to the mountain. She attempts to kill her, but is thwarted by Colm, who knocks the pistol from her hand but does not kill her. They all climb the mountain, as an act of redemption, where Dympna, losing her footing, falls to her death. Father and daughter are reconciled and Magnus Eyre, a typical Martyn character, returns to his reclusive life as a writer and teacher. He has his life's work in front of him: 'I would regenerate this starved and ruined country whose gifted people are barbarised by the dual despotism of half-civilised masters, I would make her great in the arts again, as long ago.'[8]

So, although Regina is Edward Martyn's *Hamlet*, Magnus Eyre is the chief protagonist. He is the flawed idealist, the 'Carden Tyrell'. We do not need a full script to see that we are back to Martyn's 'soul in crisis' theme, but it is not Regina/Hamlet's soul, but the soul of Magnus Eyre/Edward Martyn. Still, it has a positive ending, a change in this form of drama from Edward Martyn.

The critics were almost unanimous in their condemnation of the play in general, but few referred to its similarity to *Hamlet*. However, the reviewer in the *Leader* (almost certainly D.P. Moran) could not resist: 'There was not a laugh, nay not so much as a smile, in the whole play; even in *Hamlet* and *Macbeth* there is some comic relief; but of course

Edward Martyn would not deign to take a tip from Shakespeare – at least intentionally.'[9] Jacques in the *Independent* was fascinated by the idea of 'elective moods'. He quoted many of the lines, wondering if they were 'elective moods': 'Contemplation is greater than action: ideas dominate the world' and 'philosophies are powerless against wretched miseries'. The drama critic in the *Freeman's Journal* contended that the play should be stopped until something was done about the excessive dialogue, which was often 'desultory and sometimes rather pointless'.[10]

When Stephen F. Ryan wrote a reflective piece on this play in *Studies*, in the summer of 1958, he was very hard, but perhaps realistic, about Edward Martyn: 'The strange paradox that is Edward Martyn', he wrote, 'is best illustrated by his almost sublime opinion of his own merit as playwright. The subtly acute critic of Ibsen; the standard-bearer of what was essentially right in music, architecture and art of the church; the man who saw through so much of the sham, and hypocrisy, of his century – this same man was certainly his own worse critic.' He was outraged that Martyn had attempted to write a play 'that is *Hamlet* in reverse'. Martyn, he wrote, 'was a playwright of heroic conceit'.[11] It is difficult to argue with the notion that Edward Martyn wrote his plays for himself, and 'inflicted' them on his audience, but this 'conceit' was mitigated by the other good things that he had to offer to an Irish audience, not the least being their first glimpse of Anton Chekhov's *The Cherry Orchard*.

The Cherry Orchard came to the Irish Theatre on 23 June 1919 and ran for six nights. On 21 June *New Ireland* had published an essay by Edward Martyn, preparing the public for what was to come. He was quite sure, as Thomas MacDonagh had been over *Uncle Vanya*, that the audience might not be up to Chekhov's 'coherent incoherence', if they did not have a little coaching first. We should welcome the performance of *The Cherry Orchard*, he told his readers:

> ... for if ever the mirror of social life, in its especial inanity, has been held up to us with the sure hand of a genius it is in this curious drama. ... To see that there is nothing preposterous in what I say one has only to sit silent, and listen to the general conversation that goes on at parties, or in clubs, and hear the incoherent nonsense that flows in rivers from the mob around one [for E.M. this was the middle classes] ... the mob is incoherent, but Tchekoff [*sic*] is the delineator of incoherence.

> In fact he seems to have reduced the incoherence and absurdity of average humanity to a system. He is not concerned with the psychology of remarkable minds, which the great masters of drama have made so fascinating to the civilised remnant of humanity, who will still use the theatre as a place for intellectual enjoyment … he is a photographer of average humanity, an enormously clever constructor of films which he passes before you with a skill that makes such combinations that we are often touched with their pathos, as with their primal sadness of life.

And for his greatest accolade, Martyn told them: 'He is second only to Ibsen.'[12]

The audience was not grateful for the 'lecture', or for the play. The critics were not as hard as they had been on *Uncle Vanya*, and they admired the little theatre for attempting the play. The reviewer in the *Evening Telegraph* of 24 June had mixed reactions, mainly finding good performances, but a stage much too small for a play of this size. He concluded his longish review, nevertheless, on a positive note: 'When all is said and done, the performance of such a work is interesting, and will probably serve to drive people to read the play to see how much, or how little, is in it.' Clearly the play was worthwhile to an Irish audience, especially as the 'land question' in *The Cherry Orchard* had such resonances for the Irish situation of the period. *The Leader*, on 5 July, manifested its usual philistinism by wondering: 'Is Edward Martyn a Bolshevist?' They couldn't tell, since they did not know what a Bolshevist was. But they knew that a Bolshevist came from Russia, and that 'the latest play at Mr. Martyn's "Irish" theatre comes from Russia also'. As far as they were concerned, if 'Mr. Martyn' knew what he was doing, he would have translated this play into Irish.

This demand for the Irish Theatre to perform only Irish plays, and plays in the Irish language, was getting stronger and stronger. One wonders where Moran, the populist, thought he might get his audience? Or where he might get a scholar in Ireland willing, or able, to translate the Russian master? In the early days of the Irish Literary Theatre, and of the Abbey Theatre, leaders of the Gaelic League, such as Eoin MacNeil, had been hoping to cater for a folk audience, but the playwrights, especially J.M. Synge, were not writing for such an audience. While Synge wrote about the imagination of the peasant, he was not writing his plays for the peasants, and he did not expect them to turn up in the theatre. All the leaders of the cultural renaissance, including Padraig Pearse and Padraic O'Conaire, both of whom wrote their poetry in simple Irish, shared this view. They were more interested in a cultured audience, than a popular one.[13] For Edward Martyn, there was also his belief that a European resonance was vital in the Irish theatre, to help the nation become truly European, albeit maintaining its own unique culture. His anti-Englishness did not include any antipathy to the English language and while, as a young man, he had expressed a wish to George Moore that he would like to write his plays in Irish he knew, by 1920, this would never be possible. What he was trying to achieve, through the medium of theatre, could not be achieved by presenting poor translations of great plays to non-existent audiences.

When *The Cherry Orchard* was revived in January 1920 it got very good reviews and Brinsley MacNamara, the novelist and critic, thought it the finest thing he had seen on an Irish stage in years. The comedian Jimmie O'Dea was in the cast. But, by then, John MacDonagh was gone. Edward Martyn had appointed a new manager, Robert Herdman Pender. MacDonagh had had enough. He believed, rightly, that the Chekhov play had been a good production, and he was ground down by the poor reviews even though Darrell Figgis, in a new Dublin weekly, wrote: 'For the production John MacDonagh deserves the highest praise. It was simple and direct of composition – that difficult quality in all art, especially difficult with so many characters to compose – and the setting was equally simple and beautiful.'[14] MacDonagh was, understandably, tired of rewriting Martyn's work, but he was never disloyal. Years later he spoke of what Martyn had tried to do: 'All his plays had a fine idea and he tried to develop them on Ibsen's lines but the scaffolding to support his ideas was not always well made. His dialogue was sometimes stilted, but his fine lyrical moments redeemed every fault.'[15]

John MacDonagh had many talents and was, by 1920, making motion pictures, as well as writing and producing plays. Between 1916 and 1922 he produced no fewer than eleven films. In 1920 he was working on his great success, *Willie Reilly and his Colleen Bawn*, which remains a classic to the present day. There had been tragedy in his life and more ahead, when his young brother Joseph died in 1922, from appendicitis. In jail, during the Civil War, the complaint had been neglected, and it did irreversible damage.

Edward Martyn went back to Tillyra for the summer and the social life went on. Dinners at Coole with Yeats, and driving Augusta Gregory's friends to the local tourist spots, passed the days. But by January 1920 the Goughs had left Lough Cutra and Gregory reports: 'an exodus from the country'. In Dublin the theatre opened for its last season with the revival of *The Cherry Orchard*. When it was loudly applauded Martyn declared: 'This must not be, it will never do for us to play down to the audience.'[16] But the little theatre could not sustain the loss of MacDonagh. The 'Company' remained loyal, but they did not like the new manager and there was continuous petty infighting. They were all nationalists, with a shared history in the struggle for independence, but Pender, an Englishman, did not share their history and, while this was not the cause of the annoyance, it exacerbated it. When Countess Plunkett cancelled the lease on the premises in Hardwicke Street, in March, it spelt the death-knell for Edward Martyn's last theatrical venture.

No one ever knew, for sure, why the Countess cancelled the lease. It was rumoured that she did so because the theatre was planning to put on Eimar O'Duffy's play *Bricriu's Feast*, which ridiculed her son's poetry. *Bricriu's Feast* does not ridicule Joseph Mary Plunkett's poetry, although his novel, *The Wasted Island*, concentrates on the struggle between the moderates and the extremists in the Irish Volunteeers (O'Duffy did not support the Easter Rising). It also attacks the literary movement, and satirises 'minor poets'. It is likely that the Plunkett family did not like Eimar O'Duffy, but the loss of the lease, anyway, should not have brought the blinds down so finally on the theatre. Afterwards Martyn told Augusta Gregory that he was sorry 'he didn't build a theatre twenty years ago and put the key in his pocket'.[17]

In south Galway the summer of 1920 was hell. Edward Martyn and Augusta Gregory stayed close. For 18 July, after a day in Tillyra, Gregory reported in her diary that the castle had been raided by the military. It was suspected that Martyn had been hiding Volunteers under the rugs and books in the back of his car, on his way home from Dublin. Also, in Dublin, his flat had been raided because 'Paul Farrell [well-known actor] had borrowed his room for a rehearsal of "The Enemy of the People"', and the windows being open, the shouts and strong language in the scene of the meeting had reached the windows of Kildare Street Club, and the authorities were informed he was holding a Sinn Féin meeting. Edward was in happy mood that day, reminiscing about the tenor John McCormack, who had been one of his choir boys at the Pro-Cathedral: 'He was rather insubordinate and was put out: and he was not popular, because he used to play ball with the police.'[18] The choir was always on his mind, and he was in constant touch with Vincent O'Brien. In the midst of all the mayhem he wrote O'Brien, on 24 July, that he was reading Wagner's autobiography and finding it of 'absorbing interest'.[19]

By 30 September Gregory's diary entries were far more sombre: 'I was quite ill, could not eat or sleep after the homecoming – the desolation of that burnt forge, and all one hears ... Edward Martyn's beautiful little village hall burnt down. Two lorries of military came into Gort "firing and shouting", and the people brought out their furniture from their houses expecting the burnings to begin. "Black and Tans and police and military" burnt Burke's house ... the bodies of five policemen were carried through Gort.' Peter Glynn, a neighbour, told her 'Mr. Martyn's beautiful hall they didn't leave a stone of it.'[20] But she already knew. With the exception of a letter to Vincent O'Brien, and one to Barrett H. Clarke, the only reports we have of Edward throughout that awful summer come from Augusta Gregory. They were a comfort to each other. When they were together he brought her up to speed on who was who in Sinn Féin. He knew all the leading lights in the struggle. He told her how he had known de Valera and liked him; Roger Casement had funded the little school in Tawin, Connemara, where de Valera taught, and Edward Martyn was supposed to look after. He had fond memories, too, of Sinéad de Valera from her acting days. He preferred Arthur Griffith to them all, and thought him the only true statesman. He assured her, however, that 'Michael Collins of the Volunteer Army is the man', although he knew nothing of him.

He continued to travel up and down to Dublin in his motor. There was much speculation about why he had given up the theatre. Many knew that he was trying to sell Tillyra, and assumed he had money problems. His will, just a few years later, revealed no money problems. In May 1921 he published an article in *Banba* about the difficulties, as he saw it, in the drama. In a letter accompanying the article he wrote: 'I have thrown together in this little article all I have to say about the Drama at present. It is quite futile to talk about our work in the Theatre at present, until some change as is here hinted at takes place. Most of the people around me made development impossible, and finally made chaos.'[21] And then, in the article proper, he attacks the actors. They didn't understand what the 'drama of ideas' was about, and what was required of them. He was a reformer, and the actors were performers and, as such, only interested in 'the vanity of his or her own personality'. Although he exempted some actors from this vanity, the article, on the whole, is unfair to many people who had been very loyal to him. Also it is hardly the truth about the closure of the theatre, which almost certainly came about through a lack of energy. Edward Martyn had started the project with two ambitious and energetic men; he simply could not run it on his own, especially if the actors were undermining the authority of the new manager.

He continued to worry about money all the same. The summer of 1921 was an improvement on the previous one and, by September, settlement talks were bringing the war to a close. That month Augusta Gregory brought her two granddaughters to Tillyra and, 'Edward sent them to the castle with Owen and let them play the organ in the hall and gave us tea and was very pleasant … approves of my keeping Coole, but thinks I have great courage. … He says George Moore is very angry about Miss Mitchell's life of him[22] … but Edward says "she took the only possible way of dealing with you as Mon Ami Moore". He is anxious about money, has fears of his investment in English railways, and is crippled with rheumatism.'[23]

In December he was back in Dublin to attend the opening of John MacDonagh's play *The Irish Jew* at the Abbey. It was the last time they met. The Anglo-Irish Treaty had been signed on 6 December, and was ratified in the Dáil on the 7 January 1922. It led to the first independent government in Ireland since the Act of Union in 1800. Edward Martyn was delighted. He had written to Barrett H. Clarke in September: 'We are longing for some permanent and peaceful settlement here which will at least be favourable to the publishing of books.'[24] On 14 January Gregory noted: 'I had been to see Edward Martyn in the afternoon in his warm little flat; very crippled but more cheerful than I had seen him for a long time at the exit of the "Tans". He is all for the Treaty and blames de Valera's doings here as much as he had admired them in America. He will listen to no excuse, says "he is jealous of Griffith. I met him in Gort at the time of his Clare election I was doing my marketing and he and another, I forget who, had come to hold a meeting there and I talked to them in their motor and I said "You will get on all right as long as you hold to Griffith, and I saw a shadow cross their faces". I spoke of de Valera's honesty and his belief that he is doing the best thing for Ireland, but he wound up as he began, "It's all jealousy of Griffith".'[25] Two days later Dublin Castle, the seat of British power in Ireland, was surrendered to Michael Collins, the new chairman of the Provisional Government, but peace was short-lived.

In May 1922 Martyn wrote to Clarke, more in hope than anticipation, inviting him to Tillyra. He was expecting to spend only the summers in south Galway, and he hoped that 'you will excuse the reduced state you will find everything in. I am carrying on under difficulties in disastrous times'.[26] In this long letter to the impresario he offers to send him letters from George Moore but 'on starting to look for them I can nowhere find them. I must have burned them some years ago, although I can't remember that I did;' (it is likely that he had forgotten that he gave many of his letters from Moore to John Horgan). He also directs Clarke to his entry in *Who's Who*, where the researcher might have been amused to find that under 'recreation' Martyn listed: 'George Augustus Moore'.[27] But the times quickly became even more disastrous; there would be no visitors. On Wednesday 28 June the anti-Treaty forces attacked the Four Courts in Dublin, and civil war broke out across the country. The Kildare Street Club had been already occupied by Irregular soldiers on 1 May and Martyn thought that he might be caught in cross-fire,[28] so he made for south Galway where he was pleased to find no trouble.

Soon he was trapped in Tillyra. In July his car was stolen in Ballinasloe. He had loaned it to a family to take a man, who had gone out of his mind, to the Asylum there. It was a cold wet summer and, on 12 October, he wrote Vincent O'Brien, at 37 Parnell Square West: 'I got a stroke of paralysis and have been laid up since.' At least then he could write. In December, when he contacted Sarah Purser, his chauffeur, Owen Linnane, did the writing: 'I got a stroke of paralysis three months ago and am not fit to be moved to Dublin. ... I quite agree with you that nothing could be more melancholy than the times. We who believed in Griffith thought that all he wanted was a chance of power.[29] We little dreamed of the de Valera difficulty in the background. It became hopeless when Ireland chose de Valera to Griffith [?]. She at once dropped into the old tradition. Tim Healy, the apostle of faction, is the fitting president of such a country. I hope to see the glass when I return. I am getting Owen to write this as I cannot write in comfort yet. Affectionately yours, E.M.'

By March 1923 he was still able to dictate letters to Owen Linnane, but only just. He wrote to Vincent O'Brien: 'Father Cyril [the Provincial of the Carmelites in Dublin, to whom he bequeathed his library and such paintings as were not donated to the Municipal Gallery] is here, and is a great comfort. Goodbye I'm in fearful pain. I can hardly dictate.'[30] After that Linnane kept O'Brien informed and the latter made a visit to Tillyra in August to say goodbye. But, not surprisingly, Augusta Gregory was the person most affected and who leaves us the most detailed account of Edward Martyn's last days. In September she wrote to her sister Arabella:

> On the way back from Galway we got to Tulira about 6.30. The chauffeur had never been there before and instead of stopping at the hall-door drove a little past it, and there, in the bow window of the Library, I saw Edward sitting. I thought he would turn and look round at the noise, but he stayed quite immovable, like a stuffed figure, it was quite uncanny. I rang the bell and Dolan the butler appeared, said he was only 'pretty well', but showed me into the drawing room, and came back to say Edward would like to see me. I went in but he did not turn his head, gazed before him. I touched his hands (one could not shake them – all crippled, Dolan says he has to be fed), and spoke to him. He slowly turned his eyes, but apparently without recognition. I went on talking without response till I asked if he had any pain and he whispered, "No. Thank God". I didn't know if he knew me, but presently he whispered "How is Robert?" I said "He is well, as we all are in God's hands. He has gone before me and before you". Then I said, "My little grandson Richard is well", and he said with difficulty and in a whisper, "I am very glad of that". Then I came away, there was no use staying. I had seen a man (his nurse) behind the screen when I came in but he went away. ... Dolan had tea ready but I could not have touched anything, it seems such a house of death. Poor Edward every moment was picking at the rug over his knees. I thought the best thing to do was to write to Lady

Hemphill, as I had promised to write when I saw her in Dublin some time ago.[31]

The nurse that Gregory refers to was Laurence Burke, a medical student, for whom Edward Martyn, generous to the last, added a codicil to his will on 31 August, so that he might receive £1000, free of legacy duty, to enable him to continue his medical studies. Martyn's signature on the codicil is a simple 'x'. In early December he had an operation to remove a tumour from his brain. The surgeon in attendance was J.P. Magennis, who had played Guy Font in *An Enchanted Sea*, almost twenty years before. He lost a great deal of blood and, on 7 December, Linnane wrote to Vincent O'Brien: 'The end has come for poor Mr. Martyn. He died a most happy death. May God have mercy on him.' The death certificate reads 'cerebral compression and respiratory failure'. The date was 5 December 1923. John Dolan, 'butler in the house where his master died', was the witness.

Augusta Gregory wrote in her journal:

> Though he had been too ill to see of late and I had not been able to go and see him before because of the broken bridge and my difficulty about rough roads, I feel a loneliness now he is gone. He was from the beginning of my life here at Coole a good neighbour; he was always grateful for my husband's interest in him. He was very kind to Robert, giving him his first real gun and letting him and his friends shoot Tulira in the holidays. And then when Yeats' summers and the Theatre project began, he was constantly here walking over and staying to dine. It was George Moore who brought that work [to an end], putting his own name to *The Bending of the Bough*, rewritten by him and Yeats but on Edward's foundation. And Edward had been weak about *The Countess Cathleen* and took a wrong turning, I think, in withdrawing his support for our Theatre. Of late I was told he felt his support of Sinn Fein in the beginning had been wrong. It was on his conscience. And yet he hated, with a real hatred, England … the country people believed him to be a descendant of Oliver Cromwell – perhaps that is why they never warmed to him (nor he to them).[32]

What happened in the end clearly shocked her. On 21 December she wrote:

Yesterday's paper told of Edward Martyn's funeral; he had directed in his will that his body, like those of many of the friendless poor, should be placed at the service of Cecilia Street School of Surgery, and when it had served its purpose then should be interred in the common grave which holds the unclaimed workhouse dead. The poor body was taken to Glasnevin [cemetery, close to Dublin city] in the workhouse van with six other bodies being buried by the Union. His coffin, the same as theirs. A mass was celebrated in the Cemetery Chapel for him, and the nameless six who were to share his grave; the 'Benedictus' was sung when they were lowered into the earth by the Choir he had endowed.[33]

George Moore, too, was shocked when he came to learn of the method of disposal of Edward's body. It spoiled the pleasure he had in being bequeathed the two plays, which he believed to be rightfully his anyway.[34] There was no word from Yeats who, in November, had received the Nobel Prize for Literature.

All the papers reported his death and most of the obituaries were respectful and fair. They included most of the highlights of his life, and the controversies. He would have liked best the one in the *Freeman's Journal* which was headed 'Death of a Dramatist', and making the point that 'Guy Font' (J.P. Magennis) had attended him at the end. The *Irish Times* wrote of 'a kindly and generous man of no small intellectual ability and artistic taste'. They also reflected on his missing presence on the streets of Dublin where his 'heavy figure, full round face and short stepping gait' was a physical loss felt by many.

In the *Dublin Magazine* for January 1924 John MacDonagh paid an elegant tribute to his friend and reminded us of Edward Martyn's essential humanity:

> One would be dull indeed who did not catch a spark from that mind, stored with culture and experience; and it would be a nature bereft of sympathy that did not expand in that kindly and genial presence. He had a childlike pleasure in having someone to talk to 'I thought you weren't coming', he would say. 'Sit down and let us talk' and he would smoke his long churchwarden, and midnight would often find me still there. His

charm and grace of manner were not of this age, that courtly dignity belonged to the statelier periods in which he lived spiritually. He had a pleasant and joyous sense of humour, little suspected by those who only knew the Edward Martyn, founder of the Palestrina Choir. The main ambition of his life was to rescue Ireland from the blighting affect of English culture and ideas ... to this end he devoted his life, and money, and to-day there are signs, however shadowy and indistinct, that he did not labour in vain.

Notes

CHAPTER 1 – SMYTHS AND MARTYNS

1   *Galway Vindicator*, 29 January 1859.
2   Irish Registry of Deeds, Land Registry of Ireland Book No. 126.
3   King's Inns List, 456.
4   Burke's *Landed Gentry of Ireland*, 1912.
5   Patrick Melvin, *Irish Genealogist*, 1999.
6   Most of the information on the town of Loughrea is taken from *Lewis's Topographical Directory* 1837.
7   Edmund Yates, *Recollections and Experiences* (London: Richard Bentley & Sons, 1884).
8   *Tuam Herald*, 26 September 1840.
9   The Great Famine lasted from 1845 to 1849.
10 Denis Gwynn, Edward Martyn's first biographer, claimed that the Smyths made their fortune buying land that became available under the Encumbered Estates Act, 1849. In fact, they were very wealthy before the enforcement of this Act. James Smyth made money by using his land to the best possible advantage.
11 Impoverished Galway landlords regularly met in Loughrea to agitate for a reduction in the Poor Law rate. They argued that they were carrying all the costs of the Famine.
12 *Galway Vindicator*, April 1848.
13 The bulk of the information on the early Martyn family is taken from Jerome Fahy's *Diocese of Kilmacduagh*, and from the unpublished work of Adrian Martyn of Ardrahan, County Galway.
14 James Hardiman's *Galway*, reissued by the *Connaught Tribune*, 1926.
15 Unpublished research into the Martyn tribe by Adrian Martyn.
16 Jerome Fahy, *The History and Antiquities of the Diocese of Kilmacduagh* (Dublin: M.H. Gill, 1893).
17 Most of the Galway gentry were related to each other. One of the more interesting quirks of history that this threw up was the distant cousin relationship between Edward Martyn, first President of Sinn Féin and Edward Carson, founder of the Ulster Volunteers. Carson's mother was the great-great-great-granddaughter of Sibella Martyn of Tullira Castle.
18 Galway Diocesan Library – unsigned affidavit in box of Martyn family papers.
19 Land Commission of Ireland, Box No. 1492, Martyn papers.
20 Ibid.
21 In the end E.M. inherited most of his uncles' property and his cousin Mary Hemphill got Tillyra.
22 Registry of Deeds, Memorial Book No. 161.
23 W.B. Yeats, *Autobiographies* (London: Macmillan, 1955), 386.
24 Joseph Murphy, *The Reddingtons of Clarinbridge* (Galway: Joseph Murphy, 1999), 124.
25 Galway County Library, Poor Law Union records for 1847.

26   *Galway Mercury*, May 1849.
27   George Moore, *Hail and Farewell* (Gerrards Cross: Colin Smythe Ltd, 1985), 187.
28   Land Commission, Box No. 1492.
29   National Library of Ireland, Loughrea Parish Register.
30   E. M.'s Diary. A retrospective list of travel dates given to the writer by Jerry Nolan of London.

CHAPTER 2 – CHRIST VERSUS APOLLO

1   Sister Marie-Therese Courtney, *Edward Martyn and the Irish Theatre* (New York: Vantage Press, 1952), 12.
2   Ibid., 14.
3   After the publication of George Moore's *A Drama in Muslin* (London: Vizetelly & Co., 1886), Annie Martyn banned him from Tillyra.
4   NLI, MS 2448, Moore to Hone, Maurice Moore collection.
5   Edward Martyn, *An Enchanted Sea* (London: T. Fisher Unwin, 1902).
6   NLI, MS 4479, George Moore to his brother Julian.
7   George Moore, *A Mere Accident* (London: Vizetelly, 1887), 35. In this short novel by Moore, the characters of Norton and his mother are based, almost exclusively, on E.M. and his mother.
8   Richard Ellmann, *Oscar Wilde* (London: Penguin Books, 1988) 75.
9   Ibid., 80.
10   In 1910 Edward Martyn told Joseph Holloway that he didn't mind how gloomy a play was so long as he enjoyed 'sensation'. Holloway thought him a 'crank of the worst kind', Robert Hogan and M.J. O'Neill, *Joseph Holloway's Abbey Theatre* (Southern Illinois University Press, 1966), 137.
11   Twenty years on a marriage connection was established between Oscar Wilde and Edward Martyn when Mary Martyn, Edward's first cousin, married Peter Hemphill, third cousin to Constance Lloyd.
12   John Henry Newman joined the Church of Rome in 1845.
13   Most of the information on this period comes from Linda Dowling, *Hellenism and Homosexuality in Victorian Oxford* (New York: Cornell University Press, 1986).
14   J.J. Winckelmann is regarded as the founder of the modern study of Greek sculptures and antiquities.
15   John Adland, *Stenbock, Yeats and the Nineties* (London: Cecil and Amelia Woulfe,1969).
16   Their children, Karin and Rachel, went on to dintinguish themselves as fine scholars and members of the 'Bloomsbury set'. Karin married Adrian Stephen, Virginia Woolf's brother, and Rachel married Oliver Strachey. Mary's sister, Alys, married and divorced Bertrand Russell.
17   A.K. McComb (ed.), *The Selected Letters of Bernard Berenson* (London: Hutchinson, 1965).
18   Adland, 72.
19   Ibid.
20   Courtney, 17.

CHAPTER 3 – THE SOUL IN CRISIS

1   Adrian Frazier, *George Moore 1852–1933* (London and New Haven, Connecticut: Yale University Press, 2000), 73.
2   George Henry Moore was MP for Mayo and a well-respected landlord.

3   Courtney, *Edward Martyn and the Irish Theatre*, 45.
4   *Landowners in Ireland* (Baltimore, Maryland: Genealogical Publishing Co. Inc., 1988).
5   Brian Jenkins, *Sir William Gregory of Coole* (Gerrards Cross: Colin Smythe, 1986), 284.
6   Gregory Diaries, 22 August 1900, quoted in Lennox Robinson, *Lady Gregory's Journals* (London: Putman and Co., 1946).
7   Gregory Diaries, 1 January 1901, quoted in James Pethica, *Lady Gregory's Diaries 1892–1902* (Gerrards Cross: Colin Smythe, 1996), 296. Hereinafter: Gregory Diaries.
8   Galway Diocesan Archive, Martyn Papers.
9   Elizabeth, Countess Fingall, *Seventy Years Young* (Dublin: Lilliput Press, 1995), 52. As well as this relationship, Daisy Fingall's sister married Nevill Geary, Edward Martyn's best friend.
10 Alan Denson (ed.), *Letters from Æ* (New York: Abelard Shuman, 1961), 82.
11 NLI, MS 4479, Moore Papers.
12 Ibid.
13 George Moore, *A Drama in Muslim* (London: Vizetelly & Company, 1886), 122.
14 Moore, *Hail and Farewell* (Gerrards Cross: Colin Smythe, 1976), 185.
15 NLI, MS 4479, George Moore to Mary Moore, February 1884.
16 Sir William Geary, Bart, Barrister and one time Governor of Nigeria.
17 Frazier, *George Moore*, 23.
18 Walter Pater, *Marius the Epicurean* (London: Penguin Classics, 1985).
19 Ibid., 43.
20 Ibid., 49.
21 Ibid., 52.
22 NLI, MS 4479.
23 Denis Gwynn, *Edward Martyn and the Irish Revival* (London: Jonathan Cape, 1930), 75.
24 Ibid., 78.
25 Ibid., 75.
26 Ibid.
27 *George Moore's Letters to Edouard Dujardin* (New York: Crosby & Guage, 1929).

CHAPTER 4 – 'STRENGTH WITHOUT HANDS TO SMITE'

1   Unpublished Gregory diaries, New York Public Library: Henry W. & Albert A. Berg collection. Hereinafter: Berg.
2   Ibid.
3   Ibid.
4   Fahy, *The Diocese of Kilmacduagh*, 314.
5   It is possible that there more than just friendship between the Persses and the de Basterots. In the parish church at New Quay, in the heart of the Burren in County Clare, there is a stained-glass window dedicated to the memory of Patrick de Basterot-Skerrit. Patrick's mother was a Persse.
6   *Connaught Tribune*, 19 August 1961.
7   Augusta Gregory had a love affair with Wilfrid Scawen Blunt within two years of her marriage to William Gregory. It lasted approximately eighteen months and then they remained friends for life.
8   The Land League was founded by Michael Davitt and John Devoy in 1879 during a period of extreme agitation and violent protest. Its main aim was the protection of tenants and an extension of their rights. Its leaders held the view that the settlement of the land question would ultimately drag the national question in train. It had the support of Charles Stewart Parnell.

9   Edith Finch, *Wilfrid Scawan Blunt* (London: Jonathan Cape, 1938), 250.
10 As Governor of Ceylon, William Gregory had built up relatively happy relations between the ruling and subject peoples and had much sympathy for the causes of small nations. In 1881 he had constantly supported Blunt on the matter in the pages of *The Times*.
11 Gwynn, *Edward Martyn and the Irish Revival*, 56.
12 Ibid., 62.
13 Ibid., 68.
14 Ibid.
15 J.J. Horgan, *Parnell to Pearse* (Dublin: Browne & Nolan, 1948), 112.
16 Donal McCartney, *W.E.H. Lecky, 1838–1903* (Dublin: Lilliput Press, 1994).
17 Ibid., 125.
18 Gwynn, *Edward Martyn and the Irish Revival*, 57.
19 John Morley, *Notes on Politics and History* (London: Macmillan, 1913), 12.
20 *Gregory's Diaries*, December 1895, 99.
21 He had first visited Bayreuth in 1882 for a performance of *Parsifal*.
22 NLI, MS 2646, George Moore to Mary Moore, 22 March 1889.
23 Edward Martyn, *Morgante the Lesser – His notorious life and wonderful deeds*. By Sirius (London: Swann Sonnenscheim, 1890).
24 Thomas Carlyle, *Sartor Resartus* (London: Chapman & Hall, 1865), 268.
25 George Moore, *A Mere Accident*, 27.
26 Martyn, *Morgante the Lesser*, 18.
27 This was dangerous territory for Edward Martyn who kept the works of Arthur Schopenhauer on his bookshelves. One of the focal points of Schopenhauer's theory was that through art man may escape subjection to the will, through free aesthetic contemplation.
28 Martyn, *Morgante the Lesser*, 192.
29 Ibid., 215.
30 Ibid., 248.
31 Lewis Mumford, *The Story of Utopias* (London: Harrap, 1923).
32 Martyn, *Morgante the Lesser*, 252, 253.
33 Ibid., 254.
34 Ibid., 265.
35 Ibid., 288.
36 Walter Pater, *The Renaissance*.
37 Martyn, *Morgante the Lesser*, 281.

CHAPTER 5 – THE BEST OF TIMES

1   Gwynn, *Edward Martyn and the Irish Revival*, 99.
2   Ibid., 100.
3   *Athenaeum*, 12 April 1890.
4   *Saturday Review*, 3 May 1890.
5   George Moore, *Mike Fletcher*, 181.
6   Ibid.
7   Ibid., 46.
8   Martyn to Gregory, NYPL, Martyn File, Berg.
9   Ibid.
10 Leo Tolstoy, *The Kreutzer Sonata* (London: Penguin Classics, 1983).
11 W.S. Lilly, *A Century of Revolution* (London: Chapman & Hall, 1889).

12 Martyn to Morris – reprinted in a short article by Stephen P. Ryan in *Notes and Queries* (Oxford: Oxford University Press, July 1960).
13 Ibid.
14 Martyn, 'Wagner's Parsifal at Bayreuth', *Black and White*, 22 August 1891, 268.
15 Ibid.
16 *Paragraphs for the Perverse* is the introduction to a book of essays that Edward Martyn was working on at the time of his death. The manuscript of the book has been lost, together with the bulk of his papers.
17 Gregory Diaries, February–March 1892, 6. It was later discovered that the 'Valazquez' was not a Velazquez.
18 Ibid.
19 Count Eric Stenbock, 'The other side', in *The Spirit Lamp*, Oxford Journal, June 1893.
20 W.B. Yeats, *The Oxford Book of Modern* Verse (Oxford: Clarendon Press, 1936), ix.
21 Frazier, *George Moore*, 244.
22 NLI, MS 35786 (2), Clonbrock Papers.
23 Gwynn, *Edward Martyn and the Irish Revival*, 103.
24 George Moore, *Hail and Farewell*, 55.
25 *Tuam Herald*, 31 March 1900.
26 Edward Martyn, *The Tale of a Town* and *The Enchanted Sea* (Kilkenny: Standish O'Grady, and London: T. Fisher Unwin, 1902), 10.
27 Gwynn, *Edward Martyn and the Irish Revival*, 142.
28 *Father Mathew Record*, Dublin, April 1943.
29 Gwynn, *Edward Martyn and the Irish* Revival, 143.
30 Robert Ferguson, *Henrik Ibsen* (London: Richard Cohen Books, 1996), 387.
31 Frazier, *George Moore*, 218.
32 Ibid., 242.
33 Edward Martyn, *The Heather Field* (London: Gerald Duckworth, 1899), 218.
34 Martyn to Moore, Berg.
35 W.B. Yeats, *Autobiographies*, 426.
36 Robert Becker, (ed.), 'Letters of George Moore, 1863–1901', (Dissertation, University of Reading, 1980).
37 Finnerman, Harper and Murphy, *Letters to Yeats, Vol. 1.* (London: Macmillan, 1977), 73.
38 Horgan, *Parnell to Pearse*, 116.
39 W.J. Feeney, *Drama in Hardwicke Street* (London: Associated University Presses, 1984).

CHAPTER 6 – ALL THINGS IRISH

1 *Galway Express*, 22 June 1895.
2 Sir William N. Geary, *Nigeria under British Rule* (London: Methuen & Co, 1927), 9.
3 Gregory Diaries, May–July 1894, 29.
4 Frazier, *George Moore*, 245.
5 Ibid.
6 Gregory Diaries, April 1895, 68.
7 Geary, *Nigeria under British Rule*, 9.
8 Gregory Diaries, November 1895, 86.
9 *Savoy*, Autumn 1896 (London: Leonard Smithers), 93–5.
10 Ibid.
11 Yeats, *Autobiographies*, 385–7.
12 Ibid.

13 Roy Foster, *W.B. Yeats, A Life* (Oxford: Oxford University Press, 1997), 165.

14 John Kelly (gen. ed.), *The Collected Letters of W.B. Yeats, 1896–1900*, Vol. 2 (Oxford: Clarendon Press, 1997).

15 Ibid., 658.

16 Gregory Diaries, August 1896, 118.

17 Moore, *Hail and Farewell*, 548.

18 *Savoy*, September 1896.

19 This essay was one of the inspirational texts that brought John Millington Synge to the Aran Isles in 1898.

20 William Sharp (1856–1905) was a Scottish poet who became D.G. Rossetti's biographer. From 1893 he cultivated a second literary style which was innately feminine and wrote under the pseudonym 'Fiona MacLeod'. For many years people believed 'Fiona MacLeod' existed in her own right.

21 Foster, *W.B. Yeats*, 167.

22 Ibid. In correspondence with Edith Somerville, Violet Martin, taking her cue from Michael Morris, who had described the trip to Aran to her, speculated that Yeats was a gentleman 'but hardly by birth', while Symons was 'just a smart little practical man of letters who knows how and has no genius at all.'

23 *Savoy*, 93–5.

24 Yeats, *Autobiographies*, 427.

25 *Daily Chronicle*, 20 January 1899.

26 David B. Eakin and Michael Case, *Selected Plays of George Moore and Edward Martyn* (Gerrards Cross: Colin Smythe, 1995), 271.

27 Ibid., 294.

28 Gwynn, *Edward Martyn and the Irish Revival*, 122.

29 Letter from Rev. J.A. Martyn to Sr. Marie Therese Courtney, 25 January 1948. Given to the writer by Sister Courtney.

30 *Daily Express*, 11 February 1899.

31 Ibid.

32 Harry White, *The Keeper's Recital* (Cork: Cork University Press, 1998), 112.

33 Ibid.

34 *The Speaker*, 1895 reproduced in Gwynn, 173.

CHAPTER 7 – A 'CELTIC' THEATRE

1 Gregory Diaries, 23 February 1897, 128.

2 Elizabeth (Daisy) Fingall, by now, was the wife of Arthur James Plunkett, 11th Earl of Fingall. During her marriage, she had a close friendship with Horace Plunkett, third son of Baron Dunsany. He was a Unionist MP, who later had strong nationalist leanings.

3 Gregory Diaries, June–July 1897, 148.

4 Ibid., 148.

5 Gonne to Yeats, June 1897, *Yeats CL*, ii, 114.

6 Gwynn, *Edward Martyn and the Irish Revival*, 122.

7 Ibid., 118–19.

8 Gregory Diaries, September 1897, 153.

9 Horgan, *Parnell to Pearse*, 116.

10 Enid Layard and Augusta Gregory were close friends. They had both married older men in the diplomatic service and, both being widowed in the early nineties, were able

to offer each other mutual support. But as Augusta Gregory's cultural horizons widened, they drifted apart.

11   Gregory Diaries, September 1897, 153.
12   Yeats to Milligan, 28 July 1897, *Yeats CL*, ii, 128.
13   Gregory Diaries, September 1897, 154.
14   Yeats to Sharp, 20 November 1898, *Yeats CL*, ii, 148.
15   Ibid.
16   Gregory Diaries, November 1897, 157.
17   Ibid., 160.
18   Yeats to Plunkett, May 1898, *Yeats CL*, ii, 225.
19   Gwynn, *Edward Martyn and the Irish Revival*, 104.
20   Yeats to Sharp, 4 July 1898, Yeats *CL*, ii, 249 (n).
21   NLI, P.4645, Martyn to Horgan, August 1910.
22   *Leader*, 20 April 1901.
23   ibid.
24   Harry White, *The Keeper's Recital*, 76.
25   Reprinted in Gwynn, 174–8.
26   White, *The Keeper's Recital*, 80–90.
27   Ibid., 180.
28   Martyn to Gregory, December 1898, Berg.

CHAPTER 8 – CONTROVERSIES

1   *Dublin Daily Express*, 12 January 1899.
2   NLI, MS 1729, Henderson Papers.
3   Allan Wade, *The Letters of W.B. Yeats* (London: Rupert Hart-Davis, 1954), 304.
4   *Daily Chronicle*, 20 January 1899.
5   Edward Martyn, *The Heather Field and Maeve*, introduction by George Moore.
6   *Academy*, 11 February 1899.
7   Ibid., 20–30 January 1899.
8   Yeats CL ii, 302. Published in *Dublin Daily Express*, 28 January 1899.
9   Ibid., 346.
10   Ibid., 360.
11   Count Harry Kessler, *The Diaries of a Cosmopolitan 1918–1937* (London: Phoenix Press, 2000), 344.
12   NLI, MS 8149, Martyn to Purser, 4 March 1899.
13   *Letters to W.B. Yeats* (Finneran, Harper & Murphy), 44–5.
14   Moore, *Hail and Farewell*, 76.
15   Yeats, *CL*, ii, 356.
16   Joseph Hone (ed.), *Letters of J.B. Yeats* (London: Faber and Faber, 1999), 36.
17   Gregory Diaries, 23 February 1899, 218.
18   Richard Pine and Charles Acton, *To 'Talent Alone' – RIAM 1849–1998* (Dublin: Gill & Macmillan, 1998), 227.
19   White, *The Keeper's Recital*, 98.
20   NLI, MS 13068, Yeats Archive.
21   Gregory Diaries, March 1899, 220.
22   Yeats, *CL*, ii, 378.
23   Ibid., 384.
24   NLI, MS 13068, Martyn to Yeats, 29 March 1899.

25 Ibid., MS 30502.
26 Hone, *Letters of J.B. Yeats*, 49.
27 NLI, MS 30502, Yeats Archive.
28 Ibid.
29 Gwynn, *Edward Martyn and the Irish Revival*, 130.
30 Moore, *Hail and Farewell*, 185.
31 Yeats, *CL*, ii, Biographical and Historical Appendix, 674.
32 Ibid., 708.
33 Ibid., 675.
34 Ibid., 670.
35 Ibid.
36 Hogan and O'Neill, *Joseph Holloway's Abbey Theatre*, 6. Hereinafter: Holloway

CHAPTER 9 – A LITERARY THEATRE

1   Holloway, 6.
2   James Joyce, *A Portrait of an Artist as a Young Man* (London: Penguin Classics, 1999), 245.
3   Hilary Pyle, *Red-Headed Rebel* (Dublin: Woodfield Press, 1998), 112.
4   Holloway, 7.
5   Moore, *Hail and Farewell*, 105.
6   Ibid., 106
7   Ibid., 108.
8   Holloway, 9.
9   Yeats, *CL*, ii, 410.
10 Ibid., 411.
11 *Saturday Review*, 13 May 1899.
12 Ibid.
13 The bulk of the reviews of the plays of the ILT are to be found in the Henderson Archive in NLI, MS 7273.
14 Frazier, *George Moore*, 271.
15 George Moore, *Hail and Farewell*, 129.
16 Ibid., 139.
17 Anthony Cronin, *No Laughing Matter, The Life and Times of Flann O'Brien* (New York: Frome International Publishing Corporation, 1998), 54.
18 Moore, *Hail and Farewell*, 162.
19 Denson (ed.), *Letters from Æ*, 33.
20 Moore, *Hail and Farewell*, pp. 144, 145.
21 *The Athenneum*, 10 June 1899.
22 Becker, *Moore Letters*, 807.
23 Frazier, *George Moore*, 276.
24 Ibid., 158.
25 Becker, *Moore Letters*, 807.
26 Gregory to Yeats, November 1900, Berg.
27 Yeats, *Autobiographies*, 427.
28 Moore to Gregory, 7 November 1899, Berg.
29 The Irish Local Government Act of 1898 gave Ireland local government on the British model. They set up county councils. It was revolutionary in that it shifted local power from the landlord class to the petit bourgeoisie and it was an invaluable training ground for self-government.
30 Yeats, *CL*, ii, 464.

31   Ibid., 473/475.
32   Martyn to Walsh, 29 November 1899, Dublin Diocesan Archive.

CHAPTER 10 – POLITICAL DRAMA

1   NLI, MS 13482 (1), Martyn to Gill.
2   George Moore, *Hail and Farewell*, 305.
3   F.S.L. Lyons, *Ireland since the Famine* (London: Weidenfeld and Nicolson, 1991), 213.
4   Gregory Diaries, 227. Alice Milligan (1866–1953) was an active nationalist despite her Ulster Presbyterian background. Her play *The Last of Feast the Fianna* was staged alongside *Maeve* for the second season of the ILT.
5   Martyn to Gregory, 15 January 1900, Berg.
6   Gregory Diaries, 228, 229.
7   Ibid., 231.
8   Ibid.
9   Ibid., 235.
10   Yeats, *CL*, ii, 492.
11   Holloway, 10.
12   Gregory Diaries, 242.
13   Ibid., 243.
14   *Irish Daily Independent*, 21 February 1900, 5.
15   *Irish Figaro*, 3 March 1900, 130.
16   Gregory Diaries, 245.
17   NLI, MS 2448, Moore to Martyn, 27 February 1890.
18   *Samhain*, September 1901, 12.
19   *Daily Express*, 23 February 1900.
20   Gregory Diaries, 246.
21   *Tuam Herald*, 31 March 1900.
22   *Galway Observer*, 31 March 1900.
23   Ibid. (All the correspondence regarding E.M.'s resignation was republished in this newspaper on 31 March 1900, and in the *Dublin Daily Express*, 24 March 1900).
24   Martyn to Gregory, 5 April 1900, Berg.
25   Gregory Diaries, 247.
26   Martyn to Gregory, 15 April 1900, Berg.
27   Fingall, *Seventy Years Young*, 300.
28   *Freeman's Journal*, 16 April 1900.
29   Gwynn, *Edward Martyn and the Irish Revival*, 288.
30   *Galway Observer*, 14 April 1900.
31   *Tuam Herald*, 5 May 1900.
32   Gregory Diaries, 1 January 1901, 296.
33   *Freeman's Journal*, 16 April 1900.
34   Gregory Diaries, 275.
35   Feeney, *Drama in Hardwicke Street*, 141.
36   *Leader*, 8 September 1900.
37   Gregory Diaries, 279.
38   Ibid. And letter already cited – Martyn to Moore, 28 September 1900, Berg.
39   It was surprising that A.G. did not include something by E.M. in this book. At the time he had just published *Ireland's Battle for her Language*, a fairly creditable pamphlet and superior to some of the essays that were included.

CHAPTER 11 – THE *LEADER*

1 Yeats, *CL*, ii, 598.
2 Gregory Diaries, 297.
3 Gregory to Yeats, 23 December 1900, Berg.
4 *Leader*, 1 September 1900.
5 Edward Martyn, *Ireland's Battle for her Language*, Gaelic League Pamphlet No. 2. 1901, 3.
6 *Leader*, 6 October 1900.
7 Ibid., 20 October 1900, 119. There was one decree dating back to 1862 emanating from the Provincial Council of Cologne. It decreed that a choir which responds to an officiating priest is actually taking part in the liturgical action; therefore it cannot contain women since women are excluded from the service of the altar. This was often ignored so, in 1903, in an attempt to bring order to the chaotic liturgy of the Church, Pope Pius X, in his *Morto Proprio*, did ban women from certain church choirs.
8 Ibid., 8 November 1900, 152.
9 Martyn to O'Brien, 7 March 1914. Papers in the possession of Mrs Elizabeth O'Brien.
10 James Joyce, *Dubliners* (London: Penguin Books, 1992), 195.
11 *Leader*, 20 April 1901, 120.
12 *An Claidheamh Soluis*, 4 May 1901, 123. Douglas Hyde had published *The Love Songs of Connacht*. in 1893.
13 Rev. P.J. Joyce, *John Healy, Archbishop of Tuam* (Dublin: M.H. Gill, 1931). Apart from this unsatisfactory biography, there is no information emanating from the diocese of Tuam on the life of Healy. The secretary assured the writer (April 1999) that the archives on Healy were 'slight' and that they did not possess any personal correspondence between Edward Martyn and the Archbishop.
14 John O'Grady, *The Life and Work of Sarah Purser* (Dublin: Irish Academic Press, 1996), 95.
15 Ibid., Hughes to Purser.
16 *Leader*, 18 May 1901.
17 Ibid., 13 June 1901.
18 Ibid., 29 June 1901.
19 *Leader*, 19 January 1901, 334/335.
20 Ibid., 31 August 1901, 12.
21 Ibid., 43.
22 Ibid., 2 November 1901, 155.
23 Holloway, 14.
24 Gifford Lewis, *The Selected Letters of Somerville and Ross*, 253.
25 Gregory to Yeats, December 1900, Berg.
26 *Freeman's Journal*, 13 November 1901.
27 Gregory to Yeats, Berg,
28 John Kelly and Ronald Suchard, *The Collected Letters of W.B. Yeats*, Vol. III, 19 January 1902.
29 Edward Martyn, *The Dream Physician* (Dublin: Talbot Press, 1915).
30 *Weekly Register*, 3 January 1902.
31 *Pall Mall Gazette*, 26 November 1901, 129.
32 Martyn's unpublished essays reproduced in Gwynn, 146.
33 *An Enchanted Sea*, 146.
34 Ibid., 159.
35 *Weekly Register*, 10 January 1902.
36 Ibid., 17 January 1902.
37 Martyn to Gregory, 19 April 1904, Berg.

38   Dowling, *Hellenism and Homosexuality in Victorian Oxford*, 115.
39   Ibid., 118.

CHAPTER 12 – SACRED MUSIC AND ART

 1   Martyn to Walsh, 3 June 1901, Dublin Diocesan Archive, Walsh Papers.
 2   Horgan, *From Parnell to Pearse*, 92.
 3   Martyn to Walsh, 18 June 1901, Dublin Diocesan Archive, Walsh Papers.
 4   Ibid., 19 June 1901.
 5   Gwynn, *Edward Martyn and the Irish Revival*, 190.
 6   Martyn to Walsh, 17 September 1901, Dublin Diocesan Archive, Walsh Papers.
 7   Gwynn, *Edward Martyn and the Irish Revival*, 193.
 8   Ibid., 194.
 9   George Moore, *The Untilled Field* (Gerrards Cross: Colin Smythe, 2000), Introduction, xxix.
10   NLI, MS 10751 (2). F.S. Bourke papers.
11   Gwynn, *Edward Martyn and the Irish Revival*, 199.
12   Edward Martyn, *Paragraphs for the Perverse*, 8.
13   *United Irishman*, 2 August 1902.
14   Ibid., 16 August 1902.
15   Holloway, 16.
16   *United Irishman*, 19 April 1902.
17   Yeats *CL*, iii, 174.
18   Ibid., 178.
19   Ibid.
20   Edward Martyn, 'Placehunters', *Leader*, 26 July 1902, 363.
21   Hone, *Letters of John B. Yeats*, 46 (12).
22   Ibid., 49 (14).
23   Ibid., 54 (18).
24   Although the publication date of Elliot's *Art in Ireland* is 1902, the first reference to it in any publication is in 1906; John Horgan sent E.M. a copy of it, and they discuss the *Leader*'s review.
25   Yeats *CL*, iii, 174.
26   Ibid., 233.
27   *United Irishman*, 27 June 1903.
28   Ibid., 388.
29   NLI, MS 13483 (5). To judge, however, from E.M.s correspondence with T.P. Gill in October 1902, he worked closely with Sarah Purser on setting up the studio.
30   John O'Grady, *Sarah Purser*, 100.
31   NLI, MS 10561. Martyn to Purser, 8 September 1902.
32   *Leader*, 11 July 1903.
33   Denison, *Letters from Æ*, 46.
34   Joan Hardwick, *The Yeats Sisters* (London: Pandora, 1996), 121.
35   Padraic Colum, *Ourselves Alone* (New York: Crown Publishers, 1959), 63.
36   Ibid., 85.

CHAPTER 13 – 1904

 1   *Freeman's Journal*, 2 April 1903.

2 Ibid., 9 April 1903.

3 Ibid., 23 April 1903.

4 Ibid., 25 April 1903.

5 Anna MacBride-White and Norman Jeffares, *The Gonne–Yeats Letters, 1893–1938* (London: Pimlico, 1993), 105.

6 *United Irishman*, 6 June 1903, 378.

7 Russell (Æ) to Yeats, Denison, 47.

8 *Freeman's Journal*, 19 May 1903.

9 Æ to Yeats, Denison, 47.

10 *Gonne–Yeats Letters*, 173.

11 *United Irishman*, 20 May 1903, 377.

12 *Father Mathew Record,* June 1943.

13 *Leader*, 15 June 1903.

14 Reprinted in the *Leader*, 3 October 1903.

15 *Leader*, 10 October 1902, 101.

16 J.C.M Nolan, 'The First President of Sinn Féin', *Irish Studies Review*, Vol. 15, Summer 1996, 29.

17 NLI, P.4645, Martyn to Horgan, 26 June 1907.

18 Two of the politicians who were against the Union with Britain in 1800, although Charlemont (James Caufield) died in 1799. The dissolution of the Irish Parliament at that time is what E.M. means when he refers to 'our stolen Constitution'.

19 *All Ireland Review*, 30 May 1903, 216.

20 Ibid., 217.

21 Yeats's *The Hour Glass* and Gregory's *Twenty-five* were performed at the Molesworth Hall on 14 March by the Irish National Theatre Society, of which Yeats was now president, while Willie Fay did the production.

22 Russell to Yeats, Denison, 47.

23 *United Irishman*, 17 October 1903.

24 Annie Horniman was an old friend of Yeats from the Golden Dawn days. She was a wealthy Quaker and she funded the Abbey, partly because of her innate interest in theatre and partly because she was in love with Yeats. She was always unpopular with the company.

25 Yeats to Quinn, *CL*, iii, 541.

26 Ibid., Yeats to Gregory, 631.

27 Holloway, 40.

28 Martyn to Gregory, 19 April 1904, Berg.

29 Hone, *Letters of John B. Yeats*, 53.

30 John Ryan's introduction to *Father Ralph* (Co. Kerry: Brandon Books, 1993), ix.

31 In 1918 O'Donovan met, and fell in love with, the novelist Rose Macaulay. Although he never left his wife, they remained faithful to each other until his death in 1941.

32 Martyn to Gregory, 28 December 1904, Berg.

33 Richard Cave in the introduction to *Hail and Farewell*, 28.

34 This description of the first night of the Abbey comes from Maire ni Shiubhlaigh's *The Splendid Years*.

35 R.F. Foster, *The Apprentice Mage: W.B. Yeats, A Life* (Oxford: Oxford University Press, 1997), 344.

36 Joseph Hone, *Yeats*, 257.

37 Holloway, 52.

38 Wade, *The Letters of W.B. Yeats*, 462.

CHAPTER 14 – KING MARTYN AND THE MARTYNETTES

1 Gonne to Yeats, *CL*, ii, 192.
2 Ibid., 210.
3 NLI, P.4645, Martyn to Horgan, 26 January 1906.
4 Lyons, *Ireland since the Famine*, 256.
5 *Leader*, 13 November 1906.
6 Ibid., 23 Februry 1907.
7 Ibid., 4 May 1907.
8 NLI, P.4645, Martyn to Horgan.
9 *Leader*, 21 December 1907.
10 NLI, P.4645, Martyn to Horgan, January 1906.
11 Gwynn, *Edward Martyn and the Irish Revival*, 305.
12 Ibid., 306.
13 Ibid., 315.
14 NLI, MS 35766 (9), Clonbrock Papers.
15 NLI, P.4645, Martyn to Horgan.
16 Horgan, *Parnell to Pearse*, 117.
17 Ibid., 118.
18 Ibid., Martyn to Horgan, 9 August 1906.
19 NLI, P4645, Martyn to Horgan, June 1907.
20 *Leader*, 1 December 1906.
21 Ibid., 7 June 1908.
22 NLI, P4645, Martyn to Horgan, June 1908.
23 *Leader*, 5 September 1908.
24 Ibid., 24 April 1909.
25 Thomas MacGreevy in the *Father Mathew Record*, April 1943.
26 Moore, *Salve*, Book 2, *Hail and Farewell*, 351.

CHAPTER 15 – MELANCHOLIA

1 NLI, P4645, Martyn to Horgan, 23 November 1909.
2 Yeats, *Autobiographies*, 388.
3 Holloway, 81.
4 J.M. Synge, *Collected Plays and Poems*, Alison Smith (ed.) (London: Everyman, 1997), xvi.
5 Gwynn, 144.
6 W.B. Yeats to J.B. Yeats, 17 July 1909, Wade, 527.
7 Æ to John Quinn, Denson, 67.
8 Yeats to Gregory, Wade, 547. In 1913, however, when WBY was writing to Katharine Tynan about her memoirs, he told her: 'I am glad too that George Moore's disfiguring glass will not be the only Glass.'
9 Frazier, *George Moore*, 368.
10 NLI, MS 18275, Moore to Martyn.
11 Moore, *Hail and Farewell*, 187.
12 Edward Martyn, *Grangecolman* (Dublin: Maunsel & Co., 1912).
13 *Sinn Féin*, 3 February 1912.
14 Holloway, 134.
15 Ibid., 137.
16 Ibid., 141.

17 *Leader,* 4 June 1910, 370.
18 Ibid., 371.
19 Ibid., 18 June 1910.
20 Ibid.
21 NLI, P.4645, Martyn to Horgan, 26 August 1910.
22 *Leader,* 11 November 1911.
23 Martyn to O'Brien, 26 December 1912: letters in the possession of Mrs Elizabeth O'Brien, who kindly allowed me to read them.
24 Martyn to O'Brien, 2 June 1912.
25 NLI, P.4645, Martyn to Horgan, 26 June 1911.
26 J.H Cousins and M.E. Cousins, *We Two Together* (Madras, India, 1950), 142.
27 Holloway, 151.
28 Lewis, *The Selected Letters of Somerville and Ross,* 295.
29 Holloway, 159.
30 NLI, MS 2134, Moore to Gosse, George Moore Papers.
31 Philip Rooney, 'The Turret Room', *The Capuchin Annual 1963,* 79.
32 Ibid.

CHAPTER 16 – HARDWICKE STREET

1 NLI, P.4645, Martyn to Horgan, 29 January 1914.
2 Ibid., 27 July 1914.
3 *Irish Review,* April 1914.
4 Maire ní Shiubhlaigh, *The Splendid Years* (Dublin: Browne & Nolan Limited), 141.
5 W.J. Feeney, *Drama in Hardwicke Street,* 47. The bulk of the information on the *Irish Theatre* is taken from this book, a *tour de force* on the subject.
6 ní Shiubhlaigh, *The Splendid Years,* 156.
7 Desmond Ryan, *The Rising* (Dublin: Golden Eagle Books, 1949), 68.
8 Feeney, *Drama in Harwicke Streert,* 40.
9 ní Shiubhlaigh, *The Splendid Years,* 151.
10 Mícheál Mac Líammóir, *Theatre in Ireland,* Dublin Cultural Relations Committee 1950, 20–1.
11 *Irish Press,* 20 March 1937, 8.
12 Martyn to Boyd, 25 August 1919, Healy Collection, Stanford University Libraries, California.
13 NLI, MS 13099, Thomas MacDonagh papers.
14 *Irish Times,* 2 November 1914.
15 Edward Martyn, *The Dream Physician* (Dublin: Talbot Press, 1914), 43.
16 Ibid., 62.
17 Feeney, *Drama in Hardwicke Street,* 68.
18 Ibid., 62.
19 Ibid.
20 Ibid., 66. Grace Gifford also penned an excellent sketch of E.M kneeling down and rebuffing a very stylish woman and her dog. Title: 'Edward Martyn: "Having a week of it" in Paris'.
21 Martyn to Clark, 12 October 1914, Barrett H. Clarke Papers, held in the State University of Washington Libraries, Seattle.
22 Feeney, *Drama in Hardwicke* Street, 83.
23 NLI, P.7271, Henderson Papers. Also reviews reproduced from Feeney.

CHAPTER 17 – EASTER 1916

1 Feeney, *Drama in Hardwicke Street*, 103.
2 Martyn to O'Brien, 16 October 1915.
3 Feeney, *Drama in Hardwicke Street*, 114.
4 NLI, MS 4702, Martyn to Purser, 7 October 1915.
5 Martyn to Boyd, 25 August 1915, Healy Collection.
6 The only manuscript of this play is in the possession of Stephen Ryan, Scranton University, USA. Ryan completed a Ph.D thesis (UCD) on Edward Martyn in 1956.
7 Feeney, *Drama in Hardwicke Street*, 121.
8 Ibid., 125
9 Ibid., 129.
10 ní Shiubhlaigh, *The Splendid Years*, 164.
11 Holloway, 178.
12 Desmond Ryan, *The Rising*, 255.
13 Ibid., 259.
14 Martyn to Gregory, 19 May 1916, Berg.
15 Feeney, *Drama in Hardwicke Street*, 152.
16 NLI, P.4645, Martyn to Horgan, 5 August 1916.
17 Feeney, *Drama in Hardwicke Street*, 137.
18 Ibid.
19 Edward Martyn, *Paragraphs for the Perverse*, 5.
20 Anne Saddlemyer, *Becoming George* (Oxford: Oxford University Press, 2002), 171.
21 Ibid., 184.
22 Feeney, *Drama in Hardwicke Street*, 163.
23 Ibid., 173.
24 Ibid., 208.
25 Ibid.
26 Ibid., 198.
27 Michael J. O'Neill, *Lennox Robinson* (New York: Twayne Publishers, Inc., 1964), 113.
28 Feeney, *Drama in Hardwicke Street*, 231.
29 Holloway, 202.
30 Martyn to Boyd, 23 October 1918, Healy Collection.

CHAPTER 18 – THE FINAL CURTAIN

1 Oliver St John Gogarty, *As I Was Going Down Sackville Street* (New York: Reynal & Hitchcock, 1937), 288.
2 Lennox Robinson, *Lady Gregory's Journals, 1916–1930* (New York: Macmillan, 1947), 139.
3 Mary Kotsonouris, *Retreat from Revolution* (Dublin: Irish Academic Press, 1994), 20.
4 Robinson, *Lady Gregory's Journals*, 86.
5 Martyn to Clarke, 18 May 1922. Barrrett H. Clarke Papers.
6 Feeney, *Drama in Hardwicke Street*, 232.
7 Stephen F. Ryan, *Studies*, Summer 1958.
8 Feeney, *Drama in Hardwicke Street*, 233.
9 Ibid., 235.
10 Ibid.
11 Stephen Ryan, *Studies*.

12 *New Ireland*, 21 June 1919.

13 Declan Kiberd, *Synge and the Irish Language* (London: The Macmillan Press, 1979), 218.

14 Feeney, *Drama in Hardwicke Street*, 246.

15 Ibid., 302.

16 Ibid., 270.

17 Ibid., 275.

18 Robinson, 183. Vincent O'Brien had, in fact, discovered John McCormack and had, by this time, accompanied him on his first tour of the US from where he had sent Edward a plethora of postcards.

19 Martyn to O'Brien, 24 July 1920.

20 Robinson, *Lady Gregory's Journals*, 188.

21 Feeney, *Drama in Hardwicke Street*, 276.

22 Susan L. Mitchell, *George Moore* (Dublin: Maunsel & Co., 1916).

23 Robinson, *Lady Gregory's Journals*, 295.

24 Martyn to Clarke, 3 September 1921.

25 Robinson, *Lady Gregory's Journals*, 169.

26 Martyn to Clarke, 18 May 1922.

27 Ibid.

28 Daniel J. Murphy (ed.), *Lady Gregory's Journals, Vol. 1* (Gerrards Cross: Colin Smythe, 1978), 363.

29 Arthur Griffith had died on 12 August from a cerebral haemorrhage, and Michael Collins was ambushed, and shot dead, in County Cork ten days later. Liam Mellows, who had brought his troops to a halt in Tillyra in 1916, was executed by the Free State Forces in December. Altogether seventy-seven republican prisoners were executed in the Civil War.

30 Martyn to O'Brien, 2 March 1923.

31 Robinson, *Lady Gregory's Journals*, 29.

32 Ibid., 31.

33 Ibid.

34 Joseph Hone, *A Life of George Moore* (London: Victor Gollancz, 1936), 384.

35 *Dublin Magazine*, January 1924.

Bibliography of Edward Martyn's Writings

NOVEL

Morgante the Lesser: His Notorious Life and Wonderful Deeds. By Sirius (London: Swan Sonnenschein, 1890).

PLAYS

The Heather Field and *Maeve*, with an introduction by George Moore, (London: Gerald Duckworth, 1899). Published separately by Duckworth in 1917.

The Tale of a Town and *An Enchanted Sea* (Kilkenny: Standish O'Grady, and London: T. Fisher Unwin, 1902).

The Place-Hunters, Leader, 26 July 1902.

Romulus and Remus: or *The Makers of Delights*, in the Christmas supplement of the *Irish People*, 21 December 1907.

Grangecolman (Dublin: Maunsel & Co., 1912).

The Dream Physician (Dublin: Talbot Press, 1914).

The Privilege of Place, performed in Dublin 1915, unpublished.

Regina Eyre, performed in Dublin 1919, unpublished.

SELECTED JOURNALISM

'Wagner's Parsifal at Bayreuth', *Black and White*, 22 August 1891.

'Palestrina at Cologne', *Speaker*, 23 February 1895.

'Vittoria at Saint-Gervais', *Speaker*, 1 August 1896.

'A Celebrated Musician': Vincent O'Brien, *Dublin Daily Express*, 27 March 1899.

'The Modern Drama in Germany', *Dublin Daily Express*, 11 February 1899.

'A Comparison between Irish and English Theatrical Audiences', *Beltaine* 2, February 1900.

'The Use of a Provincial Feis', *Dublin Daily Express*, 1 September 1900.

'Catholic Church Music in Dublin', *Leader*, 6 October 1900.

'The Musical Season in Ireland', *New Ireland Review*, October 1900.

Ireland's Battle for Her Language: Gaelic League Pamphlet no. 4, 1900.

'The Palestrina Choir', *Leader*, 20 April 1901.

'Stained Glass', *Leader*, 18 May 1901

'Letterkenny Cathedral', *Leader*, 29 June 1901.

'Two Irish Artists', *Leader*, 26 October 1901.

'A Plea for a National Theatre in Ireland', *Samhain* 1, 1901.

'Art and Nationality', *Leader*, 21 February 1903.

'The New Parish Church at Spiddal', *Leader*, 13 June 1903.

'The Present State of Irish Music', *Leader*, 11 February 1911.

'Schools of National Music', *Leader*, 10 December 1910.

'The Feis Ceoil', *Leader*, 13 July 1912.

'Little Eyolf' and 'The Lady from the Sea', *Irish Review* 2, February 1913.

'Wagner's Parsifal or the Cult of Liturgical Aestheticism', *Irish Review* 2, December 1913.

'A Plea for the Revival of the Irish Literary Theatre', *Irish Review* 4, April 1914.

'Palestrina in Ireland: Reformed Choirs', *Daily Telegraph*, 4 December 1920.

BOOKS ABOUT, AND PARTLY ABOUT, EDWARD MARTYN

Courtney, Sister Marie-Thérèse, *Edward Martyn and the Irish Theatre* (New York: Vantage Press, 1956).

Ellis-Fermor, Una, *The Irish Dramatic Movement* (London: Methuen, 1964).

Feeney, William J., *Drama in Hardwicke Street. A History of the Irish Theatre Company* (Associated University Presses, 1984).

Gwynn, Denis, *Edward Martyn and the Irish Revival* (London: Jonathan Cape, 1930).

Moore, George, *Hail and Farewell,* 3 vol. (London: William Heinemann, 1911, 1912, 1914). Single-volume edition with an introduction by Richard Allen Cave (Gerrards Cross: Colin Smythe, 1976).

Nolan, Jerry, *Six Essays on Edward Martyn, Irish Cultural Revivalist* (Wales: The Edwin Mellen Press, 2004).

Setterquist, Jan, *Ibsen and the Beginnings of Anglo-Irish Drama, Vol II: Edward Martyn* (Uppsala: A.B. Lundequistska and Dublin: Hodges Figgis, 1908).

Index

Abbey Theatre, 117, 165, 180, 218, 244, 250, 217, 220, 222, 228, 234, 244, 245, 250, 254
'Absent-Minded Beggar', 135, 136
Abstentionism, 178
Acton, James, 69
Agriculture, Department of, 128
Allgood, Sara, 185, 199
An Enchanted Sea, 63, 109, 154–158, 159, 166, 181–182, 239, 257; literary aestheticism, 160
An Tur Gloinne, 130, 172, 183, 184
Antient Concert Rooms, 93, 99, 113, 115, 133
Aran Islands, 77
Archer William, 64, 67, 78, 79, 83, 100
Ardrahan, 191, 195
Arnold, Matthew, 20
Ashbourne, Lord, 135
'Asgard', 216
Ashlin, George, 27
Athenaeum, 117, 118
Ave, 104, 117

Balfe, James, 8
Balfour, Betty, 99
Ballylee Tower, 238
Bannerman, Campbell, 170
Barry, Dr. William (priest, novelist, critic and essayist), 106
Bayreuth, 48, 59, 68, 71, 82, 85, 120, 176
Beáslai, Piaras, 235

Beaumont College, 15–18
Beerbohm, Max, 102, 116, 117, 119, 226
Belvedere College, 15
Bending of the Bough, 122, 124, 125, 129, 130; question of authorship, 132–134
Benedictines, 15, 162
Bennett, Louis, 228
Berenson, Bernard, 21
Bewerunge, Heinrich, 94, 146
Blake Moore, Mary, 17, 19
Blunt, Wilfrid, Scawan. 40, 41
Bodley, J.E.C., 18
Boer War, 131
Bolshevist, 250
Bordeaux, 'Parlement' of, 40
Boucicault, Dion, 68
Bourget, Paul, 77
Boyd, Ernest, 218, 222, 230, 244
Boyle, William, 207
Burke, Florence, 86
Burke, Thomas, 4, 9, 12

Carmelite Abbey, 3
Carmelites, 3, 6, 19, 22, 105
Carlyle, Thomas, 43, 48
Carson, Edward, 215, 216, 260 n 17
Casement, Roger, 253
Cecilia Street School of Medicine, 6
'Celtic Theatre', 89, 90, 92, 95
'Celtic Twilight', 166
Chamberlain, Joseph, 45, 47, 58

Chekhov, Anton, 249

Child, Alfred, 172

Clanricarde, family of, 3; stabilising force in Galway, 4

Clarke, Barett H., 226, 246, 247, 253, 254

Clonbrock, Lord G., 135, 136, 137

Coffey, George, 105–106, 144

Coiside Gnótha, 182

Collins, Michael, 232, 247,

Colum, Padraic, 121, 173, 207, 220

Connemara, 211

Coole Park, 7, 9, 23, 25, 39, 91

Corballis, Richard, 8

Costelloe, Con., 21, 261 n 16

Countess Cathleen, 98, 101, 103; Edward Martyn's theological problems with, 105–108; Frank H. O'Donnell's attack,111–112; difficulties with staging, 113; condemned by Cardinal Logue, 116

Cousins, James H., 210

Cranach, Lucas, 120

Crimean War, 11, 20

Cullen, Cardinal Paul, 1, 96, 127

Dail Courts, 247

Daly, Denis Bowes, 3

Davis, Thomas, 111, 113, 178

Davitt, Michael, 23, 111

Déak, Franz, 178

'Dear Edward', 25

de Basterot, Florimonde, 76, 77; connection with south Galway, 40; criticism of Morgante the Lesser, 53

de Burgo, Ulick, John (see Clanricarde)

de Stackpoole, George, 15, 17, 238

de Valera, Eamon, 240, 253, 254–255

de Valera, Sinéad, (see Flanagan)

de Vega, Lope, 226

Devotional Revolution, 96

Dillon, John, 241

Dillon, Luke (Lord Clonbrock), 61

Douglas, Lord Alfred, 60

Dream Physician, First Night at the Little Theatre, 222; Edward's revenge, 223; plot and theme, 224–225; the critics, 226

Dublin Daily Express, 96, 102

Dublin Magazine, 258

Dublin Orchestral Society, 104

Dublin Cultural Relations Committee, 222

Dublin Season, 31, 32

Dun Emer Industries, 219

Dujardin, Edward, 37

Dungarvan, 109

Dunguaire Castle, 7, 238

Dürer, Albrecht, 28, 43

Durus, 40, 77; agreement to found a theatre, 88

Easter Rising, Dublin,1916, 216, 232–235, 240

Elliot, Robert, 169, 172

'England's Faithful Garrison', 177

Esposito, Michele, 85

Fahy, Jeremiah (Jerome), 72

Famine, 6

Farr, Florence, 86, 99, 103, 104, 108, 111, 114, 126

Farrell, Paul, 240, 252

Fay, Frank, 166, 219

Fay, William, 153, 165

Feis Ceoil, 73,84, 85, 141, 147

Figgis, Darrell, 251

Fingall, Daisy (wife of 11th Earl of Fingall and cousin of Edward Martyn), 88, 99; asked to persuade Martyn to quit Kildare Street Club, 138

Finlay, Thomas, S.J., 15, 107, 109, 142

Fitzgerald, Percy, 113

Flanagan, John Woulfe, 47

Flanagan, Sinéad, 167–168, 253

Flanagan, Terence Woulfe, 21

Frampton, Edward, 28

French, Percy, 229

Frongoch, Prison, 235

Gaelic League, 62, 80, 84, 142, 218, 219, 226

Gaiety Theatre, 131

Geary, Nevill, 22, 32, 35, 42, 69, 70, 71, 104; visits Maud Gonne in Paris, 188

Gifford, Grace, 205, 226, 230, 231

Gill, T.P., 95, 96, 105, 117, 128, 130, 133

Gladstone, William E., 23

Gleeson, Evelyn, 172, 219, 220

Gogarty, Oliver St. John, 246, 247

Gonne, Maud, 87, 93, 111, 155; National Council, 176, 177, 180; resigns from National Theatre Society, 181; files for divorce from John McBride,188

Gough, Lord G., 191–194

Grangecolman, 206–207, 240

'Green Hungarian Band', 191

Gregory, Augusta: early life at Coole Park, 25, 27, 28; south Galway gentry, 39; trouble for Wilfrid S. Blunt, 40; shares intellectual pursuits with Edward Martyn, 47; distains Yeats's 'stories' of Martyn told him by George Moore, 68; in London with Edward and Nevill Geary, 69–71; meets Yeats and Symons at Tillyra, 76; in Durus in July 1897 (decision to found a theatre), 88; Yeats comes to Coole, 91; helps Edward with 'Celtic Party', 91; sympathy for Edward over rewriting of *The Tale of a Town*, 120–124; defends Edward over *The Bending of the Bough* and sympathises over success of same, 130–133; reluctantly helps Martyn with letter of resignation as D.L., 137; regrets Edward cutting away from the theatre project, 142; good wishes for the production of *An Enchanted Sea*, 159; putting on her plays during Lent, 180; writing to Yeats disparagingly about Edward, 185,

196; worries about Edward in Dublin in April, 1916, 235; anguish over Robert Gregory's death, 241; close neighbours in troubled times, 1920, 252–253; lonliness after Martyn's death, 257, 268 n 39

Gregory, Robert, (William's father) 40, Gregory Robert (son of William and Augusta), 98; death in Great War, 241

Gregory, William, 9, 23; brings his bride to Coole Park, 25, 263 n 10

Griffith, Arthur, 151, 165, 170, 177, 180, 185, 191, 197, 276 n 29

Gwynn, Denis, 194, 260 n 10

Gwynn, Stephen, 156

Hail and Farewell, 25, 201, 204

Hardwicke Street, 220, 222, 228; used for training Irish Volunteers, 235; 236, 240, 245; Countess Plunkett cancells lease, 252

Harrington, Timothy C., 93

Hauptmann, Gerhard, 103

Healy, John (Bishop of Clonfert), 84, 140, 148, 149, 209–210, 269 n 13

Healy, Tim, 192, 194

Heather Field, 65–69, 78, 82–83, 101–102, 115–118

Hellenism, 20, 22, 28, 159, 160

Hemphill, Andrew, 247

Hemphill, Lady (Andrew Martyn's daughter), 247–248

Hemphill, Peter, 32, 170

Holloway, Joseph, 112; report of first night of Irish Literary Theatre, 113; 116, 131, 152, 165, 181, 207, 219, 228, 232

Hone, Joseph, 186

Hone, Nathaniel, 151

Horgan, John, 178, 189, 190, 192, 195, 202, 210, 211, 215, 217; rewarded for loyalty and friendship, 236; 240, 255

Horniman, Annie, 181, 183, 198, 199,206, 271 n 24

Hughes, John, 149
Huysmann, Joris-Karl, 37
Hyde, Douglas, 24, 62, 117, 118, 134, 167, 170, 228
Hyde-Lees, George, 238

Ibsen, Henrik, 63, 67, 100; 'drama of the mind', 109; influence on *The Heather Field*, 156; 166, 240
Irish Literary Theatre, 94, 98, 99; Martyn threatens to withdraw support, 105; Bishop Healy blesses, 108; inaugural performance, 111; 112, 116, 120, 122, 123, 250
Irish National Club, 109
Irish National Dramatic Society, 165
Irish Review, 217–219, 226, 236
Irish Theatre: foundation of, 218; a suitable home, 220; no peasant plays, 222; Joseph M. Plunkett resigns, 231; last remaining director, 232; where nationalism and internationalism meet, 244; a European resonance, 251
Irish Volunteers, 215, 216, 220

Jesuits, 18, 22, 107
Jowett, Benjamin, 20, 21, 22
Joyce, James, 113, 146
Jubilee Celebrations, 87

Kelly, Anna, 222
Kessler, Count Harry, 103
Kettle, Laurence, 215
Kildare Street Club, 115, 140, 159, 175, 192–195, 200
Kilkenny Moderator, 96
Killaloe, 151, 152
Kilmacduagh, 94
Kilroy's Hotel, 6
Kinvara, 40, 72, 238

Labane, 26, 30, 37, 94, 170
Land Commission, 69, 139
Land League, 23, 40, 44, 109, 262 n 8
Layard, Enid, 83 265 n 10

Lecky, W.E.H., 44
Leo XIII, 148
Letterkenny, 150
Linnane, Owen, 214, 255, 257
Lisdoonvarna, 12
Lloyd, Constance (wife of Oscar Wilde), 32
Logue, Cardinal Michael, 116, 141
Loughrea, 3, 10, 12, 40; consequences of famine, 10; foundation of cathedral, 84; 148

Macan, R.W., 20
MacBride, Major John, 188, 232
MacBride, Sean, 188, 239
MacDermott, Charlotte, 2
MacDermott, Anthony James, 2
MacDonagh, John, 226, 228, 231; interned in Frongoch, 235; keeps theatre alive, 236, 238–240, 247; last meeting with Edward, 254, 258
MacDonagh, Joseph, 238
MacDonagh, Thomas, 218, 219, 230, 231; in Jacob's Biscuit factory during Easter Rising, 232; execution of, 235, 249
MacGreevy, Thomas, 63, 200
MacLeod, Fiona (William Sharp), 77, 87
MacLíammóir, Mícheal, 220, 222
MacNamara, Brindsley, 251
MacNeill, Eoin, 215, 250
Maeterlinck, Maurice, 156
Maeve, Moore claims authorship, 67; central theme, 78; help from Arthur Symons, 78; William Archer's critique, 79; 88, 100, 128, 130; inaugural performance, 131–132, 166
Magennis, J.P., 257
Mahaffy, J.P., 161, 162, 168
Markievicz, Casimir, 206
Markievicz, Constance, 206
Marriage Settlement, 11
Martín, Eamon Bui, 8
Martin, Violet (Martin Ross), 152, 213, 265 n 22

Martyn Adrian, 260 n 13

Martyn, Andrew, 148, 170

Martyn, Annie: early years, 2; marriage settlement, 11; sending Edward to Oxford, 19; ungracious with the tenantry, 25; 36, 87, 90; death, 94

Martyn, Edward: Birth, 5; embryonic aesthete, 15; the Jesuits, 17; influence of Walter Pater, 19; Oxford years, 20–23, the young squire, 27; life provides copy for George Moore's novellas, 30; crisis of confidence in Hellenism, 34; reluctant landlord, 40; *Morgante the Lesser*, 49–52; passion for Wagner, 57; questions Unionist heritage, 62; introduction to Ibsen drama, 63–65; W.B. Yeats at Tillyra, 73–77; guarantor of a 'Celtic Theatre', 90; changing relationship with Augusta Gregory, 91; mother's death, 94; meets Vincent O'Brien, 96; choir for Dublin, 98; success of *The Heather Field*, 114–116; influence on Metropolitan School of Art, 130; first night of *Maeve*, 131; controversy over *The Bending of the Bough*, 133–134; offers resignation as J.P. and D.L., 135; sale of land to Land Commission, 139; campaign for choir in the *Leader*, 145–147; friendship with Bishop John Healy, 148–149; Yeats and Gregory sorry to see him go from theatre project, 155; paucity of artistic values in Irish Catholic Church, 161; Martyn as satirist, 167; protests visit of Edward V11, 174–177; likes Arthur Griffith's 'Hungarian Policy', 178; reprimanded by Standish J. O'Grady on 'Republican simplicity', 179; negotiating patent for the Abbey, 181; a missionary for art, 183; first night at the Abbey, 184; chairman of the National Council, 189–190, leaves Kildare Street Club, 195; friendship with John Horgan, 195–196; resignation from Sinn Fein, 197; melancholia, 202; Moriarity correspondence, 208; *Hail and Farewell* confrontation, 214; violence on the street of Dublin, 216; a plea for the revival of the Irish Literary Theatre, 217; no peasant plays, 218; friendship with Thomas MacDonagh, 220; Articles of Agreement for Irish Theatre, 222; Rabelaisian strain, 225; presentation of 'Cupid and Psyche' poster. 226; still friends with George Moore, 230; listening to the guns in April, 1916, 232; reports to Augusta Gregory on fateful week, 235; looks like a money changer in the temple, 238; advises W.B. Yeats on Ballylee Tower, 238; realization of other's peoples interpretation of *An Enchanted Sea*, 238; lack of dramatic craftsmanship, 243; Dublin Drama League, 244; Trying to sell Tillyra, 246; Is Edward Martyn a Bolshevist? 250; Black and Tan invasion in Gort and life in south Galway, 1920, 252–253; paralysed by stroke, 256; last meeting with Augusta Gregory, 256; death 257–258.

Martyn, John (Edward's father), 'a man with a past, 6; life and responsibilities at Tillyra, 7–9; civic duty, 10; marriage to Annie Smyth, 11; death, 12

Martyn, John (Edward's brother), 24, 27

Martyn, Oliver, 6

Martyn Richard, 7

Mason, Robert, 3

Masonbrook, 1, 3; early childhood of Edward Martyn, 5; John Martyn's familiarity with, 11

Massinger, 3

Maturin, Charles, Robert, 3

McCormack, Count John, 253

Mellows, Liam, 235

Meltzer, C.H., 140

Meynell, Wilfrid, 155–158

Mill, John Stuart, 20

Milligan, Alice, 91,130, 131, 209, 268 n 4

Mitchell, Susan L., 104, 113, 127

Monck, Sarah, 3

Monck-Mason, Robert, 3

Moran, D.P: 'The Philosophy of Irish Ireland', 142; attacking Yeats, 151; dislike of Sinn Fein, 189; ridiculing Edward Martyn, 191; personal attack on Yeats and Martyn regarding *Deirdre*, 196; Moriarity correspondence, 208–209

Morley, John, 45, 46, 56, 61

Morgante the Lesser, 49–52

Morris, Michael (later Lord Killallin), 55, 56, 77

Moore, George Augustus: description of Annie Martyn, 11, 17; reflection on Edward's sexuality, 13; Edward's confidences, 15, 16; return from Paris, 24; uses Edward's life in fiction, 34, 54; observations on Edward's Christianity, 38; editing Edward's creative work, 42; Edward confides in him re. nationalist instincts, 62; Augusta Gregory's dislike of, 68; controversy over introduction to *The Heather Field* and *Maeve*,100–102; rage at Edward's behaviour on *The Countess Cathleen*, 107; disappointment on arrival in Dublin, 115–117; *The Tale of a Town* turns into *The Bending of the Bough*, (relationship with Edward cools) 134; friends again,144; assessment of Edward Martyn's contribution to the cultural renaissance,163; pleasure in visits to south Leinster Street, 195; satirised in *The Dream Physician*, 223; anger over Susan Mitchell's 'life', 254;

Augusta Gregory blames him for Edward's disaffection from theatre project, 257; shock at manner of disposal of Edward Martyn's body, 258

Moore, George Henry, 24

Nation, the, 111

National Council, 174–178, 189, 198, 199

National Literary Society, 134

National Theatre, 154, 155

National Theatre Society, 181, 185

New Ireland Review, 142, 148

Newman, John, Henry, 19, 20

Noble, George (Count Plunkett), 240

Norman Tower (at Tillyra), 19, 20

O'Brien, Vincent: Edward discovers in Carmelite Church in Dublin, producing Palestrina's *Missa Papae Marceli*, 96; Bishop Walsh considers him for choirmaster, 126; with Edward in Bayreuth, 150; Edward pushes for his appointment, 161; generous legacy, 202; 211, 230, 236, 252; keeping in touch, 255–257

O'Brien, William P., 198

O'Conaire, Padraic, 251

O'Connor, Una, 219, 226

O'Dea, Jimmie, 251

O'Donnell, Frank, Hugh, 109, 111–112

O'Donovan, Jeremiah (Gerald), 32, 84, 128, 149; gives up ministry, 183, 271 n 31

O'Duffy, Eimar, 228, 252

O'Grady, Standish, James, 96, 123, 134; reminds Edward why he doesn't sit comfortably with Sinn Fein, 178–179; 195, 211

O'Hanlon, Henry B., 242

O'Kelly, Seamus, 242

O'Leary, John, 175

Ó Raifteiri, Antoine, 141

Oxford Catholic Club, 21

Paragraphs for the Perverse, 58, 215, 264, n 16
Palestrina Choir, 96–98, 126, 147–148, 161–165,182
Parnell, Charles S., 47, 48, 58, 178, 195
Parnellism and Crime 44
Pater, Walter, 18, 33, 34, 160
Patterson, Annie, 84
Pearsall Smith, Robert, 21
Pearse, Padraig, 211, 212, 228, 232, 234, 251
Pearse, Willie, 226, 235
Pender, Harold, 252
People's Protection Society, (see National Council)
Persse, Augusta, (see Gregory)
Persse, Algernon, 39
Persse, William, 39
Pigott, Richard, 48
Pinero, Sir Arthur Wing, 100
Piper's Club, 167
Place-Hunters, 167
Plan of Campaign, 47
Plunkett, Countess, 220, 252
Plunkett, Horace, 86, 92, 95, 106–107, 118, 128, 131, 149, 152
Plunkett, Joseph Mary: wants an Art Theatre, 218; resigns as director of Irish Theatre, 231–232; execution of, 235
Portumna Castle, 4
Primrose League, 131
Privilige of Place, 231, 274 n 6

Quinn, John, 141, 170

Raglan Road, Dublin, 14
Reddington, Thomas, 9
Reddington, Christopher, 45
Redmond, 93, 215, 216, 241
Regina Eyre, 'a female Hamlet', 247–249
Robinson, Lennox, 121
Romulus and Remus, 198–199, 236
Rooney, Philip, 213

Rotunda Rowdies, 176
Ross, Robert, 106
Roxborough Castle, 39
Ruskin, John, 18
Russell, George (Æ), 30, 91, 102, 112, 118, 149, 155, 172, 173, 204
Ryan, Cyril, 32, 105, 256
Ryan, Stephen F., 249

Saint Brendan's Cathedral, 148, 149, 170, 172
Saturday Review, 102, 116
Schola Cantorum, 97, 164
Scott, W.A., 182, 238
Sharp, William, (Fiona MacLeod), 87, 92, 94
Shelbourne Hotel, Dublin, 26, 31, 32
Shiubhlaigh, Maire ní,185, 205–206, 218, 219, 220, 222, 224, 226, 232
Sinn Fein Movement, 197, 203, 240
Sidhe, 172
Smith, Mary Pearsall, 21
Smyth, Annie (see Martyn)
Smyth, James: beginnings in Loughrea, 1; buys Masonbrook, 3; 5, 11, 12, 13
Smyth, John, 84
Smyth, Louise, 10
Sommerville, Edith, 212
The Speaker, 97
Spiddal, 150
Stenbock, Count Eric, 21, 22, 61
Strindberg, August, 231
Sweetman, John, 174
Symons, Arthur, 21, 72; summer in south Galway, 1896, 74–79; 81, 151, 167
Synge, J.M., 82, 180, 185, 203, 250

The Tale of a Town, 88, 118–123, 126, 167
Théâtre Libre, 99
Theatre of Ireland, 199

Tillyra, 7, 8, 10, 11; doubts on restoration, 23; 26–28, Daisy Fingall's 'pleasing castle', 28; W.B. Yeats and Arthur Symons visit, 72–76; Edward reluctant to return, 231; Yeats brings Georgie Hyde-Lees, 239; anxious to sell, 246

Tolstoy, Leo, 54, 103

Trench, Fanny, 135

Tribes, 6

Ulster Volunteer Force, 215

Wagner, Richard, 43, 56, 57, 61

Wakefield, Edward, 1

Walsh, Bishop William, 126, 147, 161–162, 170

Whitman, Walt, 21

Whitty, May, 114

Wild Geese, 2

Wilde, Oscar, 2, 18, 19, 22, 32, 42, 60; first trial, 71; death in Paris, 127; 159; subject of dinner-table talk at Tillyra,196

Wilson, Woodrow, 240

Winckelmann, Joachim, 20, 43, 52, 261 n 14

Yeats, Jack B., 140, 69, 173

Yeats, John B., 61, 104, 114, 168

Yeats, Susan Mary (Lilly), 172

Yeats, W.B: revelations in *Autobiographies* regarding authorship of *The Heather Field* and *Maeve*, 67; complex relationship with Martyn, 73; seduced by the modern comforts of Tillyra, 76; persuades Edward to set the scene for 'cabbalist and shared visions', 76; meets Augusta Gregory in Tillyra, 76; trip to Aran Islands, 77; decision, at Durus, to found a theatre, 88; anxious about Martyn's 'depression', 92; brings J.M. Synge to Tillyra, 95; Martyn's disquiet over *The Countess Cathleen*, 103; organises theological response to Martyn's problem, 105; attack from Frank Hugh O'Donnell, 111; writes to the *Morning Leader* re. 'blind bigots of journalism', 116; moves into Tillyra with George Moore to re-work Martyn's *The Tale of a Town*, 121; persuades Maud Gonne to recruit Martyn on to the National Council, 175; worries about Martyn getting 'The Mechanics', 181; assessment of Martyn's creative ability, 187; keeping Edward informed on Maud Gonne's marriage breakdown, 188; dining at Tillyra, 196; sympathy for Edward re. Sinn Fein, 203; speculation on George Moore's intentions in *Hail and Farewell*, 204; Edward Martyn pays homage to, 217

Zola, Emile, 32